# PARENTCARE

# PARENTCARE

## A Commonsense Guide for Adult Children

# LISSY F. JARVIK, M.D., Ph.D.
# & GARY SMALL, M.D.

WITHDRAWN

CROWN PUBLISHERS, INC.
NEW YORK

*Publisher's Note:* This book contains case histories derived from interviews and research. The relevant facts have not been altered. However, names and other identifying details have been changed. While the book discusses certain health and legal issues regarding aging, it is not intended as a substitute for professional medical or legal advice.

**Library of Congress Cataloging-in-Publication Data**

Jarvik, Lissy F.
   Parentcare : a commonsense guide for adult
children.

   "How to help your elderly parents cope with the
problems of aging."
   Includes index.
   1. Parents, Aged—Care—United States.   2. Parents,
Aged—Services for—United States—Directories.
3. Aged—Care—United States.   4. Aged—Services for—
United States—Directories.   5. Adult children—United
States—Family relationships.   I. Small, Gary
II. Title.   [DNLM: 1. Family—popular works.
2. Geriatrics—popular works.   WT 120 J38p]
HQ1063.6.J37   1988        646.7'8              87–17165
ISBN 0-517-56765-2
10  9  8  7  6  5  4  3  2  1
First Edition

TO OUR PARENTS

# CONTENTS

# PREFACE

Five years ago, Lissy Jarvik said to Gary Small, "I have an idea for a book." Small thought to himself, "No way!" He and Jarvik had just finished editing a volume on psychiatry and aging—the project had taken up much more time and energy than expected, and now he wanted to focus on producing the scholarly articles that are the mark of a professor. Books had too many words! Small politely declined her offer to collaborate.

But Jarvik persisted. Every week or so, Small received a note scribbled on a piece of scratch paper: "This book will be much shorter than the other one." "We won't have to edit or rewrite the work of others—we'll write it ourselves." "It will be for a general audience, not an academic one." And the topic seemed irresistible.

More than forty years ago, Dr. Benjamin Spock began to guide parents as they cared for their children. Now Jarvik and Small would guide adult children as they cared for their parents. Other books had approached the topic from different vantage points and had often oversimplified the problems, infantilized the parents, narrowed the focus, or presented too scholarly a format for the lay reader. Their book would be practical, helpful, comprehensive, and authoritative. Small began to weaken.

Jarvik brought years of experience and insight to the project. A professor of psychiatry at the UCLA School of Medicine, she had been a pioneer in the field of aging. Her research, first at Columbia University, then at UCLA's Neuropsychiatric Institute and Brentwood VA Medical Center, had led to a deeper understanding of the natural effects of aging on the mind as well as a more precise definition of the two diseases that most often afflict the elderly—senility and depression. Small would offer a younger person's perspective. After training in psychiatry at Harvard's Massachusetts General Hospital, he had recently come to UCLA, where Jarvik had been his mentor in the psychiatry of old age. An assistant professor of psychiatry at UCLA, Small was on the threshold of his own academic career. They would span two generations in personal and clinical experience.

In their work with older patients, they were struck by the level of involvement of the patients' adult children. It was usually the adult child who made the initial contact, telephoned during an emergency, or sought advice. That would be their audience—not the parents, but the grown-up children.

Small finally agreed, and over the next five years they spent many weekends and holidays exchanging ideas, manuscripts, and stories, and many late nights writing. The project was as lengthy, complex, and time-consuming as Small had feared. But it was also much more rewarding and fun than he had anticipated. Jarvik knew all along that it would be.

# 1

# THE SANDWICH GENERATION: Don't Parents Take Care of Children — Not the Other Way Around?

*It is well known that one mother can take care of ten children, but ten children cannot take care of one mother.*

Ancient proverb

Have you ever felt that your relationship with your parents was not working? Do you ever get angry at them without understanding the reason? Do you miss the old days when they looked after you? Do you find that it gets harder and harder to call your parents to ask how they are doing—especially on weekends when you have free time? Have you read all the books about how to take care of your children, but never really found anything practical or helpful on how to deal with your parents? Do you feel ambivalent about helping them? If your answer to any of these questions is yes, if you have ever had difficulties in your relations with your parents, then this book is for you. You are not alone! This book was written for all of us whose relationships with our parents have been troubled, and especially for those who have become involved in parent-care.

Biology, history, and society have decreed that parents take care of their children, not the other way around. We are born our parents' children, and, barring some misfortune, our parents will take care of us from the moment we are born until we are old enough to take care of ourselves—or, until they think we are old enough to take care of ourselves. And then, supposedly, we are old enough to take care of our own children— old enough and mature enough to become parents ourselves.

Such has been the parenting cycle from generation to generation throughout the ages—until the end of the twentieth century, when things began to change. With improved living conditions and countless breakthroughs in medical technology, from the polio vaccine to the Jarvik-7 heart, survival rates have spiraled. Not long ago, anyone reaching the age of 60 was considered to have arrived at "old age," which in 1940 was the average man's life expectancy. Today, the average man can expect to pass his seventieth birthday and the average woman to approach her eightieth. The percentage of people over 65 years of age has nearly tripled—from 4 percent at the turn of the century to more than 11 percent today. Even more impressive are the gains for those over the age of 85. In 1940, there were 365,000 people over 85 in the United States; by 1980, the figure was 2.2 million. But along with increased survival comes chronic illness. Although we can expect our parents to live to riper ages, we also anticipate that more of them will suffer a greater number of chronic illnesses for longer pe-

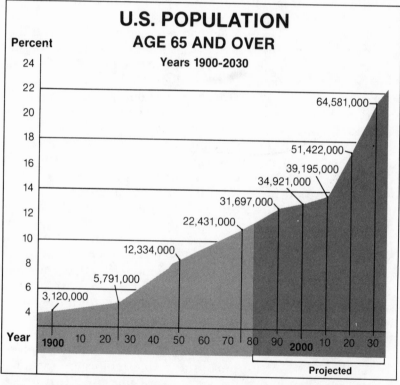

Percentage of American population age 65 and older from 1900 to 1975, with predictions for 1980 to 2030. (From US Bureau of the Census, 1984.)

riods of time than parents of any previous generation.

Meanwhile, exponential advances in technology have brought more rapid and effective communication and transportation and have simultaneously increased and decreased the distances between adult children and their parents. It can take far less time to cover a given geographic distance now than ever before. Just a hundred years ago, a person traveling on horseback might cover the 40-mile journey between New York City and Bridgeport, Connecticut, in five hours. Today, in five hours we cover the 2,400 air miles between New York and Los Angeles. (Of course, it may take another five hours to get to and from the airport with our luggage.) Although more adult children live far away from their parents now than did a hundred years ago, instantaneous telecommunication and jet travel have jolted our concept of distance. Along with such changes, adult children are called upon increasingly to assume greater parenting functions for their parents, whom the illnesses of old age force into dependency. Providing transportation, food, shelter, clothing, and companionship—as well as counsel—has become commonplace for adult children of older parents.

At first, we, the adult children, give willingly of our time, but sooner or later it begins to dawn on us that we, too, may not be far from 60 or 65. How much time is left for us to enjoy all those recreational and vocational pursuits we have patiently postponed year after year after year? When will our time come? And, when it comes—if it comes—will we still be able to enjoy the activities we have dreamed about? Or will we be too old? Too old to go skiing, skating, surfing, or even sailing? Too old to travel to Alaska, to China? Too old and too sick to climb that mountain, to penetrate that cave, to explore that ocean floor, to soar into space? Too old, too sick? Or, perhaps, no longer alive?

Even though men who reached their sixty-fifth birthday in 1980 could expect to live another 14 years, and women another 18 years, many people do not live even to reach 65. How do we know we will not be among those who miss the chance to follow their fancies—miss that chance because we are wedged between two generations grappling for care? We are, indeed, the "sandwich generation," sandwiched between our children's and our parents' needs. Even though most parents, most of their lives, need only tender loving care—a phone call, an errand, a thoughtful note, a helping hand—many of us resent our parents' intrusion into our busy lives.

In the Western world, our parents' generation is living longer and we adult children are having our own children later in life. All of a sudden we find ourselves faced with two generations competing for attention. Many of us in this sandwich generation feel cheated, deprived of self-fulfillment, robbed of the opportunity to indulge in pleasures that we have come to look upon as our rights. And it is not only time—it is money, too. Just when we are about to finish paying for the last of our children's college tuition, when we take stock of our remaining resources and decide that we can risk taking that long-postponed vacation, just then we are called upon to help defray the costly dental work Father needs, or the hearing aid that, according to the doctors, Mother must have. Cutbacks in Medicare, Social Security, and other government programs, together with our parents' own dwindling financial base, have curtailed their access to health care, housing, transportation, and similarly vital resources.

Over the next few decades, as the "baby-boom" generation matures, it may well face a crisis. We have heard the figures many times. Following World War II, an unparalleled increase in the U.S. birth rate occurred. In 1946–47, the number of births in the United States reached a new high—3.9 million, an increase of about a million over the previous year and higher than any prior year since 1900, the year that the United States Bureau of the Census began recording birth statistics. Already, the first of these baby boomers are beginning to confront the responsibilities of parentcare. As they approach middle age, they are fulfilling—more or less successfully—their role of parents to their children. Satisfied or not, they were prepared—at least in some measure—for this role, but they have not been prepared for the role of parents to their parents. None of us has been prepared for that role—not historically, not biologically, not psychologically. How can we cope with this reversal of parenting roles? Throughout this book, we will look at the options. We will suggest paths through the thorny maze of unresolved conflicts, smoldering discord, and ill-understood problems.

In many ways, parenting aging parents resembles parenting young children, but there are important differences. Nowadays, most children born are wanted—and often deliberately planned—by parents who look forward to their birth with eager anticipation. By contrast, most of us lament, rather than delight in, the prospect of having to care for helpless parents; and most parents, too, dread the day when they may be helpless and need their children's care.

Another difference between the helplessness of the child and that of the parent is that the developing child becomes more and more independent, while the deteriorating parent becomes more and more dependent. Moreover, the child knows no world outside the one we provide; our aging parents often bring into our homes a perspective of the world that differs greatly from our own, accompanied by disapproval of the lifestyles we have chosen. The ensuing conflicts put stress on both parent and child. The parent often tries hard to adapt to the child's way of life, to refrain from unfavorable comments, to suppress disparaging gestures. The conflicts are reminiscent of an earlier time, and some of the principles established for dealing with our adolescent children apply to interactions with our aging parents, but others are unique to late-life interactions.

As adult children we often resent having to be the support, strength, and sustenance of the very people upon whom we counted for our own support, strength, and sustenance. Painfully we begin to realize that our pillars of support have crumbled—that, in essence, we have been abandoned by the people whose perennial power we have taken for granted. Reversing the parental relationship calls for definitive separation from the parent, and requires dealing with the anger and sadness that accompany any separation or perceived abandonment. It has been said, "Maybe nature makes old people cantankerous, especially when they are sick, so we won't miss them so much when they die!" What a shocking and frightening thought that is! Frightening not only in its callousness, but also because we fear our parents' death. What will life be like without them? And beyond that thought, their illness and death foreshadow our own. We will have to learn to accept the reality of both—as the generations before ours have done. But we will also have to accept the reality of a new developmental stage in life, that of providing parentcare, of parenting our parents.

The extraordinary stress of caring for children and parents—simultaneously or sequentially—is a phenomenon of our times. Parentcare—unexpected, unplanned, unnatural—is bewildering and oppressing to a multitude of middle-aged and younger adult children who are emotionally and financially unprepared to cope with this reversal of roles. Often the true nature of the problem is disguised. It may surface in marital discord for the adult children, or depression and anxiety in their parents, or both. As long as they are healthy and financially secure, however, parents' needs are often minimal. Susan's story of her mother offers an example in which a small dose of parentcare was all that was needed. Susan's help not only got her mother through a crisis, but it improved her mother's daily life long after the crisis.

"Mom had always been a dependent lady. Dad took care of all their business affairs, paid the bills, did all the driving, never expected or wanted her to work, even when money was tight and it would have helped. Mom devoted her life to taking care of her husband, children, and family. Dad was more outgoing and liked to have his pals over to the house to play cards. Mom always prepared the refreshments, but never seemed interested in the card games.

"Because Dad had done so much for her, I never realized how dependent Mom was in practical ways, until he died. Even though she could hardly face the idea of living alone, she moved into her own apartment, knowing that moving in with us would not work out.

"She was grieving in those early months and did not think she could go on without Dad. I was often tempted to give up, too. I even tried to persuade her to move in with us, but she refused. Yet she was so lonely.

"A letter came from her landlord saying that the rent had not been paid for three months; he wondered if she was planning to give up her apartment. I was shocked to learn that the reason Mom hadn't paid was that she had never written a check! Dad had taken care of all their business affairs. I discovered that he had given me the power of attorney not only to conduct his business and eventually wind it down, but to be able to take care of Mother and her personal affairs after he was gone. It never occurred to me that she wouldn't pay the rent.

"I noticed a slight positive change in Mom's attitude on the day I insisted she learn how to write a check. At first she would only consent to signing her name. It seemed crazy, but I left samples of checks and had her practice. In the beginning, I balanced the checking account to make it easier for her.

"Three other widows lived in her apartment complex. I gave our phone number to her next-door neighbor, who seemed to be the outgoing type. I asked her to please look in on Mom now and then, and not to hesitate to call us at any time. She and the other neighbors began spending time with Mother—they had been reluctant to get too close while Dad was alive. They all liked to play cards, and imagine my amazement to find Mother playing gin rummy one afternoon, keeping score, no less. 'When did you learn to do that?' I teased. 'Well, it really wasn't so hard. I used to watch your father play, but never thought to join in, nor was I asked,' she replied. In ensuing months, she learned to play poker, kaluki, and pan, and was delighted that she knew how to play games I did not. The ladies became good friends. They would check with each other daily, and take turns hosting tea or card games; they would chat outdoors while knitting or sewing, and exchange tidbits about the children and grandchildren.

"They heard about a local senior citizens' club in the neighborhood, but since none of them could drive, they were concerned about getting there. Hiring a cab was out of the question; their generation never paid for such extravagances. I called some of the other daughters, and we arranged a car pool for 'grandmas,' taking turns driving our mothers to and from the club, to lectures, and to outings. In later years, we arranged a guided tour of Hawaii—for many, the dream of a lifetime come true. I saw my mother, at the age of 71, become an independent and confident grown woman. Her conditioning and background had programmed her for her role of wife and mother, without any other expectations, and my father had liked her that way. His death actually gave her an opportunity to change."

Not all of us will be as successful in parentcare as Susan. Yet there are a remarkable number of similar stories. And other widows emerge into the world from the shelter of marriage even without their children's help.

Some parents never require assistance from their children. They are the fortunate few who remain physically and mentally healthy and have the financial resources to take care of themselves throughout their lives. Such parents may even continue to care for their children long into the children's adult years. But families differ. Healthy, wealthy parents may use their money and resources to control their children, or may feel that their children no longer deserve their generosity during adulthood.

Throughout the world, attitudes toward parentcare differ. Certain cultures revere and respect the elderly. In the Orient, the oldest son is expected to care for his parents and bring them to live in his home when they can no longer care for themselves. In early times in Western cultures, a family's wealth was measured by the number of children, who were in turn their parents' chattel and ultimate social security. Children were expected to heed the Fifth Commandment or its variants in other religions: "Honor thy father and thy mother, that thy days may be long upon the land. . . ." Not many of us realize that this commandment is one of the few of the Ten Commandments stated positively, admonishing that "thou shalt" instead of "thou shalt not."

In the United States, before the Social Security Act was signed into law in 1935, adult sons who were gainfully employed were responsible for their parents and could be held accountable for their debts, medical care, and housing. Statutory responsibility of adult children for their needy parents continues to exist in many countries. And, even though parents are no longer entitled by law to their children's care, today most parentcare in the United States is actually delivered by the adult children, especially the daughters. Women have traditionally assumed nurturing tasks, and working as homemakers has given them more flexible time than men. But recent trends for women to enter the work force may increase the burden of parentcare for both men and women.

Not only are more people living longer, thanks to modern medicine, and enjoying more healthful lifestyles, but they are more youthful-looking, more active, and probably healthier now in their sixties and seventies than previous generations were in their fifties. Even so, no one has attained immortality as yet. And one day we realize that our parents, too, are mortal. The signals vary. You may have felt a knot in the pit of your stomach when your father collapsed in the store and the emergency-room doctor told you he had suffered a stroke. Or you may have felt a chill run down your back at the funeral of your last grandparent. Or perhaps it was finding your mother asleep in front of the TV when she should have been watching the baby. Or it may have been that story your father told over and over and over again. Or perhaps his battle with alcohol resurfaced after his first attack of angina. Whatever your signal, it is likely that many parents who live beyond age 85 will eventually become disabled to such an extent as to require significant help.

Small families make the job of parentcare difficult. The problem is most difficult for an only child. But even when there are several children, it is often just one who assumes the major burden of parental care. It may be the youngest child, the one who is with the parents in their later years, the one whom they most resist "letting go," especially if that child is a daughter. A jingle comes to mind that youngsters used to sing while jumping rope: "Give me a son, and he'll go to his wife! Give me a daughter, I'll have her for life!"

Upper-income families and white-collar workers are likely to hire caregivers and provide separate housing for their parents. Eventually, many of these parents end up in nursing homes or other types of extended-care facilities. Are these parents abandoned, rejected, discarded by their children? It is an old fear stated in the Bible: "Cast me not off in the time of old age; forsake me not when my strength faileth" (Psalms 71:9). In fact, most children in the United States today continue to care for their parents until that care exceeds their physical, financial, and emotional resources. It is often only at the time when the caregiving adult child (or that child's spouse or children) becomes overwhelmed, ill, or otherwise incapacitated that the parent requiring total care is placed in a "long-term care facility," such as a nursing home—and, typically, the adult child is plagued by guilt, remorse, and self-reproach. It is startling just how many such incidents are described whenever the topic of parentcare is mentioned.

And what about the low-income worker or the impoverished, unskilled laborer who does not have the funds for extended care? Sometimes the parent can be accommodated in a county or city home, but often only after months or years of waiting to get into one of these overcrowded facilities. What about such parents? Are they better off in the midst of their loving families than are the isolated, socioeconomically more advantaged parents? Sometimes they are; often they are not. These families tend to have few resources. Often the parents are home alone all day, and typically the families find their physical, emotional, and financial resources depleted by the demands arising from the total care requirements of their infirm parents. The families have little money and little time; often nearly every family member is working two jobs just to secure what we in the United States today have come to define as the essentials. The stress may engender disease and family disruption—as it does in families at higher socioeconomic levels. When the situation becomes extreme, the inescapable togetherness in crowded quarters with depleting resources may lead to elder abuse—a phenomenon akin to child abuse, not limited to any one socioeconomic group, and just now beginning to gain public attention. The old, frail parent clamors for attention, exhausting the caregiver's nights as well as days—just like a frail young child. And again, like the frail young child, the frail old parent is defenseless—physically weak, often mentally impaired, isolated from society at large, and totally dependent on the caregiver. More than one-quarter of all persons living beyond the age of 85 need help in walking; more than one in ten needs help in dressing; even worse—embarrassing, if not degrading—one in ten needs help to use the toilet. Beyond that, one in 20 hardly ever gets out of bed and nearly one in 25 has to be fed by someone else.

Of course, such total dependence rarely occurs overnight; usually it develops gradually, the parents becoming just slightly more needy and less providing as the years go by, until one day we realize that we go to them for help less often than they seek assistance from us. A multitude of conflicts unfolds during this transition.

In the following chapters we will explore how some adult children cope with the conflicts, how they deal with this new developmental role of becoming their parents' parents, a role for which none of us has been prepared, either at home or at school. In particular, we will look at the lives of certain adult children and their families, in order to learn from their experiences what may be useful for our own lives.

## 2

# RELATIONSHIPS:
# How Can We Get Along with Our
# Parents?

*Nothing astonishes men so much as common
sense and plain dealing.*

Ralph Waldo Emerson

"My parents still treat me like a child. No matter what decisions Steve and I make, they always have something negative
to say. When it was time for us to buy a house, they gave us a
dozen reasons why the one we chose was not right for us. And
you know how hard it is to find a decent house. The kitchen
wasn't big enough; the location was too far from the school;
we'd need an extra bedroom for the kids; and, of course, it was
too expensive—not a good investment. You can imagine how
nervous they made us feel; we would have been scared enough
without their digs. Whenever they babysit, we find that Mother
has rearranged the kitchen drawers or closets, and Dad has
done the same in the garage. If I protest, they tell me how
lucky I am to have them nearby to help. It's true, but they're
going through *my* closets, *my* kitchen! I was married at nine-
teen and unprepared when my firstborn arrived a year later. I
did rely on them in those early years; I couldn't have done
without them. But now I'm always on edge when they're
around, about to explode, and then I feel like an ungrateful,
mean little girl. Steve's parents are angels compared to them.
I never thought I'd say that about my in-laws."

Do Marilyn's complaints ring a bell? Have you or your
friends had experiences like hers? Have you felt nervous, tense,
torn apart, ready to dissolve into tears or burst into an angry
shouting match with your parents?

Marilyn's situation may not exactly fit your own, but frustration, anxiety, and guilt far too often characterize relationships between adult children and their parents. What can you
do to avoid these feelings? How can you adjust to the changing relationships with your parents? How can you help them

*11*

to adjust, help them see you as an adult? And, as an adult, how can you find new and better ways of getting along with your parents? We suggest that you try the six steps of "The Commonsense Approach to Problem Solving."

## STEP 1. MOOD METER READING

You might think about your emotional responses as if you had a built-in meter registering feelings at any given moment in any situation. The meter swings back and forth throughout the day, but tends to rest in the neutral zone. At one extreme, it registers the most positive feelings: joy, warmth, satisfaction, excitement, pleasure, and contentment. At the other, it measures the most negative feelings: anger, dread, despair, fear, anxiety, and pain. At times, some of these feelings are tolerable, but when they become too intense or too unpleasant, the tendency is to avoid them.

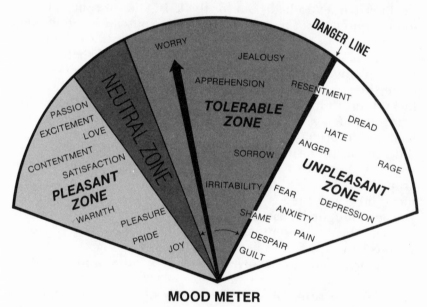

**MOOD METER**

Reading your Mood Meter is a crucial first step. For example, your mother may remind you too often that you are already 35 years old and still have no children, but you may have learned to keep your Mood Meter close to the Neutral Zone by ignoring her remarks and changing the subject. When she makes the same comment in front of your wife, however, you may not be able to suppress the feelings any longer and your meter might then swing past the Danger Line into the Unpleasant Zone. Whenever the meter does move into the Unpleasant Zone, it is time to move on to Step 2.

## STEP 2. PERSONAL REFLECTION

When your Mood Meter has passed over the Danger Line, it is a signal that the time has come to sort out the reasons for the intense negative feeling. Is your meter registering a feeling that originates in the current situation, the present-day problems with your parents? Or is your feeling left over from the past—perhaps resentment dating back to old conflicts with your parents? Or is it some combination of the two—present and past? For example, Marilyn was angry when her mother said in front of Marilyn's guests, "I can never find anything in your kitchen!" To Marilyn, it meant, "You're a lousy housekeeper! You're a slob! Your things are always in a mess. You can't do anything right." And Marilyn was ready to scream or cry. Her feelings were intensified by "skeletons in the closet," by unresolved past conflicts that were mostly forgotten but could be reactivated by related present-day conflicts.

There are several clues that feelings may not simply relate to current, everyday problems. The following are some telltale signs of "closet skeletons":

*The feeling seems too intense for the situation.* Marilyn's mother said the same kinds of things all the time, yet this time her feelings were intolerable.

*Others comment that you are overreacting.* One of Marilyn's guests, for example, an old friend, followed Marilyn into the kitchen and told her to calm down. "You know your mother, she always finds something to criticize. It's nothing to get so upset about."

*You cannot get rid of the feeling.* No matter what you do, it persists. You think about the words—about what you could or should have said. You ruminate and recall other times when you said or did the "wrong" thing—lots of other times. Marilyn would rehearse saying, "Mother, if you continue to rearrange my cabinets, I'm not going to let you stay with the children." She could never get the words out. A good thing, too. So immature a response can only aggravate ill feelings, heighten resentment. It signifies tit-for-tat: "You hurt me, so I'm going to hurt you. I'll get back at you, I'll show you who has the power around here." An eye for an eye and a tooth for a tooth may be an effective way to keep enemies in check, but it is no way to heal old wounds.

*Your emotional reaction seems stereotyped.* Every time her mother walked into any room of her house, Marilyn felt a tightness in her throat and her heart would pound—even before her mother uttered a single word.

When you experience similar telltale signs that you may be reacting to painful experiences suffered in the past, rather than to the present situation alone, take it as your signal to reflect. For example, when Marilyn was told by her friend that she was overreacting, she had been ready to scream; instead, she stopped and reflected. A picture flashed into her mind: she saw herself, when she as 11 years old, just having come home from school, her mother standing in her room, in front of her chest of drawers, with every drawer open. "Why can't I ever find anything in your room?" The anger rose up inside her. The room was a mess—but it was Marilyn's room, not her mother's. She could make a mess in her room if she wanted to; it was none of Mom's business. That was how she had felt then, more than 20 years earlier. And that was how she had continued to feel ever since. Somehow, though, after visualizing that scene, she did not feel so angry anymore.

To get a better idea of how to use personal reflection, it is often helpful to begin by recording some of the feelings that register on our Mood Meters, together with various possible causes, both past and present. For example, Marilyn's list might begin like this:

| Mood Meter Reading | Possible Causes | |
| --- | --- | --- |
| Anger: | PRESENT | PAST |
| Unpleasant Zone | Mother: "I can't find anything in your kitchen!" | Memory (11 years old): Mother in room |

## STEP 3. RECOLLECTION

If you are not doing so already, you may find it helpful to make an inventory of strategies that you remember worked successfully in the past. Many strategies or psychological defense mechanisms can be used to cope with depression, anger, jealousy, pain, and other feelings in the Unpleasant Zone. A few of them are listed in the chart below.

### COMMON PSYCHOLOGICAL STRATEGIES

| Potentially Destructive Strategies | Alternative Terms |
|---|---|
| Pushing it away | Denial, repression, suppression |
| Giving it away | Projection |
| Getting sick | Somatization |
| Redirecting it | Displacement |
| Backing off | Avoidance |
| Not getting angry, getting even | Passive-aggressiveness |
| Loving them to death | Reaction formation |
| Not getting mad, getting sad | Self-blame, internalization |
| Playing the martyr | Masochism |

| Potentially Constructive Strategies | |
|---|---|
| A place for everything and everything in its place | Obsessive-compulsiveness |
| Thinking instead of feeling | Intellectualization |
| Planning ahead, asking for help | Anticipation |
| Laughing instead of crying | Humor |
| Doing something constructive | Sublimation |
| Getting it off your chest | Ventilation |

*Pushing it away (denial, repression, suppression).* One way to deal with a feeling is just to forget it exists. When you refuse to acknowledge the feeling, whether you are doing it consciously or subconsciously (i.e., without immediate awareness), you are using this strategy. If you ignore the fact that your father's memory is deteriorating, you may be denying feelings of fear about what it may mean. Using this defense may protect you from awareness of the fear that he may be developing Alzheimer or some other disease, but it may also endanger your father's health by delaying potential medical treatment.

*Giving it away (projection).* You can avoid accepting your own feelings by passing them on to someone else. Marilyn would have been projecting, had she responded to her mother's criticism by saying, "Mom, you're upsetting Dad when you talk to me that way—that's why he left the room." Dad had actually gone to the bathroom, and it was really Marilyn who was upset and would have liked to leave the room. Because she could not accept her own feelings, she would have been projecting that her father was upset.

*Getting sick (somatization).* Another way to escape a feeling is to get sick. Our bodies often express those emotions that are hidden from our awareness. For example, when you are embarrassed or angry—whether you acknowledge it or not—your face may turn red. And, no doubt, Marilyn's face turned red when her mother rearranged her kitchen cabinets. If she had not responded in some way to release that emotion, within minutes or hours of the incident she might have lifted something and wrenched her back, or had an asthma attack, or cut her finger when she sliced the rolls for the barbecue. Her mother, on the other hand, might have had angina pains, or felt dizzy, or had a migraine headache after Marilyn "talked back" to her. These are ways in which we use physical pain to distract us from emotional pain.

*Redirecting it (displacement).* Have you ever been angry at your husband about an incident that was important to you, perhaps when he forgot to buy you a gift for your anniversary? If you said nothing, but instead exploded with rage when he asked you to do something minor, like buying him a copy of the *Wall Street Journal*—then you were using displacement. Essentially, displacement is redirecting feelings from a primary event to an unrelated situation. To use this strategy, if you are mad at Mom, just yell at your son (instead of your mother) when he comes into the room, "How dare you walk around without shoes! Go and put them on immediately." Or attack your daughter with, "I don't want to see you with that boy

Howie anymore—he drives a motorcycle and hangs around with a tough crowd." Maybe you will scream at the poor dog when he grabs your slippers. All of us use displacement from time to time because it is easier to focus on minor issues than to allow the major one to stir up deeper feelings in us.

*Backing off (avoidance).* Backing off from whatever stirs up the feeling will diminish its intensity. "Whenever Dad gets into his moods, the best thing to do is just stay out of his way." Overuse of this strategy, however, can eventually lead to your severing any continuing relationship with your father. Ignoring your mother's critical remarks may start out as a strategy of denial, but used excessively it becomes avoidance. Sooner or later it needs to be confronted, or the relationship could be jeopardized.

*Not getting angry, getting even (passive-aggressiveness).* For some of us, expressing anger and aggression directly is unacceptable. When instead, we express these feelings indirectly and often ineffectively, we use the passive-aggressive strategy. Maybe your wife "forgot" to buy decaffeinated coffee, so your folks had to "do without" at the family picnic because they could not drink regular coffee. You can be sure your wife is serious about hating those Sunday picnics. Perhaps you were twenty minutes late to drive your in-laws to the airport, and told them it was the traffic on the freeway rather than your tennis game that detained you. (You do not understand why they have to be there an hour before departure time, anyway.) This type of behavior is passive-aggressiveness.

*Loving them to death (reaction formation).* Reaction formation is a term used to describe what we do when we express, often excessively, the opposite of what we feel. Have you ever turned down an invitation to a family dinner because you could not stand being with certain relatives, and ended up inviting them to your house instead? "We would love to have you over." You may be overcompensating for guilt about saying no, or for feeling dislike for your relatives. Do you always voice agreement with your father-in-law about politics, even though you really disagree? Perhaps it has to do with the $3,000 he lent you to help pay your taxes; maybe you feel that you owe him more than just the money.

*Not getting mad, getting sad (self-blame, internalization).* Some of us who cannot express anger openly do not get even, we get sad or depressed. If we do, we may be "hurting ourselves" by turning the feelings inward and getting depressed. Have you ever gotten so angry at one of your parents that you started crying? They may have ticked you off to the point where, if you really expressed your anger, you could have hurt them. Your father needles you about losing your job, and you think to yourself, "If he does that one more time, I'll strangle him!" But the next time he needles you, you do not get mad; instead, you feel sad.

*Playing the martyr (masochism).*   Martyrs are sufferers for a principle. Too often, the principle is really an expression of hostile feelings, and thus effectively induces guilt in someone else. Mothers do not have a monopoly on martyrdom; children can be talented martyrs too. Can you think of the last time you played martyr? How about, "It's okay, Mom, I don't mind giving up my Sunday (even though it is my only day off). I would love to take you shopping."

Although the above strategies are commonly used by most of us, they may be harmful at times, rather than helpful. Sometimes it is a matter of the degree to which the strategy is used. If you always used self-blame, you would be chronically depressed. If your exclusive strategy were somatization, you would never get out of bed.

Sometimes it depends on the context. If your doctor told you that you needed penicillin to treat your pneumonia, and you ignored his recommendation, denying you were sick could endanger your very life. On the other hand, athletes' denial of physical exhaustion and pain can give them that extra burst of energy to help achieve peak performance. Several studies report that heart-attack patients who deny the life-threatening aspects of their illness may be more likely to survive than those who are excessively aware of them. Do cancer patients who survive tend to deny the seriousness of their disease, "willing" themselves to get well? And is denial of physical illness more prevalent among those who get cancer in the first place? These questions remain to be answered.

Although all strategies, when overused or used in the wrong context, can aggravate instead of resolve conflicts, there are certain strategies generally considered more helpful and psychologically more adaptive than those previously discussed. They are listed in the following paragraphs.

*A place for everything and everything in its place (obsessive-*

*compulsiveness*). Some people attempt to ward off anxiety and other unpleasant feelings by keeping life's details in order. Strictly speaking, *obsession* refers to an intrusive thought or idea; *compulsion* to the impulse to act. Many successful people, those who are able to get a job done, have some degree of obsessive-compulsiveness. When excessive, however, the strategy can be crippling.

*Thinking instead of feeling* (*intellectualization*). If you do not want to "feel" something, you can "think" something in its place: "When Dad was hospitalized with chest pain, I was too busy managing his business to feel scared. Once he got better and returned to work, that's when I went to pieces." Often this strategy is useful temporarily in helping us to get an important job done. Used too long or too often, however, it puts us at risk of becoming excessively detached from our feelings.

*Planning ahead* (*anticipation*). One way to deal with worry about future events is to plan. Sometimes this strategy helps us to prepare realistically. For example, knowing your father always falls asleep after family dinners, you could plan to bring some work or reading along so you will not get angry at him during his nap. But anticipation, too, can become an unhealthy preoccupation, as when worry about the future makes people lose sight of the present.

*Asking for help* (*anticipation*). This is another form of anticipation. Try asking for help; you may be pleasantly surprised. In our society we have become accustomed to avoid asking for what we want. Yet we expect others to know, as if they could read our minds. Since they usually do not read our minds, they often fail to give us what we want from them and leave us disappointed, angry, frustrated, resentful, sad. We blame them, and they do not even suspect that we do—or why. We needlessly endanger our friendships as well as our good relations with our parents for want of asking.

*Laughing instead of crying* (*humor*). When we use humor, we openly express a feeling without much personal discomfort or unpleasant effects on others—provided, of course, the humor succeeds. Norman Cousins wrote a popular book based on the premise that laughter is a good form of medicine. Sometimes humor provides welcome relief from a tense situation. After everyone has tasted Mom's "slightly spicy" soup, you ask sheepishly, "So, are we having fire extinguishers for dessert?" Sometimes humor conveys sadness. Often it is an effective way of defusing anxiety and bringing people together.

*Doing something constructive (sublimation).* Probably the most efficient and creative strategy is to redirect or sublimate forbidden impulses into socially acceptable channels. Football and tennis are examples of games that help the players sublimate aggressive impulses. Sometimes housework or heavy gardening may function in the service of sublimation. Having the family get into a game of Trivial Pursuit the evening when you and Mom "went after each other," could have been another example of sublimation.

*Getting it off your chest (ventilation).* During the 1960s, many people viewed this strategy, which sanctions open expression of our feelings, as the panacea for social conflict. Even though telling others how we feel may clarify that feeling for us and lead to mutual understanding, it does not always result in conflict resolution.

Nor is there any guarantee that using any of the other strategies will automatically resolve every problem. We need to have a repertoire of defense strategies available to us, and be flexible enough to use those most appropriate to each situation. How can we do that? We can start with a Commonsense Checklist, like the one at the end of this chapter. It holds answers to the questions, What worked in the past? What did not work? If nothing worked and you have not come upon any new strategies, this may be the time to consult a friend, a family member in whom you can confide, or a professional, such as a psychiatrist, to help you recognize and cope with painful emotions.

Once you have assembled a selection of useful strategies in the Commonsense Checklist, you are ready for Step 4 of the Commonsense Approach to Problem Solving—reassessment of the situation.

## STEP 4. REASSESSMENT

This is the step we take to reassess a situation in terms of our expectations and their congruence—or incongruence—with reality. On a practical level we may ask ourselves, "How much am I capable of giving to my parents? How much do I feel comfortable taking from them?" For example, if you are annoyed by what you perceive as your parents' incessant demands that you spend more time with them, how much time are you willing to give—maximum and minimum? Eight hours each week? Zero hours?

Reassessment involves reflection and understanding of your own feelings about giving and taking. How much are you willing to give? How much is available from others who may be able to help? A crucial part of reassessing the situation is to learn about available resources (also see chapter 12). You may want to make two lists when carrying out this step: one list is of your parents' specific needs, and the other is of potential resources to meet those needs. Can others in the family help out—grandchildren, siblings, cousins? What about social services, community programs, friends, or neighbors?

Julia is a 54-year-old divorcée who has always been the "perfect daughter," whether it was picking up the folks from the airport or taking care of Dad's daily needs—shopping, laundry, meals—when Mom was in the hospital for surgery. Julia, rather than her younger sister Rachel, did all the work, partly because Rachel lived several hundred miles away. When Rachel's job forced her to move back to their hometown, she still failed to chip in, and Julia found herself resenting Rachel's apparent unavailability (Mood Meter Reading: resentment, anger). Julia recalled that when she was in her teens, her younger sister had seemed to get their parents' affection and attention because she was "so pretty," without having to do anything, while Julia had had to earn it by being "so good" (Personal Reflection). She had been unaware of this memory until now—at least on a conscious level—having learned to do everything for her parents automatically, without thinking about it. In fact, she would object whenever Rachel did attempt to help out (Recollection). Through Reassessment, Julia realized that Rachel indeed could help out now, that Julia no longer needed to compete with her sister, and that Rachel's help would not only relieve her burden of parentcare, but her jealousy and resentment as well, since she would no longer be doing more than her fair share.

Reassessing the situation often involves setting boundaries, something we all do; in fact, many animals do it instinctively. The next time you are at the beach, observe the sea gulls establishing their feeding territories. If one bird intrudes into another's territory, it creates havoc. We humans do the same with our relationships. The trouble is, too often we fail to personally reflect and explicitly establish boundaries, needs, and desires.

Depending on the particular problem at hand, the specifics of how you reassess a given situation will vary. Reassessment may not be a simple step; it requires some degree of self-knowledge. You have to know what, in fact, you do want. Many people reach an impasse at this step. Sometimes fine-tuning our abilities for the first three steps (Mood Meter Reading, Personal Reflection, and Recollection) will sharpen our skills at Reassessment. If you still get stumped, this might be a time to consult a friend or professional.

## STEP 5. NEGOTIATION

Now that you have identified your own feelings, and have at least begun to sort out the sources of those feelings—now that you have some idea of how much you are willing to give to your parents, and how much you are comfortable in taking from them—it is time to talk. Negotiation is an active process—not only in that you and your parents are telling each other how you feel and how you perceive the situation, but also in the way you listen. And don't forget to listen and listen and listen some more. Don't think you really know how your parents feel until you have heard them out.

*Active listening* means that (1) you listen to what your parents are saying, (2) you listen to your own feelings respond to what your parents are saying, and (3) you actively refrain from blurting out your initial response; you wait to hear them out fully, and think before you speak. Two thousand years ago, Publilius Syrus admonished, "Keep the golden mean between saying too much and too little."

Because negotiation will involve dialogue with your parents, you may need to return to some of the earlier steps in the Commonsense Approach to Problem Solving. For example, your mother may tell you again, during the negotiation step, that it is about time you settled down and got married. Her remark might swing your Mood Meter over the Danger Line; if so, you will need to return to Step 1, Mood Meter Reading. You may then need to identify the feeling, recall strategies effective in the past in dealing with that feeling and so on.

## STEP 6. COMPROMISE

Successful negotiation results in reasonable compromise. Even though both we and our parents will have to give up something, many conflicts can be resolved in such a way that both parties are satisfied. Each has gained and each has given up something. This last step may seem self-evident: "Of course, we've got to compromise." The trouble is that too often you may assume beforehand that either you or they must give in. "Haven't they been the ones who gave in all those years when we were growing up?" Or maybe *you* always gave in, and they were rigid and uncompromising. Regardless of your old, familiar ways of relating, you and your parents have changed over the years. Your roles now differ. If you expect and anticipate that you yourself will be the one to give up the most, even if you never have done so in the past, the results of your negotiation may be less painful than if you arrive at that conclusion unprepared.

Now that we've described the six steps, let's take one more look at them:

1. Mood Meter Reading—What am I feeling?
2. Personal Reflection—Why do I feel this way?
3. Recollection—How did I deal with the feeling before?
4. Reassessment—What am I willing to give and give up?
5. Negotiation—It is time to talk and actively listen.
6. Compromise—Prepare to give up something, to give in.

Your parents, too, may find the Commonsense Approach to Problem Solving a useful one. Remember, they have their own Mood Meters and strategies of coping, probably similar to your own. Marilyn's meter jumped into the Unpleasant Zone when her mother rearranged her kitchen drawers. Her mother's Mood Meter may have entered the same zone when, for example, Marilyn commented on her erratic driving.

For some people, the six steps may seem either too rigid or too simplistic. But they can be helpful guides until you become familiar with your feelings and the strategies available to deal with them. The six steps can also be helpful in situations not involving your parents. In fact, most psychotherapists and counselors use some variation of these steps in their practices. They can be useful tools to help us through many a conflict.

To start, write down the six steps, keeping them handy in your wallet or pocket or next to the telephone. Remember them as you read through the rest of the book, and as we examine in more detail the dilemmas, the joys, and the pains adult children experience when they care for their parents.

## COMMONSENSE CHECKLIST

| Situations that swing my Mood Meter into the Unpleasant Zone | Strategies that have *not* worked for me | Strategies that have worked for me |
|---|---|---|
| 1. | | |
| 2. | | |
| 3. | | |
| 4. | | |
| 5. | | |

# 3

# TIME:
# How Can We Stretch It?

*We always have time enough if we will but
use it aright.*
                    Johann Wolfgang von Goethe

Goethe's quotation may have been true in its time, but is
it true today? The late twentieth century is quite different from
the early nineteenth. No matter how we juggle our schedules,
we never seem to have enough time. Do you have enough
hours in the day to complete all your chores and have time for
pleasures, too? Have you ever made out a list of "Things to do
today," ended up with 23, and found that the whole day went
by and you barely finished four or five? Do you feel as though
you are being crushed by demands from your employer,
spouse, friends, children, community, and parents, too? Have
you ever forgotten to wear your wristwatch and panicked? How
can you give time to everyone and still have some for yourself? Where do all the hours go? Do you remember the robot-
like figure of Charlie Chaplin in the early silent films, rushing
from place to place, nonstop, expressionless, like a mechanical, wound-up doll? Do *you* ever feel like that?

Alvin Toffler defines the title of his book *Future Shock* as
"a time phenomenon, a product of the greatly accelerated rate
of change in society." He is concerned about the social and
psychological effects of the technological revolution that char-
acterizes our modern culture. His premise is that this accelerated and extraordinary "pace of life" deeply influences our
behavior and elicits strong and contrasting reactions. Some
relish the pace; others hate and resist it. He maintains that this
pace of life divides humanity and triggers "bitter misunder-
standing between parent and child, between Madison Avenue
and Main Street, between men and women, between American and European, between East and West." Many cultures and
countries also resist that pace. Our Mexican neighbors are often
ridiculed for their *mañana* temperament: "What's the rush? You
can do it tomorrow." That is their attitude, in contrast to the

Yankee motto, "Never put off until tomorrow what you can do today." Have you taken a look at your schedule lately? If you did, you might find that your schedule made you anxious, and that anxiety could be illustrated on a Time Meter, not unlike the Mood Meter. As you have more and more to do, your Time Meter swings to the right and, like the Mood Meter, registers greater emotional discomfort. Only a few hours of free time? A few minutes? No time? Anxiety . . . dread . . . panic!

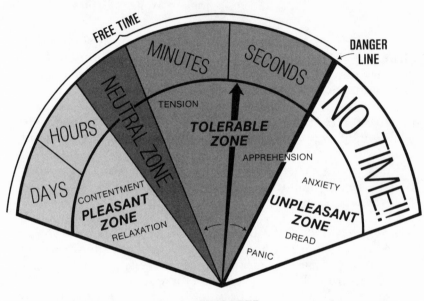

**TIME METER**

Finding time to spend with parents creates one of our greatest sources of anxiety. Parents often seem to complain that they don't see enough of their adult children, and those children end up feeling guilty if they do not respond to the complaints. Donna, a 45-year-old housewife, certainly felt that way. As Donna describes it, "When I was a child, my mother cooked, cleaned, shopped, sewed, ironed, baked, and always had time to sip some tea or sit on the porch or chat with a neighbor. Sure, her house was smaller than mine, but I have all the modern time-saving devices from washing machine to corn popper to microwave, and I don't have a minute to myself." Where do all the hours go? Today, 24-hour schedules include endless chores without a minute to spare for errors, break-downs, illness, or other emergencies. "There's always something to be done," Donna continues. "Car pools, errands, marketing, Little League, orthodontists, doctors, cleaners, music lessons—and that's for everybody else. I'm the last one on the list, and there's just no time left for me."

Working mothers report even more complicated grievances. "I have to work full-time because we need the money," says Marlene, a 38-year-old mother of two and vice-president at a savings-and-loan. "But I'm still expected to do the marketing, cooking, and cleaning, and look after Jack and the kids—and be available to my parents, too. It's like having two full-time jobs, and I'm a bitch because of it!" For women in this century, there has been a dramatic increase in time spent working outside the home. In 1900, the average number of years a woman spent in the labor force was 6.3. By 1982 that figure had more than quadrupled, to 27.5 years.[1] Today, most married women are homemakers *and* maintain paid jobs. Women are also usually the ones to care for their elderly parents as well as their husband's parents. How can these women find time enough for their husbands, children, and jobs, and for their parents too? And how do they withstand the emotional pressures caused by the time demands of such busy lives?

Many parents dread being dependent on their adult children, asking for their attention and time, but often they have no alternative. For others, their dependency is only temporary. Henry and Mary offer their point of view: "We recently moved to Atlanta from New York City to be near our children," Mary reported. "We don't like being so dependent on our children and grandchildren, but we're lonely and have no friends here yet. We decided that as we got older, and as Henry reached 65 and was forced to retire, we wanted to be near our youngest child and his family. Sometimes we feel like intruders when we hang around our son's house on weekends. We don't know what the future holds in store for us, and we're frightened."

"When I was forced to leave my job," Henry added, "the move seemed right. New York has been our home all our lives, but our parents are gone, our friends and relatives are retiring and moving south or out to California. What are we supposed to do?" These parents, in relatively good health and accustomed to their children's absence, may become more independent and spend time on their own as they adjust to their new environment. Others, who are ill or handicapped, may not fare as well.

Another couple, Bob and Katherine, expressed their concerns: "Our son and his wife keep themselves and their children busy to avoid us. We gave them everything, we worried about their health, their loves and their psyches, we lived through their 'hippie' period. They were supposed to be gentle 'flower children.' We never thought they would be so insensitive when we needed them. It was so different with our own parents. We loved them, respected them, worried about them, and took care of them until they died. And they never had much time for us. They were too busy working just to keep us fed, clothed, and sheltered. Now that we need our children, they're not around. It's not fair!"

Fair or not, the cultural and moral changes of the past two decades have been more rapid than those of the preceding two centuries. Both young and old are still struggling to adjust. For most of us, the time pressures have become overwhelming. More than 200 years ago, Benjamin Franklin warned us, "Dost thou love life? Then do not squander time, for that is the stuff life is made of." We need to reexamine our day-to-day schedules, our lifestyles, and our plans for the future. As our children grow into adulthood, the amount of time we need to spend with them will gradually diminish. By contrast, as our parents get older, as their friends die or move away, and as they become less able to care for themselves, the amount of time we need to devote to them will increase. Because adulthood is delayed in the young, demands from both generations often overlap.

That is your dilemma—how will you handle it? When, oh when, will there be time for you? When will you ever get to read those books you put aside? When will you get to attend all those classes you have postponed? When will you ever take those dream vacations? When will it be your turn? "Time's running out!" Sandwich Generation, indeed!

The "aged dependency ratio" (i.e., the percentage of persons age 65 and over in relation to persons age 18 to 64) is expected to double in the next 50 years. But don't panic! It may not be as bad as you think. Actually, your parents are in better shape than their parents were; they'll live longer and remain healthier than parents of previous generations. They may even achieve their greatest successes in their later years. At age 76, Ronald Reagan is the oldest U.S. President ever. The late Henry Fonda, at the same age, won an Academy Award for his performance in *On Golden Pond*. In his nineties, George Burns still entertains millions. We hope that our parents will live that long and remain healthy and independent. In reality, however, few parents do. Their time is limited, and its limits may impinge on our relationships with our parents.

That is what happened to Donna, the housewife who complained about time pressures. Her parents and their need for her attention were at the core of her anxiety about time. When she took a few moments to reflect on her life, Donna was pleased. She and Jim had been reasonably happy for their 19 years of marriage. His law practice was going well. She enjoyed her job, and their three children were "good" kids. But her doctor had referred her to a psychiatrist because of a rash. To her, it was just a nuisance, an itchy rash on the upper part of her body. But her doctor thought it was neurodermatitis, a rash caused by nervousness. Still, Donna knew she had to do something, because none of the medications had worked. She felt anxious when she first saw the psychiatrist. Before she knew it, she had told him of frequent headaches, difficulty in sleeping, and feelings of depression. "I'm in a mental vacuum," she lamented, "and I feel like it's going to consume me. I'm impatient and short-tempered these days—I'm not my usual self." She barely alluded to her parents. She did, however, have a list of complaints about her husband's neglect and lack of understanding.

Donna reported her activities on a typical weekday as follows:

6:30–8:30 A.M.: Showers, dresses, prepares lunches for children and self; makes breakfast for everyone; drives car pool.

8:30–9:30 A.M.: Returns home; loads dishwasher with breakfast dishes; makes beds, calls parents to check on their health and hear what they need that day; Mother requests a ride to doctor in afternoon; off to her job in car—a 15-to-20-minute drive. (No allowance for a possible traffic delay or flat tire, or an extra-long conversation with Mother.)

9:30 A.M.–12:30 P.M.: Works as a legal secretary for semi-retired attorney.

12:30–1:30 P.M.: Lunch hour—shops for clothing for children.

2:00–3:15 P.M.: Leaves work early to pick up Mother for doctor's appointment. While waiting at office for 2:15 appointment, she balances her checkbook, reads mail, writes overdue letter. Doctor delayed—Donna leaves to pick up 3:30 car pool.

3:30–5:00 P.M.: Delivers children in car pool; drops off Jeff, her 13-year-old, at orthodontist. Picks up Mother and returns her to her home; Dad gives her a list of errands for the following day, since his car will be out of commission for another week. Stops at market. Picks up Jeff, who complains because she is late.

5:00–6:30 P.M.: Prepares dinner; helps Benjie, her 9-year-old, with homework while making salad; shortens dress for Amy, her 11-year-old; makes various phone calls; sets table.

6:30–7:15 P.M.: Serves the family dinner the minute Jim arrives home from work. (He is annoyed because she forgot to pick up his shirts at the laundry, and complains about the hard day he had at the office.) Takes call from Mother, who is angry about Donna's father, her new medicine, and her "inconsiderate" doctor. Donna takes a sedative, and by the time she returns to the table, everyone has finished eating. Jim leaves for a meeting, and she begins to cry, and spends the next 15 minutes yelling at Benjie for not finishing his homework.

7:15–11:00 P.M.: Cleans the kitchen. Takes several phone calls, and finally sits down to watch TV while folding clothes from dryer. Jim returns from meeting feeling talkative and amorous. She rejects him, partly out of anger, partly because of fatigue.

Reports of other days were monotonously similar. Sunday always meant her parents visited, wanting to spend time with the grandchildren. They came early, stayed late, and usually brought their laundry to do so they would not have to go to the Laundromat. Whenever a crisis occurred, such as her parents or the children getting sick, her days were even worse. Sometimes she was jealous of Jim; he seemed to have so much more free time than she did.

Jim had his own view of their situation. When he went with

Donna to her psychiatrist for a joint session, he complained that he felt his needs came after Donna's parents', and after the children's. As a result, he worked longer hours, indulged in sports, and fell asleep exhausted before the TV most nights. He said he had never told Donna how he felt because "after all, my in-laws have been good to us, and Donna loves her parents like crazy." He added sadly, "I don't know why Donna is so unhappy all the time." Jim said that many times he had offered to take Donna away for a vacation alone, even a short weekend, suggesting that she was tired and overworked. "She always has an excuse," he said. "Her folks would be hurt if she left, or she worries about the children needing her."

Donna was depleted and depressed; she seemed unable to care for her own needs, and was unable to say no. She was the epitome of the woman described by Betty Friedan in *The Feminine Mystique*, the woman who accepts her responsibility as the provider of happiness and fulfillment for her family, without concern for her own growth or needs. The happy housewife, mother, and daughter roles were supposed to be enough—and despite the women's movement of the late sixties heralded by Betty Friedan's book, most women continue to accept this philosophy, and men reinforce it.

If Donna were to use the six-step Commonsense Approach to Problem Solving, she might do it as follows:

*Step 1. Mood Meter Reading.*

Donna would realize that her meter wavered all during the morning while she rushed around to complete her unreasonable schedule. It settled in the Unpleasant Zone when her mother told her that she needed a ride to the doctor. Donna neglected to pay attention to those feelings.

Donna's Mood Meter passed over the Danger Line again when her mother called at dinner. Donna ignored her signals and displaced her anger onto Benjie and Jim—a common but ineffective strategy (displacement). She might have been better off politely curtailing the conversation, telling her mother that she was eating and would call back later. This would have given her time to move on to:

*Step 2. Personal Reflection.*

After dinner, with Personal Reflection, she would realize

she was angry and that her strategies were not working. What were the possible reasons for her discomfort? Her husband and children had criticized her when she made every effort to please them; no one had helped her with household chores; her dinner had been interrupted by phone calls; she was not getting her reward for being a "good girl," for doing for others; she allowed herself to be manipulated; she ignored her needs. Some feelings were also connected to the past. They had to do with her realizing that she always acted as an intermediary for her mother. She recalled her teens, when she had often fought with her father because of her mother's constant complaining about him. Realizing that her feelings had to do with both the past and present, she moved on to:

### Step 3. Recollection.

Donna was using a number of strategies that seemed ineffective—getting sick (she had neurodermatitis), avoidance (she took sedatives), and self-blame (she got sad instead of mad), to name a few. What alternative strategies could she recall?

Donna did remember that back in high school, if she had too much homework and asked for their help, Mom and Dad would give her a hand. Mom would iron her clothes and pack her lunch, and Dad would often pick her up after school so she would not have to spend the extra time needed to walk. Could she possibly *ask* her parents for help now? Of course she could. They were always happiest when they were doing something for her or the children. Could she ask her father to help with the car pools and her mother to baby-sit once in a while?

Could she ask for more help from her husband and children? She knew her job was important to her; it gave her a sense of self-worth as well as extra spending money. Was she overloading herself so that she did not have to be with her husband, children, or parents? At this point she took out her Commonsense Checklist and recorded her feelings and strategies.

## DONNA'S COMMONSENSE CHECKLIST

| Situations that triggered Donna's Mood Meter | Strategies that did *not* work for Donna | Strategies that did work for Donna |
|---|---|---|
| Nonstop schedule; Mother's unexpected doctor's appt.; Dad's car out of use; car pool deadlines (anxiety). | Got sick (somatization)—neurodermatitis, headaches, insomnia. | Avoided martyrdom, asked for help. |
| Incomplete, rushed shopping; Jeff's complaint about Donna's lateness; Dad's requests (resentment). | Pushed it away (denial), ignored feelings. | Did something constructive (sublimation), went to work. |
| Continuous chores—dinner, laundry, phone, Amy's request for hem, Jim's complaint re shirts (guilt). | Loved them to death (reaction formation), tried to do too much for everyone. | Sat down and talked to family (open communication). |
| Disruptive call from Mother during dinner; complaints about doctor and Father (discomfort and irritability). | Pushed it away (suppression), took sedative (avoidance). | Set limits, rearranged timing of mother's telephone calls. |
| Dinner interrupted; Jim and children finish dinner without Donna (depression). | Got sad, not mad (self-blame), began to cry. | Talked to family, asked for help, set limits. |
| Jim and children leave Donna alone at table (anger). | Yelled at kids, rejected husband (displacement). | Planned ahead (anticipation), reorganized chores, communicated, got professional help. |

*Step 4. Reassessment.*

Donna had never assessed how much time she was willing to spend with or for her parents. Thinking about it, she knew she was not willing to give up the daily phone call. She liked talking to her parents; she did want to know how they were doing. As she thought about them, she wondered if things had gotten worse since Dad's retirement. Were there, perhaps, some activities in the community that could help to fill some of Dad's time—and possibly something for her mother, too? Then her parents would not have to count so heavily on her. Could she ask her brothers to call or visit more often? Could she ask her parents to baby-sit, which would allow her to take a weekend with Jim?

Donna decided that she would be willing to devote one or two hours a week to helping her parents with chores—shopping, doctors' appointments, any emergencies—and she wanted to spend another three to four hours with them just for pleasure time. But she would have to get those hours from some other place, and that would require a rearrangement of her schedule. She would have to get Jim and the children to pitch in with household chores, and her father to share some car pooling.

Adding up the hours saved, she came up with five to six extra hours each week. The more she thought about it, the more Donna realized she had options, and the possibilities challenged and exhilarated her. She was now ready to move on to:

*Step 5. Negotiation.*

Donna still had anxiety about confronting her parents. She and her parents talked often, but rarely would they speak candidly about their feelings. Donna began by saying, "Mom, Dad, I need to talk to you about something that has been bothering me. [She identifies her own needs rather than blaming her parents.] You know I love you both and want to be available to you as much as I can [a positive statement preceding a negative one], but I'm having trouble juggling all my hours; I'm exhausted and cranky all the time because I never seem to have enough time for everyone [a clear statement of her problem]. I still need some suggestions from you, so that we can all get what we need from each other [she points out their worth]." This kind of approach is more likely to elicit constructive communication than would accusing her parents of being too demanding, but it must be combined with *active listening*.

Though her parents' first comments were critical, they eventually were relieved by her words. Through active listening, Donna learned something about her parents. Dad seemed to feel that he was not worth much without his job. He felt clumsy, unneeded, and sad. They argued and nitpicked all day. Mother had been her own person, to do as she pleased, visit with friends, shop, not account to anyone. Suddenly, Dad was around all day; she felt guilty if she left him alone, and angry when she stayed with him.

These talks did not end after one meeting, and the resolutions came about slowly. Donna realized that her parents had felt a great loss and change in their lives with her father's retirement, and that they might need some extra attention until they got over the crisis and adjusted to their new lifestyle.

### Step 6. Compromise.

By learning how to listen to one another in Step 5 (Negotiation), Donna and her parents agreed to talk about problems as they came up in the future, rather than avoid them. Donna asked her parents not to call between the hours of 5:00 and 8:00 P.M., except in a true emergency. Her parents asked to see the grandchildren at least a few hours a week, and asked Donna to let them do something for her and her family every now and then. By reorganizing her time and asking for help from her husband, children, and parents, Donna found that she spent less time with her parents than before, but it was time they all enjoyed. She gained some leisure time for herself, and minor emergencies no longer turned into crises. So the six steps of the Commonsense Approach to Problem Solving not only helped Donna improve her time management, but also strengthened her relationship with her parents.

In addition to the Commonsense Approach, what can we do to make the most of a 24-hour day, to decrease the many demands on our time? Also, knowing that our parents will not be around forever, how can we organize our schedules more effectively so that we have more time for them now? Here are a few additional hints that have helped others in the struggle with tight daily timetables.

*See it in writing.* Write down what you actually do each day. At first, this may seem to be a trivial exercise; you may think "I know what I do each day—I don't need to write it down." You may feel as if you really do not do all that much, that your day is made up only of "little things." But little things add up.

Writing down your schedule will put your time into a different perspective. You may be surprised by how much you are trying to do. Be sure to include in this itemized list not only actual activities but also all those things you promised you would do, for yourself as well as for others—all the things on your mental "to do" list. Remember that new sprinkler system you promised yourself for the past three months you would install? Or, what about cleaning your parents' garage? It is essential that your list include such promised activities because they weigh down your "psychological time schedule"; they are on your mind, nagging away, contributing to your time pressure and feelings of guilt.

*Set priorities.* If you know you are pressed for time, you are left with one rational solution: decide what is most important and least important, and what should go in between. This process, unfortunately, may necessitate your uttering one of the syllables in the English language that seems to be the most difficult for active, ambitious people: "No." Get used to it. Adult children need to say it often.

Setting priorities is difficult for a host of reasons. Sometimes we do not want to disappoint others. Sometimes we really do like doing what we ought to give up. Specifying priorities involves admitting to ourselves that we have limits, that we can do only so much.

A list of "set priorities" may look something like this:

*Priorities for week of May 2:*

1. Personal needs—get at least three hours of exercise, walking, tennis, or aerobics.
2. Spouse's needs—set aside time to go to the theater with him/her.
3. Job requirements—finish personnel report by Thursday.
4. Parents' needs—pick up bookshelf for Dad.
5. Community service—try to get neighbors to attend fund-raiser.

Your specific priority list will be different. The important thing is to have one, and to realize that it will almost always be in flux. From day to day and week to week, the order of priorities will change. And, as you become more adept at using the six steps of the Commonsense Approach to Problem Solving, the order may begin to look altogether different. Regardless of the changes, a ranked list will more often than not help you set the priorities that are best for you.

If ordering priorities is not enough, you may have to go on to:

*Rearrange.* For example, a 48-year-old college professor, with all his activities written down, mapped them out geographically. He saw that with a few appointment switches he could cut 45 minutes each week from his commuting time. He also noticed that one of his weekly shopping errands could easily be done during his Friday lunch break—one less trip, 30 minutes saved. Small stuff? Perhaps, but it adds up. He began to notice that his parents' demands on weekends irritated him less than before. He was beginning to enjoy his more leisurely schedule, so he went on to try some other changes, such as:

*Invest.* Sometimes investing time or money or both *now* can pay off later. What can you invest in? What about a new bicycle for your son so he can get himself to school, and you can drop out of the car pool? What about that home computer your kids have been pestering you to get? It might save time balancing the accounts. What about a bookkeeper? Could you afford one for a few hours every couple of weeks? What about some taxi vouchers for your folks? What about a telephone for your car? It may sound extravagant, but in the long run it may save you much-needed time and really be a bargain. Time invested in the Commonsense Approach to Problem Solving saves time lost to frustration, hurt, and anger.

*Make time for yourself.* Of course, you can't literally *make* time, but you can set aside time, on a regular basis, just for you. Take 20 minutes each morning as a quiet time—time to be alone, to meditate, to take a walk, to exercise, to think. Some people may feel that this will only create more pressure by taking up extra time. On the contrary, quiet time often creates more time for you by recharging your emotional battery, which allows you to be more productive the rest of the day. Give it a try. You may gain more than just time. You may gain some peace of mind, some energy, and the opportunity to get to know yourself just a little better. And, as you get to know yourself better, you cannot help but get to know others better, too—your spouse, your friends, your children, and yes, even your parents.

When it comes to time, there are indeed limits. Given only 24 hours each day, the six steps of the Commonsense Approach to Problem Solving can be an effective tool in helping you to make the most of your time.

"We always have time enough if we will but use it aright." Perhaps Goethe's quotation remains true even today. To us it makes sense . . . *common* sense.

---

### REASSESSING YOUR TIME SITUATION

- Think through the six-step "Commonsense Approach to Problem Solving."
- See it in writing: write out your weekly schedule to get a realistic perspective of how you spend your time.
- Set priorities: practice saying no.
- Rearrange: try to reorganize your commitments creatively.
- Invest: spend time or money now on something that will save you time later.
- Make time for yourself: get off the treadmill at least once a day.

# 4

# MONEY:
# How Do We Use It?

*It is not money as is sometimes said, but the
love of money that is the root of all evil.*

Nathaniel Hawthorne

Between adult children and their parents, money can be a
symbol of power or strength, a means of expressing love and
caring—or a symptom of festering emotional wounds. If you
and your parents can begin to ask a few questions about
money—questions about the expectations, needs, and resources each of you has—then you may find that money is no
longer a "root of evil" in your relationship, but rather a source
of mutual support and gratification.

Yet we cannot make up our minds about money. Is it a root
of evil or a source of bounty? Money can represent so much or
so little to us; and it can generate intense feelings, both positive and negative. Money is a symbol of the things we can acquire with it. Some of these are fundamental to our survival—
food, shelter, safety, and comfort. Is it evil to want to survive,
to feed ourselves, to have shelter? Why is there such disdain for
money? Perhaps it is because so many of us desire so much of
it, much more than we can have. Do we feel guilty about having it? Why do we want so much money? What can money buy?

It can buy a lot. Money can buy life itself. The federal
government spends more than 2 billion dollars each year on
dialysis for 80,000 patients with kidney failure—adding
hundreds of days to their lives. For approximately $130,000,
the patient with liver disease can purchase an unknown number of additional days through transplant surgery. To the
transplant recipient, money means life; to the donor, it can
mean profit. "KIDNEY FOR SALE—from 32-yr-old Caucasian female in excellent health. Write to P.O. Box 654." So read a
classified ad in a New Jersey newspaper.

Money can buy power, as demonstrated by the Rockefel-
ler, Carnegie, and Kennedy families. Money can buy time.

"Remember that time is money," Ben Franklin advised young tradesmen in the eighteenth century. Money can also buy all those things that make life more pleasurable: that refrigerator with the automatic icemaker, that vacation in Tahiti, or that new sports car. And money can be used to manipulate and control, especially in families.

Our society's economic values often seem bizarre. Rock stars are paid in millions, policemen in thousands. Today, first-year professional basketball players are paid an average of $200,000, while public school teachers earn approximately one-tenth that amount. In 1984, the cosmetic industry's product shipments totaled $12.3 billion, a hefty sum in comparison to the $3.4 billion spent on our children's school lunch program, or the $60 million the federal government spent on Alzheimer disease research in 1986.

Defined as "a medium of exchange, a measure of value, or a means of payment," money takes on the importance of what we value in our lives. Tocqueville observed that he knew of no country "where the love of money has taken stronger hold on the affections of men" than it had in the United States of America. That statement seems to have lost none of its validity in the 150 years since it was made. Today we can ask people about their most intimate thoughts and activities, but we still cannot ask them how much money they make. That is considered rude and makes us feel uncomfortable.


## MONEY AND PARENTS

Since money has so much meaning in our lives, it will certainly play an important part in our relationships with our parents. While most of us were growing up, our parents took care of our financial security, from comic books to college tuition, from our first allowance to our first automobile. Did they give us too much, or too little? How many strings were attached? Did they make us feel guilty about taking money? Did they feel guilty about not giving us enough?

As our parents get older and earn less, we may find ourselves giving them money. Remember how good you felt that first time you treated your parents to dinner, or bought them a gift? Too often, the giving and taking are not simple matters between children and their parents. Francis Bacon said, "The joys of parents are secret, and so are their griefs and fears." We might say the same about children. Some children may even fear their parents' money.

Parents may use money to control us. It may be the last weapon they have, now that we are adults. "If you don't move back to Houston, we'll write you out of the will!" "We spent all that money on your education, and now you want to be a rock musician? You can forget about the loan for your condo." Now that we are adults, they can no longer restrict our television watching or impose curfews, but they can withhold the money. In today's society, many children remain at least partly dependent on their parents for financial support far into adulthood. Today's children may accept such support when they are already well into their twenties or even their thirties. With the escalating cost of housing in urban centers, there are ever fewer young couples who can afford a first mortgage without help from their families. And they face all the emotional complications that accompany such help.

Our parents may use money to buy our affection. They may feel that we are preoccupied with our own lives, with our spouses, our kids, and our jobs, and they may be giving us money to buy more attention. Or they may give money to assuage their own feelings of guilt. Perhaps your father spent most of his time at work during your childhood; he may now be giving you money as compensation.

In some families there is a philosophy that "what is mine is yours." As generous as this sounds, anger and resentment may be smoldering beneath the surface. Even though the outward message is "Take all you want," each person has an expectation of what the other deserves. You may be taking more from the "community pot" than what your parents believe you deserve. At the other extreme are those families where no one shares anything—"all for themselves." Some parents make their children pay room and board during their teens. This may reflect an economic necessity, or their way of teaching their children the value of money, or outright stinginess. Sometimes, "being careful with money" is a euphemism for being a miser. Children of such parents may feel unjustly denied and may grow up to be stingy themselves. They often treat their own children in a similar way, and when their turn comes to manage their parents' finances, they may take revenge.

Some children actually defraud their parents. One elderly woman's daughter and son-in-law accused her of being severely paranoid, "totally out of it." They claimed they were helping her budget her money; the mother insisted they were really stealing it. Many adult children do help elderly parents manage financial matters; many have to balance their parents' checkbooks for them, and some parents, instead of being grateful, falsely accuse their children of defrauding them. In this particular case, however, the mother turned out to be right, not paranoid. The daughter and son-in-law were taking her Social Security and pension checks and using them for their own purposes, not the mother's. They gave the mother an allowance of $5 per week and forced her to continue living with them.

In a recent study, the National Council on Aging found that more than two out of three people are concerned that they will not have enough money to live on when they get old.[1] In 1981, more than half of all men age 65 years and older had incomes of less than $9,000 a year, while over half of those between 50 and 59 years of age had incomes of $20,000 or more.[2] As the average lifespan has increased, the amount of money our parents put aside has become less and less adequate. The familiar stereotype of the old miser may be more reality than fantasy, a reality based on necessity. In 1980 the U.S. Census Bureau found that the average 65-year-old man could look forward to another 14 years of life, and the average woman to 18 years. As they age, our parents may have to be miserly to survive.

Both parents and children need to admit that money is an important part of their lives. They then need to put away some of their emotional connections with money so they can objectively manage their finances. A return to the six steps of the Commonsense Approach to Problem Solving may be helpful for at least a little while. When the feelings are under control, then we can begin to look at some of the following facts as they affect us all.

## THE FINANCIAL REALITIES OF OLD AGE

Between the ages of 35 and 55 years, we are most likely at our maximum earning power. Moreover, our parents' annual income is probably lower than ours. The bottom line is that we may be in a position to give to or withhold money from our parents, rather than the other way around. How can we give to them without offending them and creating resentment? It may help to ask first if we really want to give to them, and then if we can afford the added expense. Though we may be at our maximum earning capacity, we probably also face our maximum spending requirements. We may be saving or paying for our children's college tuition, an amount that could approach six figures per child in the next few years. We could be burdened by mortgage payments, repayments of educational loans, or installment loans taken out to furnish our homes, finance our cars, or establish ourselves in business or professional endeavors. Besides all these expenses, we should be investing in our own retirement (see chapter 9).

Older people often have less money than younger people. Many retired people live on fixed incomes that may have to last them a long time. As people live longer, the portion of their lives spent earning money has decreased relative to the time spent in retirement. That is true for men and for working women, but will become increasingly true for women in general, as more long-lived women enter the labor force. People 65 years of age or older *who live alone* have lower incomes than their single counterparts under the age of 65. Seventy-five percent of the people who lived alone and were over age 65 received incomes of less than $10,000 in 1981. About one in four of the single elderly received less than $4,000 per year![3] In addition, any money saved rapidly loses its value during inflationary times.

If your parents are 65 years of age or older, their greatest source of income will generally be Social Security. In 1981, Social Security furnished more than one-third of the income of couples in this age group, and nearly one-half the income of people living alone.[4] If they lack additional funds—such as personal savings and pensions—they may be less well off than either they or you would like.


## WHAT CAN WE DO?

In many families, money is a major source of conflict, and the underlying issues may not just be control or power. Perhaps incomes are inadequate for day-to-day and year-to-year living expenses. Perhaps enough money is available, but family members have unresolved emotional conflicts about how that money should be managed. Below are six key questions to help you assess and solve emotional problems concerning money.

## HOW TO SOLVE CONFLICTS ABOUT MONEY

| Ask these questions | Try these approaches |
|---|---|
| 1. What are your expectations? | Walk through the six-step Commonsense Approach to Problem Solving. |
| 2. What are your parents' expectations? | Ask them. Suggest the six-step Commonsense Approach to Problem Solving. |
| 3. What are the actual resources? | List them: PARENTS' ASSETS  YOUR ASSETS |
| 4. What are your actual needs? | FINANCIAL  EMOTIONAL |
| 5. What are your parents' actual needs? | FINANCIAL  EMOTIONAL |
| 6. Can you match needs and resources? | Use Negotiation and Compromise. |

## 1. What Are Your Expectations As the Adult Child?

The first step in understanding the feelings about money in your family is to get some idea of how much money you anticipate for yourself, if any. Did you grow up in a home where there was always enough money, so that you were never motivated to earn your own? Did your parents always give you enough money, and now, as an adult, you expect them to continue giving you money? Many baby boomers, who grew up in a time of plenty, feel cheated when confronting leaner times: "I can't believe it—it's impossible for us to buy a house without our parents' help. They had no problem when they were our age." Other adult children expect economic support to continue throughout life, and feel resentful if their parents cannot provide it. Their resentment escalates if their parents turn to *them* for help. Most have expectations about their parents' will. How much do you think they plan to leave you? How would you feel if they left you less or more?

We have all heard or read about family feuds originating with, or fueled by, the terms of a will. Stella's story provides an illustration. At the time of her parents' death, Stella had to come to terms not only with her own expectations, but also with those of her brothers.

"When I was a teenager," Stella reminisced, "I worked every day after school, and gave part of my earnings to help my parents. I paid for all my own clothes and school supplies, and rarely asked for anything from them. I thought that was the way you helped your family. We sure didn't have much. But my brother Harry, who was 16 years older than I, was just the opposite. He never helped out. Instead, every time our parents accumulated a little extra money, they gave it to him."

In fact, both of her brothers had borrowed money from their parents with promises to pay them back—promises they had never kept. The one time Stella had asked for money, when she and her husband needed a loan to help with the down payment on their house, they were handed a regular payment schedule, with interest! They repaid the loan within two years, but Stella never forgave her parents—not for requesting repayment of the loan, but for insisting on the interest.

As the years went by, Stella and her brothers became alienated; their wives, in particular, never got along with Stella or their mother-in-law. Stella was left with the entire responsibility of looking after her parents. Harry and Ralph would drop by now and then to see them, but that was it. After Stella's father died, her mother did poorly. She suffered from heart disease that progressively made her weaker. During the last two years, Stella hired a live-in caregiver for her mother. When her mother's savings were getting dangerously low, Stella asked Harry and Ralph to repay some of their earlier loans. They did so grudgingly, intermittently, and with ill grace. Harry would bring over the cash himself. Ralph humiliated his mother by sending checks his wife had signed.

In her mother's will, Stella was left all personal belongings, which consisted of a few pieces of jewelry and a TV set that she and her brothers had bought their mother for her eightieth birthday, three years earlier. The day of her funeral, Ralph and Harry asked that Stella and her husband arbitrate which of the brothers would get the TV set. After all, they had shared in the cost.

"Their timing couldn't have been worse," Stella recalled. "My husband and I were furious. Before the earth had even settled on her grave, they were picking over her belongings. Always takers—and they wanted us to arbitrate!"

Stella's Mood Meter registered rage. What were her options? She could push the feeling away—deny it—and go ahead and arbitrate. The trouble with this strategy was that it would increase Stella's anger. Using a different strategy, Stella could displace the feeling and take out her anger on the TV by smashing it. With this strategy, Stella might experience some relief from her rage, but her brothers would become enraged, she would feel guilty, and everyone would be deprived.

What did she actually do? She watched, without a word, as her husband went into their files, pulled out all their canceled checks for the past 12 years, and showed her brothers how much he and Stella had contributed to their mother's care. No one spoke about any of her belongings after that, but the silence was loud.

For Stella, it was a much better solution than allowing herself to continue in her martyrdom. After so many years of conflicts with her brothers, "loud silence" may have been the closest they could get to one another.

## 2. What Are Your Parents' Expectations?

Your parents, too, will have expectations about money. Their expectations, like yours, are invariably colored by their pasts. Some may feel that because they provided for you throughout your early years, it is your turn now to provide for them. For others, the thought of taking money from their children is anathema. It represents a sign of weakness, a source of humiliation and shame. For parents as well as for children, the expectations may be unspoken, even if not subconscious. The Commonsense Approach to Problem Solving may help both parents and their adult children to gain awareness of their expectations about money.

Dennis's story is a good example of the potentially damaging effects of parental expectations. Although seemingly happily married for 12 years, he and his wife, Sherrie, were beginning to have problems. Dennis was financially successful, a vice-president in his father's business; with two lovely children and a beautiful home, he and Sherrie seemed to have everything. Yet, for reasons they could not explain, they were unhappy.

At their first meeting with a marriage counselor, Dennis announced, "I'm here only because my wife threatened to leave me if I didn't join her." They were an attractive couple, dressed in the latest fashion. Sherrie commented sadly, "I might as well be single. Dennis has no interest in anything but his work. He never gets home from work before seven-thirty or eight o'clock, always complaining of how tired he is. If a phone call from his father doesn't interrupt our dinner, he has to call Dad right afterwards, even though they just left each other before coming home. There's always a heated, lengthy argument on the phone. Then he starts to pick on the kids or me. He barely has any interest in sex. Something's wrong with him!"

Dennis threw his hands up in a hopeless gesture, indicating his disapproval of Sherrie's narration. "I work my butt off every day so my wife and kids can wear expensive clothes, live in a new home, join the country club, and attend private schools. We have two fine cars, go out to fancy places, take costly vacations, and we wouldn't have any of it without my father. None of our friends has the financial security we have at our age. She's never satisfied."

In subsequent weeks, as more of their history unraveled, Dennis poignantly told of his earlier aspirations. "I used to love to paint and had a flair for the piano. I had to fight for piano lessons, and I dreamed of being an artist or a musician. I could spend hours at the piano, when Dad wasn't around. I wanted to go to Europe and visit all the art museums after high school, but my folks said that would be a wedding gift, if I married 'the right girl.'

"My dad has this wholesale furniture business that he and my grandfather built into a huge success. From the time I was able to understand, that was all I ever heard: 'You'll have a business to go into. You'll never have to worry.' I would have to work there after school. I hated the place. To this day, I can't stand the smell of furniture oil. But I was the only son, and even though Dad put my sister's first husband into the business, he threw him out when they divorced. He said I could go to college if I majored in business administration. Otherwise, college would be a waste of money.

"I felt important because I was one of the few guys in high school and college who had a lot of money to spend on girls. I used to think that was the only reason they went out with me. I met Sherrie during my second year in college, and quit to work with Dad so we could get married sooner.

"The folks were great. Dad raised my salary and made me a junior partner. He made the down payment on our home and furnished it from top to bottom. And I finally got my trip to Europe. The next few years were pretty good, with the kids coming and all. Dad kept giving me a bigger share in the business. But I wasn't on easy street, that's for sure. Although I do a good job, he's always telling me to do things differently. He even has something to say about the clothes I wear. Last week he bought me a dozen new shirts and ties. Sherrie gets angry when I wear them to work instead of the ones she bought me. Sometimes I feel like they're both pulling me to pieces."

The marriage counselor asked whether Dennis could be unhappy in his work, and whether he ever felt that his father might be controlling him with money. Dennis rejected these suggestions at first, although he did admit feeling angry and frustrated when his father talked of plans for his grandson in the business.

Dennis did have a lot of money, but with miles of strings attached. In his family, the formula was MONEY = CONTROL. And the control was beginning to span the generations. Dennis had to work hard to keep his Mood Meter from straying into the Unpleasant Zone. His marriage was suffering, and the emotional energy required to keep the status quo was sapping his strength and even his libido.

Dennis eventually became aware of how money had become so intimately intertwined with his family relations. He clearly had new business to take care of—the business of sorting out his life apart from his father's. Sherrie, too, had to take a good look at herself to begin to understand why she had been so passive and accepting of the situation for so many years. She learned how to express her dissatisfaction with Dennis more directly, so she no longer had to threaten to leave him when he wouldn't do what she wanted. As their relationship strengthened, their dependency on Dennis's father diminished, and, remarkably, Dennis's father became less controlling.

### 3. What Are the Actual Resources?

What are your parents' sources of income? You may not be able to ask them because they may not wish to discuss their finances with you. This can be a very volatile issue. If you ask them, they may think you are after their money or that you know something about their health—either physical or mental—that they don't. They may feel manipulated and helpless. Many times the discrepancy between expectations and resources is so large that emotions become overwhelming. If you find you cannot discuss each other's assets and income, try answering the next two questions about needs. If you anticipate trouble in these areas, too, go back to the six steps of the Commonsense Approach to Problem Solving.

Inquiring about actual resources, then, may be most difficult. In some families it may mean that you and your parents take out the calculator, consult the accountant, lawyer, or financial manager, and actually look at the numbers. In others, it may be quite simple.

Several realities need to be considered, including wills, trusts, and estate and tax planning. If your parents have property, a business, or complex financial holdings, they, or you, or all of you together may want to seek professional economic advice from a lawyer, accountant, or financial planner. Tax attorneys with expertise in estate planning can be valuable to all of us. An automobile accident or other catastrophic illness may leave one of our parents—or one of us—incompetent and helpless for many years. And, once such an accident has happened, financial planning becomes much more difficult. We should do it *now*—before we need to. Planning for the deaths of our parents, or for our own death, is painful and may strain our relationships—but money may strain parental-filial relationships at any time.

### 4. What Are Your Actual Needs?

"I need everything I have and more." Perhaps you feel that

way, but answering this question involves differentiating
"needs," or necessities, from "wants." At the most basic level,
necessities are food, clothing, and shelter. Everything else falls
into the category of "wants." Ranking your "wants" may be
helpful in setting priorities as to which ones are more "necessary" than others. Saving for a child's college tuition may be
more important than a Mediterranean cruise. Perhaps remodeling the kitchen or bathroom can be put off for a year or two.
What about mortgage payments or car loans? These kinds of
questions will help you to see discrepancies between your needs
and your expectations or desires. In addition to financial needs,
what are your emotional needs in relation to money? For example, you may have a psychological need for your parents to
care for you financially. It may make you feel secure and safe.

## 5. What Are Your Parents' Actual Needs?

Your parents will have to ask themselves the question you
just asked yourself. Or you may have to ask it of them, for
them. They may be approaching retirement and planning to
cut back on expenses. They may feel they no longer need that
three-bedroom house, now that the children have moved out.
They may suffer from chronic illness that requires medical expense. Do they have to hire home help? What about health insurance premiums, rent, or the cost of a nursing home? And
they too have emotional as well as financial needs in relation
to money. Do they have a psychological need to continue to
care for *you* financially, even though they no longer have the
money to spend? They, too, may have a mismatch between expectations and needs.

## 6. Can You Match Needs and Resources?

Here is the question that often requires the Negotiation
and Compromise steps of the Commonsense Approach to
Problem Solving. Answering this final question may bring you
and your parents closer together, or push you farther apart. We
think the risk of the latter is minimal if you have come this far.
Are they poor or rich or in between? Will you have to support
them, or will you inherit money from their estate? Your parents, with or without your help, may have to seek legal advice
about their estate and wills. Both you and your parents should
have knowledge of some basic information about such legal
documents as wills and trusts.

\ *will* is a legal document that states how we would like to
·e of our property after death. It determines who will re-
_     e property, how the estate will be distributed, who will
b( d(_.₁gnated to supervise the distribution (the executor or
executrix), and when the distribution will take place. Drawing
up a will gives each of us the opportunity to make these important decisions, thereby allowing us to assert our prefer-
ences, reward those we love, provide for family needs, plan for
taxes to help heirs minimize tax losses, and provide for charities. If a person dies intestate (without a will), a probate court
divides the property according to state law. This court decision
may differ from the deceased person's wishes. Not having a will
also means that the court chooses the estate's executor. A will
should be stored in a safe place, and copies in a separate safe
place. For a will to be valid, a person must be mentally competent and not be coerced to sign. If there is any doubt, legal—and at times medical—documentation becomes essential
to forestall invalidation of the will after the person's death.

Though not required, legal advice from an attorney with
experience in estate law is generally desirable when drawing up
a will. Laws vary from state to state, and change over time; the
specific form and language for a valid will can be complicated.
For example, many states mandate the distribution of community property, defined as earnings acquired during marriage by the work and efforts of either spouse. Financial advice
from an accountant can also be valuable.

Even before your parents seek professional advice, it may
be helpful if they first list their assets. Personal property (books,
clothing, jewelry, etc.) as well as real estate and business in-
vestments should be included. Liabilities may need to be sub-
tracted from the total. Once they have an idea of the amount
and type of property, the next step is to decide on its distribution. They may want to make a list as follows:

| Assets | Value | Distribution |
|---|---|---|
| House | $100,000 | Spouse |
| Car | 5,000 | Daughter |
| Savings bonds | 1,000 | Nephew |

After your parents have listed their assets and how they would

like to distribute them, the next step would be to get professional legal advice.

The importance of having a valid, up-to-date will cannot
be overemphasized. Without it, a court will have the responsibility of dividing the property. Your spouse may have to share
the estate with relatives. Children may have to share equally,
even if one child needs more than others. Taxes and other fees
may deplete assets. Wills should also be reviewed at regular intervals, since new laws are passed, assets increase or diminish,
and decisions about distribution may change over time.

Another way your parents may manage and protect their
assets is through a *trust*. A trust is a legal way of giving a designated person or institution, known as the "trustee," rights to
administer all or a portion of a person's assets. The trustee
must manage that part of the estate according to the terms of
the trust. A trust can be used to provide income to other family members in lower tax brackets and distribute wealth to heirs
while possibly reducing taxes. A *testamentary trust* is one created
in a will, and only comes into existence, after the death of the
person who created the trust, known as the "trustor." The
trustee may be given the power to manage the funds at his or
her discretion, or may have to follow rigid prescriptions. In a
*living trust*, a trustee is appointed to manage the trust while the
trustor is alive. The trust may be structured to continue to
function after the trustor's death.

There are at least two types of living trusts: A *revocable living trust* can be canceled by its creator; an *irrevocable living trust*
is less popular, because its terms cannot be canceled or
changed. Living trusts offer several advantages, including the
possibility of carefully planned financial management during
the person's lifetime, and reduced estate and income taxes
when the first person of a couple dies. A trust can protect your
parents' property both during their lifetimes and after their
deaths. For example, under one state's law, Jean and Trevor
set up a living trust and transferred into the trust all their
property except a small checking account and their life insurance policies. They designated themselves as trustees and could
manage the trust's assets as their own. There were no tax benefits as long as both were alive, but six years later, when Trevor was diagnosed as suffering from Alzheimer disease, an
unexpected benefit of the trust became apparent: the assets in
the trust were protected and not subject to claims for hospital,

health care, or other costs. Of course, the specific benefits of setting up a trust will vary among states.

A trust may also avoid probate. Under another state's law, a trust would have helped Alison's situation. A well-to-do widow, Alison had named her grandchildren as sole heirs in her will, because her children had predeceased her. She had carefully planned to maximize and simplify her estate for the grandchildren. She sold her house, which made up the bulk of the estate, and set up the sale in such a way as to collect the proceeds over a four-year period, thus minimizing the tax bite. But she died after two years, and the purchaser decided to stop payments and sue the estate for damages. He claimed that some defect in the house had presumably been uncovered after Alison's death. It took five years to settle the lawsuit. During that time, not a single cent could be distributed to the grandchildren. The executors were warned by the probate court that they would be personally liable if they were to distribute any funds. Even though each grandchild's share eventually ran to six figures, they had no funds for five years to help pay their college tuition, living costs, or even medical bills. Although executors cannot distribute estate funds without permission of the probate court, trustees can distribute trust funds without anybody else's permission, subject to periodic reporting to and review by the courts.

Many parents have few assets to leave to their heirs. They may be forced to use up their savings during retirement and see all of their assets wiped out by medical, hospital, and other health-care costs. Many fail to take advantage of public resources. It is unfortunate how many middle-class parents and their adult children are ill-informed about public benefits (see Appendix 7). It may take ingenuity and persistence to find out about these benefits, which could be substantial. Many times, past distortions get in the way. For example, your parents may consider it shameful to accept public aid, which they equate with charity, visions of almshouses, poorhouses, and breadlines.

Even though, in the latter half of the twentieth century, we have removed much of the indignity once associated with public aid, and even though many of the baby-boom generation consider public assistance their right if and when they need it, many middle-class children and their aged parents share the view that dependence upon the public purse is the brand of failure. These disparate views can be another source of conflict between them.

Whether a source of conflict and control or a symbol of security and love, money strongly influences our interactions with our parents. The guidelines in this chapter should help to resolve financial conflicts. Rather than deplete our relationships with our parents, money can enrich them.

---

**REASSESSING FINANCIAL SITUATIONS WITH PARENTS**

- Ask these questions:
    1. What are your expectations as the adult child?
    2. What are your parents' expectations?
    3. What are the actual resources?
    4. What are your actual needs?
    5. What are your parents' actual needs?
    6. Can you match needs and resources?
- Use the six-step Commonsense Approach to Problem Solving.
- Seek professional legal and financial advice when needed.

# 5

# FOOD:
# Have We Given It Enough Thought?

*It's good food and not fine words that keeps me alive.*

Molière, *Les Femmes Savantes*

Food is an essential part of life and an important aspect of any kind of care, whether of children, patients, or parents. Hunger is one of our basic drives, and one of the first natural instincts in all humans is that of sucking for intake of nourishment. Food continues to play a vital role throughout life, and not only to keep us alive physically; it has come to assume enormous symbolic significance as well. Just look around. Food is served at almost every social and professional gathering. Courtships, friendships, and other new relationships are often begun and nurtured by "breaking bread" together. Many a financial merger, contract, or corporate venture is negotiated over lunch or dinner. In an informal survey of college professors, we learned that the teaching conferences having the highest attendance were those that served free food. The topic of food in any group usually elicits hearty response, stimulates conversation, or engenders debate.

Food is a symbol of love and an expression of concern. Just as providing food for their young was our parents' first obligation, as they age we may find it our task to make sure they are fed, and fed properly.

Expert advice on the nutritional needs of the elderly, however, is nearly nonexistent. Even though a new diet book appears on the best-seller list nearly every week, diet and nutrition books specifically for older people are hard to find. Our nation's medical schools have generally neglected the topic. A dozen years ago, the entire curriculum on nutrition in some medical schools consisted of a single hour, and during that hour medical students were taught only to identify the four food groups: milk, meats, fruits/vegetables, and breads/ce-

reals. Many of today's medical schools still lack a formal curriculum on nutrition; some schools merely distribute a booklet
with general nutritional information. By contrast, most medical schools make their students spend more than a dozen hours
each week for an entire year studying human anatomy. As a
result, most doctors know much more about the organs of cadavers than about the fuel that keeps the living body going.
Even though facts are scarce, opinions abound, in line with
Montaigne's observation, "Nothing is so firmly believed as that
which we least know." Acquiring some familiarity with the experts' current thinking is a useful strategy in preparing for
possible dietary problems that our parents may come to face.

At one end of the spectrum are parents who remain
healthy and sociable as they age; they will cook for themselves
and attend to their own nutritional needs. At the other end are
parents who become seriously ill; professionals will care for
them. The adult child may have to take care of everything in
between, from a depressed, widowed father who refuses to eat
or cook for himself, to a hypertensive mother who denies that
she has to restrict her salt intake or change her cooking style.

When other sources of pleasure diminish with age, food
gains ascendancy as an ever more important source of pleasure and security. If our parents live long enough, their hearing and vision are likely to become impaired; their ability to
chew may decrease if they lose their teeth; their mobility will
diminish; their self-worth and independence may vanish. One
of the few pleasures remaining to our parents may be that
which they derive from food.

On a recent visit to a nursing home, a young man was invited to stay for dinner, and took a resident's seat. That resident became verbally abusive when he saw a stranger invading
his dinner spot—his territory. To him, the intruder was threatening to steal one of the few entitlements he had managed to
retain in the face of all his losses. The ritual and routine of
meals were gratifying constants in his life; they meant security,
comfort and care, just as they did when he was a child.

## PARENTS AND FOOD: WHAT CAN WE DO?

*Remember that food is essential to both physical and psychological
well-being.* For most people, food increases in value as other

sources of gratification decrease. Most of us, at least three times a day, partake of the social and biological ritual that is eating; it provides both pleasure and nourishment. People enjoy the taste, smell, color, and texture of foods. Mealtimes should also provide an opportunity to relax and talk with others. For many of our parents, they do not. Some eat alone or not at all. Some (especially men who live alone) lose interest in eating because they have problems buying and preparing food. A poor diet can result in lack of energy, malnutrition, and physical illness.

---

## MAKING MORE OUT OF MEALS

- Invite your parent out to breakfast, lunch, or dinner, or over to your house on a regular basis—perhaps weekly or monthly—depending on needs and resources.

- If your mother enjoyed cooking for the family, perhaps she would like to have your family over to her place for meals. These meals, too, could be arranged on a regular basis.

- If your parent does not like to cook, but prefers to stay at home, offer to bring over take-out food, or cook there.

- If your parent has special dietary restrictions, keep them in mind when preparing meals at your home, or bringing dessert or other food when you come as the guest.

- To break up the routine of eating alone, your parent could try eating in different places in the apartment or house, such as the living room or outside on the porch.

- Neighbors or friends might start a "potluck" group in which everyone brings a prepared dish.

- Check with local agencies to find out if their neighborhood provides meals for other people at a community center, church, or school (as many do, often free or at low cost). These meals offer not only adequate nutrition but a chance to be with other people as well.

- For the disabled parent who has difficulty getting out, home delivery services such as "Meals on Wheels" may be available locally.

---

*Watch for pronounced or sudden changes in your parent's body weight.* Changes in a parent's dietary habits, physical appearance, and body weight can be a clue to physical or psychological illness. Has your mother, who has always been a bit chubby, suddenly become thin? Is your father running to the tailor to have his pants let out? Such changes in body weight should be red flags, warnings that there may be serious physical or psychological problems. For example, weight loss may be a first symptom of depression or cancer. Weight gain may also indicate depression, or it may be a symptom of heart failure. Although most fluctuations in body weight do not result from serious illness, it is best to check with the doctor.

*Become familiar with your parent's nutritional needs.*    Many middle-aged children have parents with one or more physical illnesses that affect their diet and nutritional needs. Are they obese or too thin? Do they have hypertension, diabetes, osteoporosis, or arthritis? The adult child can often be helpful by learning about foods that need to be restricted and foods that are beneficial, given their parent's specific health problem. Although some claims made about links between diet and disease prevention are exaggerated, diet is one controllable factor in disease risk. Smoking, alcohol consumption, and exercise are others. The following discussion relates to the most common ailments that may afflict your parents as they age, and those that may be influenced by dietary factors.

*Do we have to get fat as we get old?*    Obesity is a problem at any age, but in old age it is worse because of its association with other illnesses, including adult-onset diabetes, hypertension, heart disease, arthritis, gout, and even accidents. It may be especially hard to lose weight late in life because of complex interactions between early eating habits, diminishing activity and exercise levels, lowered caloric requirements, reduced metabolism, and ever-decreasing sources of pleasure.

*Is there a miracle diet that can keep our parents from gaining weight along with their years?*    Despite numerous claims from many sources about diets that prescribe everything from grapefruit to soy beans, the most reliable way to lose weight is to eat less. Sensible weight-loss programs involve an overall reduction in daily caloric intake along with a well-balanced diet and moderate exercise. Some form of aerobic exercise helps by raising a person's metabolic rate, increasing energy expenditure, and suppressing appetite. For any sensible program to be effective and safe, however, it must follow a predetermined schedule. A common problem with many diets is that they are too severe; the dieter experiences hunger and deprivation, with the ensuing drive to "make up for lost calories." People tend to go on and off these diets, so that a graph of their body weight over time tends to resemble a roller coaster. A commonsense diet plan, by contrast, yields a body-weight profile resembling a slight downward grade with small plateaus that gradually level off. The keyword should be *moderation*.

---

### SOME PRACTICAL GUIDELINES FOR A MODERATE DIET PLAN FOR PARENTS

---

- Look through diet books; pick the one that appeals to you; and consult your physician.
- Choose a modest goal, perhaps one pound per week. Overly ambitious goals yield the "roller coaster" effect.
- Avoid fried, fatty foods and sweets.
- Avoid large quantities of food.
- If you break your diet, do not be discouraged. Expect an occasional binge.
- Keep portions small.
- Eat slowly; savor every bite.
- Avoid second helpings.
- Avoid diet pills.
- Expect plateaus in weight loss.
- Do not waste your money on expensive special diet foods. Some are reasonably priced, others exorbitant. Read labels carefully; often, specially marketed foods differ from regular brands only in price and not in fat content or calories.
- Avoid between-meals snacks; try taking a drink of water instead.

---

Aside from general weight-loss diets, your parents may need more specific nutritional advice:

*How does cholesterol affect the heart?*   Foods high in cholesterol and saturated fats can be harmful to people prone to atherosclerotic disease, which results from the deposition of cholesterol and other fatty (lipid) substances in the walls of blood vessels. It used to be called "hardening of the arteries." These substances form deposits called atherosclerotic plaques and can make the smaller arteries in the heart, brain, and other organs too narrow for the blood to circulate easily. Eventually, too little blood is supplied to where it is needed. If too little blood goes to the heart muscle, one consequence is angina pectoris—the chest pain that people experience, especially

---

### SOME FOODS HIGH IN CHOLESTEROL
### AND SATURATED FATS AND
### POSSIBLE SUBSTITUTES

---

| High | Low |
|------|-----|
| Butter | Margarine, vegetable oil |
| Red meat | Fish, poultry |
| Eggs | Soy bean products |
| Homogenized milk | Nonfat milk |
| Most cheeses | Pot cheese |

---

when walking up a flight of stairs, exercising, or traveling at high altitudes. Another may be a heart attack. Sometimes a blood clot forms, or a piece of the atherosclerotic plaque breaks off and travels inside the blood vessels until it hits a narrow spot. If it closes off the vessel altogether, the tissue supplied by that vessel dies. If the tissue happens to be a piece of heart muscle, the person suffers a heart attack, or myocardial infarction (called an MI in medical jargon); if it is a part of the brain, the person suffers a stroke (known as a cerebrovascular accident or CVA). Coronary artery disease accounts for nearly 50 percent of deaths in the elderly, and strikes six out of ten people aged 70 or older.

Heart failure (the inability of the heart to pump enough blood to meet the body's metabolic demands) affects 3 to 4 million Americans, and 75 percent of them are 60 years of age or older.[1] The most frequent causes of heart failure are high blood pressure (hypertension) and coronary artery disease.

Among the risk factors for coronary artery disease are age, sex (men are more vulnerable), and heredity, as well as some factors related to diet, especially for people under age 50. Obesity, if defined as 30 percent higher than average weight, appears to increase the risk of coronary artery disease. Elevated blood sugar from uncontrolled diabetes may also increase the risk for coronary artery disease. Hyperlipidemia (increased fat level in the blood) is an important risk factor related to diet and age as well as heredity. Cholesterol and triglyceride levels seem to increase with age, but the exact interplay among the factors of age, cholesterol level, heredity, body weight, and diet are complex and not completely understood. Nonetheless, most experts recommend cholesterol restriction, especially for people with other risk factors for coronary artery disease, and common sense is on the side of limiting dietary cholesterol at all ages.

*How does diet affect hypertension?* Hypertension (high blood pressure) is a potentially fatal, debilitating illness. In one large-scale investigation conducted in Framingham, Massachusetts, and known as the Framingham Study, ordinary hypertension was defined as blood pressure (measured in millimeters of mercury) above 160/95. In that study, almost one-quarter of the men (22 percent) and one-third of the women (34 percent) between 65 and 74 years of age suffered from hypertension.

Hypertension can lead to heart attack, stroke, and chest pain (angina pectoris), as well as pain in the legs while walking. Exercise and medications are often used to treat hypertension, but dietary adjustments focusing on salt (sodium) restriction and weight loss may be the first approach. They have been used effectively, and most experts agree that modest sodium restriction (to an intake of 60 to 100 milliequivalents (mEq) per day) is a safe way to lower blood pressure in many patients. Although it may seem impossible, it *is* possible to restrict salt intake. Old habits *can* be broken.

Ellie's story provides one example. Her widowed father developed hypertension and complained for weeks on end about his new diet. He became so preoccupied with it that food and its preparation preempted all conversation. In the past he had relied heavily on prepared foods, but found that the easiest-to-prepare meals—the ones you just pop into the microwave—contained fat and preservatives high in sodium. And even if he disregarded the expense and took the trouble to find a specialty store that carried prepared low-salt and low-fat foods, he assumed they would taste awful.

So he decided to ignore the diet, go back to his old habits, and eat out or use prepared foods. Not surprisingly, his blood pressure climbed again. His doctor was concerned, and even Ellie's father began to worry and told Ellie about it. At this point, Ellie decided to do some cooking for him. She got in touch with the American Heart Association, got some advice from them, and purchased their cookbook. She cooked once a week, large enough amounts to put away and freeze an extra few days' supply. Since she knew her father's taste well (and was a good cook), he thoroughly enjoyed her meals. Of course, when he came to Ellie's house, she made sure she followed his dietary restrictions in preparing meals. On those days her whole family ate low-salt, low-cholesterol food, and was none the worse for it. Ellie also got a list of restaurants serving meals in accordance with American Heart Association guidelines.

---

### TIPS ON LOW SALT DIETS

- Check labels; the Food and Drug Administration (FDA) recommends that foods be labeled with salt content. Many commercial foods are being prepared without sodium, or with very little.

- Do not buy foods containing any form of sodium, such as baking powder, baking soda, brine, or monosodium glutamate.

- Do not add salt during or after cooking.

- Use fresh spices instead of salt to flavor food, such as basil, thyme, lemon, garlic, oregano, onion, dill, and dry mustard.

- Avoid these foods:

| | |
|---|---|
| potato chips | lox (smoked salmon) |
| pretzels | sardines |
| sauerkraut | pickles |
| soy sauce | catsup |
| olives | ham |
| frankfurters | canned tomato juice |
| sausage | some frozen or canned vegetables |
| herring | pudding and cake mixes |

---

*Can calcium prevent bone thinning?*   Nutrition researchers have established that certain nutrients (e.g., protein and fiber) can increase calcium requirements. Since the amount of calcium absorbed from the digestive system tends to decrease with aging, there may not be sufficient calcium available to maintain the body's skeleton. Osteoporosis (bone thinning or degeneration) results, and may lead to fractures, pain, disability, and the inactivity that promotes further loss of bone. Nondietary factors are also important. In women, for example, lack of estrogen following menopause contributes to bone thinning.

Although research has not answered all the questions, it does suggest that increasing calcium intake will halt osteoporosis. Experts thus suggest that postmenopausal women supplement their diet with calcium. Daily supplements of up to 1.5 grams of elemental calcium are often recommended, and though they are twice as high as the 800 mg per day Recommended Daily Allowance or RDA, established by the Food and Nutrition Board of the National Research Council, they are safe for most people at all ages. A physician needs to be consulted, however, since people with a disease such as tuberculosis should not follow this recommendation and persons on estrogen supplements need to reduce the dose, 1.0 gram of calcium generally being recommended for them. While most of the calcium preparations on the market contain calcium carbonate, some nutritionists believe that compounds containing calcium citrate may be preferable. This is especially true for the elderly since calcium citrate absorption does not depend on stomach acid, which is reduced in many older persons. Calcium citrate preparations are thus less likely to lead to calcium oxalate kidney stone formation in individuals susceptible to such formation.

*Can some foods prevent cancer?* Given the inability of medical technology to cure most cancers, interest has grown in preventive measures. Cigarette smoking accounts for nearly one out of three cancer deaths in the United States, and is the most common cause of preventable cancer. What about vitamins and other nutrients in our diets? If we ingest more of them, are we less likely to develop cancer?

Diets high in fiber may decrease the risk of cancer of the colon. High-fiber foods such as fresh fruit, vegetables, and bran have other effects: they help control constipation, a common complaint of older people, and may help to reduce blood pressure, blood sugar, and weight. Various types of fiber have different actions. For example, wheat bran increases bulk of stool; other fibers may not. Though foods are often labeled as to whether they contain fiber, rarely does the label specify the *type* of fiber. Increasing the amount of fiber ingested, however, may have negative as well as positive consequences. Thus, for some people, even moderate amounts of fiber may interfere with digestion and absorption of proteins, fats, and calcium.[2]

*Does a spartan diet prolong life?*     Dr. Roy Walford has done extensive studies on the effects of caloric restriction on laboratory animals. In brief, eating fewer calories than is customary for these laboratory animals resulted in increased life span and decreased frequency of diseases associated with aging. That is true particularly if the dietary restriction is introduced early on and very gradually so as not to "shock the system." Though adequate studies have not yet been carried out in humans, Dr. Walford recommends some caloric restriction. In fact, he restricts his own intake and fasts at least a day a week. But any diet control program must be done sensibly and carefully, keeping in mind specific nutritional requirements; otherwise, disease may result. People who severely restrict intake without attending to specific dietary needs will suffer from malnutrition and may develop such illnesses as beriberi or scurvy.

*What's wrong with junk food?*     Eating "fast" food or "junk" food has become an accepted pastime for millions of Americans—the habit has even spread beyond the United States and become an international craze. In most countries today, the tourist visiting urban centers can readily locate those familiar, fast-food chains by their blazing logos—despite the foreign lettering. A 1980 U.S. Gallup poll found that one out of three people surveyed had "eaten out" the day before, and of these people, one out of four had eaten fast food.

For most of us, "fast food" means food that is prepared prior to purchase and immediately ready to eat, while "junk food" may have a slightly more general meaning, taking in all foods that are primarily high-fat, high-sugar, and low-protein: potato chips, fatty burgers, candies, ice cream, and other sweets. Many people, though, use the terms interchangeably.

No one knows exactly how much fast food is eaten by people as they get into their sixth or seventh decades and beyond, but these types of food are considered particularly unhealthy for the elderly, given their high risk for physical illnesses that require special diets. Though fast foods do have some nutritional value, taste good, and may be inexpensive and convenient, they are also *inadequate* as sole sources of nutrition.[3] They have sufficient carbohydrates, but not proteins, and they contain excessive amounts of fat.

The basic strategy for keeping the "junk" in the junk food from hurting you or your parent is to not overdo it. If you eat lunch at a fast-food restaurant, plan on low-calorie, low-fat meals for breakfast and dinner. Much of the extra fat (and calories) comes from the way the food is prepared, and frying is the most fattening method of preparation. Moderation, again, is the key, so go easy on the french fries (180 to 280 calories per order), and neither you nor your parents need be deprived altogether. Avoiding soft drinks, with their high content of sugar, and substituting fruit juices or milk (for those who are not lactose-intolerant) will help. Cautious people will also avoid soft drinks with artificial sweeteners, since it takes years to find out how injurious they may be to our health.

Until more is known about dietary requirements as well as the effects of dietary excesses, deficiencies, and imbalances in older adults, it seems wise to keep an open mind about diets and nutrition. It is vital, of course, that we remain alert to the detrimental—or even fatal—consequences of vitamin and mineral depletion (e.g., unsupplemented weight-loss diets), and of some dietary supplements (such as amino acids).

Some adult children will have to assist their parents in meeting nutritional needs. Others will be luckier; their parents will remain healthy and independent. Regardless of the specific circumstances, food and eating are essential parts of our lives with our parents. Giving it enough thought, therefore, will only make our lives with them more satisfying and fulfilling.

## PARENTS AND FOOD—WHAT TO KNOW AND DO

- Remember that food is essential to physical and psychological well-being.

- Watch for pronounced or sudden changes in your parents' body weight.

- Help your parents make the most of meals:
  try to dine with them often
  respect their dietary restrictions
  encourage them to make dining a social event

- When weight reduction is necessary, help them to follow a moderate diet plan, to avoid the "roller coaster" weight-loss effect.

- Know the substitutes for high-cholesterol foods.

- Know how to substitute low-salt for high-sodium foods; know how to avoid extra salt.

- Know how to keep some fiber in the diet.

# 6

# SEX:
# Do They Really Do It—Now?

*Kids think parents old and dull*
*On matters lewd or sexual.*
*They, of course, don't know the truth—*
Libido *is perpetual!*

Gertrude Small,
unpublished poem (1971)

You may be wondering why you need burden yourself with concern about your parents' sex life. That would seem to be one area of their lives you should not have to worry about. It is none of your business, just as *your* sex life is none of *their* business. You wouldn't want them intruding in your sex life. "What I don't know won't hurt me. Besides, I'm sure they don't do it anymore." Don't be too sure. In fact, many people do remain sexually active well into their eighties and nineties. Nonetheless, it is important that you know some of the sexual changes that occur with advancing age, and as a result of some diseases. You may have an opportunity to talk to your parents about their concerns, and someday you yourself may be able to use the knowledge you gained about the effects of aging on sexual performance. Correct information is the first step toward alleviating, and often preventing, a problem.

It is difficult for children at any age to imagine their parents engaged in sexual intercourse. But now that those parents are so old—"over the hill"—past 50, 60, 70 . . . it seems impossible. Passion and romance in our culture seem to be only for the young and beautiful. Despite the new sexual freedom, the "adult" books, the explicit movies, and despite discussions of birth control and the prevalence of legal abortions and free clinics, ignorance about sex continues, and a reluctance to talk about the subject persists, especially among parents and their children. While teenage pregnancies abound, providing testimony of sexual promiscuity, sexual dissatisfaction is rampant. One survey published about a decade ago analyzed responses

67

of well-educated and "happily married" couples in their mid-
to late thirties.[1] Both men and women reported sexual dysfunction: 40 percent of the men cited problems with erection
or ejaculation, while 63 percent of the women noted problems
centered around arousal or orgasm. Lack of interest, or inability to relax, was reported by 50 percent of the men and 77
percent of the women. Some people may be having more sex
at earlier ages, but many at all ages seem to be enjoying it less.

Sex is one of the three basic drives common to all animals,
the others being hunger and thirst. It is a healthy and satisfying outlet that brings about a release of physical and psychological tension, and can be a pleasurable culmination of
intimacy when shared with another person. It has been the object of taboos in every religion and culture, and has been reg-
ulated and controlled by both. For example, the ancient
Buddhists believed that frequent intercourse depleted the life-
sustaining *ch'i* (essence or sperm), and as a result, casual sex was
disdained by them and each sexual act was thought to reduce
a person's life span.[2] By contrast, the Taoists had a more moderate view:

> We do not struggle against the natural tendency of man,
> and [yet] we are able to obtain an increase in longevity. Is
> that not pleasant?[3]

We have come a long way toward sexual sophistication, but
many "moderns" still blush and are uncomfortable when they
hear a "dirty" joke or are privy to some scandalous sexual information.

Do you remember your parents' embarrassment when one
or both of them attempted to discuss the "facts of life" with you
in your teens? Maybe they gave you a book to read or avoided
the subject altogether, and you were too shy to ask. They
probably never had the privilege of such a discussion, and had
to learn from life experience or from friends who were just as
uninformed or misinformed as they were. The miracle is that
most people seem to manage their sexual lives reasonably well,
despite such mystique and lack of information.

What were the sexual messages when you were a child?
Did your parents touch and hug each other? Did they hug and
kiss you and your siblings? Were sexual subjects open for discussion? Were you punished when they found you masturbat-

ing? Freud believed that many emotional problems in adult life result from unresolved early-childhood sexual conflicts. Astute psychotherapists know that patients often resist discussion of their sexuality, even when it is a major cause of concern. And most physicians are just as happy if the elderly (and not so elderly) patient never brings up the subject. Although, to date, a few states require that health professionals be trained in the evaluation and treatment of sexual dysfunctions in order to be licensed to practice their specialties (for example, medicine and clinical psychology in California), the adequacy of the training varies and is generally too limited, considering the immense psychological and cultural barriers to open discussions about the topic. Physicians are often reluctant to volunteer information about sex unless patients ask, sex therapists being the exception. At cultural and psychological levels, sex remains taboo. An important way to remove this taboo for us and for our parents is to acquire accurate information.

## SEX AND AGING

Our aversion toward sexuality among the aged found support in early studies that reported a decline in sexual activity and interest with age.[4] The early sex researchers, such as Masters and Johnson, had much to learn about young adult sexuality and failed to focus on the elderly. A telling example is the number of pages Kinsey devoted to the subject; out of 1,646 pages, three were devoted to older men, four to older women.[5]

These early studies measured statistical frequencies and collected physiological data. The finding by Kinsey that intercourse frequency in people 60 years old was once every two weeks compared to the rate of two to three times per week for 20-year-olds was interpreted as supporting the idea that sexual interest and activity necessarily declined with age. Moreover, the emphasis on physiological losses raises the inevitable question, "Why bother having sex at all if you're old?"

Yet, recent studies point out that an elderly person's sexual activity and interests are consistent with those in earlier adulthood.[6] In fact, for many, sexual response improves. Why such discrepancies?

There are a number of reasons. For one, older people today, like younger people, have been influenced by the "sexual revolution." Also, today's elderly are healthier, more active physically, and have more leisure time than those studied 40 years ago. The major reason for the differences, though, may be that those early studies just emphasized the physiological and statistical changes rather than looking at the individual's experience and perception of sex.

When researchers finally did focus on the experience of sex, the findings contradicted the stereotypes of old age and sex. For example, using a 50-item, open-ended questionnaire, sex researchers gathered replies from 800 people aged 60 to 91 years. What did they find?

- 95 percent said they liked sex
- 99 percent would like to have sex if it were available
- 99 percent of the women said they were orgasmic most of the time or always
- 93 percent considered touching and cuddling important
- 75 percent were as sexually satisfied now as in younger years
- 91 percent approved in principle of older people having sex and living together unmarried
- 82 percent accepted masturbation in principle, but only 46 percent said they masturbated[7]

Although people may not be completely truthful about themselves when answering a questionnaire, these responses are intriguing. Despite our society's negative attitude toward sex among older people, sexual feelings do endure through most of life. Biologic responses may slow down as tissues wear out; sexual activity may be altered or impeded by the many physical illnesses that accompany old age; but sexual feelings and fantasies are independent of these changes. They can and do endure. The physiological intensity of the response may diminish, but subjective enjoyment persists. And the sexual habits and behavior established in earlier years seem to set the pattern for those of later years. If your parents enjoyed sex when they were young, they are likely still to enjoy it when they are old.

In many ways, sex is no different from other bodily functions. Muscles need to be exercised to keep their tone, and sexual responses seem to benefit from active and regular use. "Use it or lose it" has no upper age limit. A major problem that the elderly face when they are widowed or divorced is the unavailability of suitable partners. Since women outlive men by nearly a decade, single women in their sixties, seventies, eighties, and beyond have a harder and harder time finding suitable mates. For every four women 55 years of age and older, there are approximately three men in the population. By the time women reach the 85-plus age group, there are only two men for every five women. And most of these women are widowed, while most of the men are not. An estimated three out of four men 65 years of age and older are married, compared to less than half of the women in that age group.[8]

Society's message to the older generation is that sex and romance do not apply to them. And adult children are just as insensitive to their parents' needs as is the rest of society. "My father is a dirty old man," Natalie told the social worker at the retirement home. "My mother isn't even gone a year, and those witches in his apartment building are out to get him. Last week when I stopped by with some groceries, I found one of them in bed with him at two o'clock in the afternoon. I hope this place monitors such activities and he can find some male friends. He was so dependent on my mother—I can't see him living alone." The social worker smiled and said, "Actually, I wish we had the facilities to encourage our residents to enjoy intimate relationships. But we don't have enough space here for the privacy they would need. Did you know we have dances and other mixed social activities for our male and female residents?" Needless to say, Natalie responded to the social worker's candor by not including that home in the list she presented to her father.

Natalie's reaction was a typical child's denial of a parent's sexuality. Men, more than women, find it difficult to live alone, and ordinarily children can accept their father's sexuality more readily than their mother's. To a large extent, the double standard is still with us. In fact, children usually benefit if their elderly parent finds a mate. It reduces loneliness and eases the burden for them when the parent becomes sick or infirm. Many elderly widowed or divorced men and women enjoy intimacy, but are reluctant to marry because they do not want to

## MYTHS AND FACTS ABOUT
## SEXUAL RESPONSE IN OLDER PEOPLE

| MYTH | FACT |
|---|---|
| Sexual feelings and fantasies are not normal for older people. | Sexual feelings and fantasies are normal and healthy and may continue until death. |
| Gray hair, sagging bodies, and wrinkles reduce sexuality and desirability. | Maturity and experience may minimize the importance of physical appearance; sexuality and desirability do not necessarily diminish with these changes. |
| Masturbation is harmful and "not nice" for older people. | Masturbation is safe and normal. |
| Sexual gratification comes only through intercourse, especially for older people. | Manual and oral stimulation are acceptable and pleasurable alternatives to sexual intercourse. |
| Sex is dangerous if you have been sick or had surgery. | Pain and bodily malfunction can deter sexual function, but in many cases sexual activity can be resumed; alternate methods and positions can be used. |
| Older people lose their ability to enjoy sex. | Older people need not lose their ability to enjoy sex. |
| Satisfying sex must always end in intercourse and orgasm. | Hugging, kissing, stroking, and giving pleasure to a partner can be sexually gratifying, without culminating in either intercourse or orgasm, regardless of the person's age. |

be vulnerable to another loss, to assume the burden of caring for an ailing spouse, or to face the financial entanglements resulting from a legal union and the controversies about inheritance that might ensue. You may be struck by Natalie's lack of respect for her father's privacy. Many adult children feel it is okay to drop in at a parent's home anytime, especially if it used to be their home, too. These same children would be incensed if a parent dropped in at their home without notice. After all, *they* have a right to privacy!

Human sexual behavior is influenced not only by emotional reactions but by many other factors, ranging from biological endowment to cultural and religious background, marital status, developmental and age-related changes, and physical and psychological health, as well as interpersonal relationships.

## CHANGES FOR WOMEN

Menopause—cessation of menstruation—often leads to uncomfortable physical symptoms. Although most women cope, many experience sweating, hot flashes, depression, and nervousness. Reduced and slower vaginal lubrication and decreased elasticity may cause painful intercourse, resulting in anxiety and diminishing sexual activity. These symptoms can be treated with estrogens. There is, however, controversy about the use of estrogens to treat menopausal symptoms, given the potential side effects. Chronic bladder and vaginal infections, too, can temporarily interfere with sexual activity. Some women experience a sense of loss when their child-rearing days are over. Others feel emancipated when the fear of pregnancy ends, and subsequently find their sex lives more fulfilling.

In addition to the normal age-related changes, women often have to deal with the consequences of surgical interventions. Even though sexually significant surgical procedures can be carried out at any age, they become more frequent as women get older. Removal of the ovaries (oophorectomy) can produce menopausal symptoms, but many of the symptoms remit with estrogen treatment. Removal of a breast (mastectomy) can lead to grief and depression and a decrease in sexual interest and activity. In a study of 77 women who had undergone mastectomy, 12 percent had thought of suicide following the surgery, yet only 6.5 percent had sought psychotherapeutic help from a mental health professional.[9] Removal of the uterus (hysterectomy) does not lead directly to menopausal symptoms, but can have a profound psychological impact. The uterus represents a woman's ability to procreate, her nurturing and maternal functions. With its removal may come a sense of loss and grief—sometimes augmented by a sense of worthlessness and feelings of sexual unattractiveness. The emotional reactions following such surgical procedures are often complex, with an intermingling of the woman's sense of body mutilation, and often fear of death or further morbidity, especially if the procedure was a cancer treatment.

### CHANGES FOR MEN

As men reach their sixth decade and beyond, they too can expect sexual changes. Although most men cope with such changes, many do not. Erections become less rigid, delayed, and/or partial. When they ejaculate, there is a reduction in force and volume of fluid emitted. They may experience a delay before orgasm (prolonged plateau phase). After orgasm, the penis becomes flaccid more rapidly than in younger men, and the refractory (recovery) period before the next erection and ejaculation is prolonged. Men do, however, maintain the capacity for erection throughout life. Kinsey and his associates discovered decades ago that three out of four men at 70 years of age maintain potency and that approximately half of 75-year-olds do also.[10]

Tragically, some aging men move from adequate sexual function to varying degrees of dysfunction and impotence simply because they do not understand the changes that aging imposes. They entertain the false belief that the physiology of old age must lead to a radical decrease in sexual function or even abstention altogether; that their lessened sexual drive and occasional impotence is just the beginning of a rapidly progressive decline; that such physical changes as hair loss or weight gain necessarily mean lack of attractiveness to potential sexual partners. Many uninformed older wives suppress their own sexual needs and avoid sex with their husbands so as not to embarrass them because they may have difficulty getting an erection and maintaining it.

Often, prostate surgery in older men can affect their sexual performance. Anxiety and doubt about sexual potency and desirability after surgery can lead to a self-fulfilling prophecy. The surgical trauma from transurethral prostatectomy (removal through the urethra), however, does not necessarily affect the physiological capacity for erection. It is important for the patient to be aware of potential changes following surgery—for example, ejaculation may become retrograde into the bladder rather than through the penis. This should not affect the physical pleasure, but not seeing the ejaculate fluid can so frighten the patient as to traumatize him psychologically and inhibit his sexual activity. Physicians may be remiss in failing to discuss this potential change after surgery.

## ILLNESS AND SEX

With age comes the likelihood of multiple physical illnesses, along with the drugs to treat them and the side effects of those drugs. In general, illnesses tend to decrease sexual interest and function. There are exceptions. Sometimes patients suffering from Alzheimer disease and related brain disorders experience a disinhibition, with increased and sometimes inappropriate sexual interest and display (hypersexuality). For example, a previously shy and very proper person may masturbate in public or make sexual advances to strangers. In many situations, though, physical or mental illnesses tend not to interfere with an enjoyable sex life. Knowledge of these illnesses and how they can impair sexual function may help partners adjust and maintain sexual activity.

The following chart lists some common conditions that may affect your parents' sex life. At times it is hard to predict what influence an illness will have. Hardening of the arteries of the brain (cerebral arteriosclerosis) may cause loss of sexual desire or heightened and inappropriate sexual behavior. Hardening of the arteries in the genitourinary system may impair the blood flow directly to the penis, leading to impotence. Strokes often cause paralysis, with changes in physical appearance that may make the victim less attractive sexually to the partner. Patients with heart disease, on the other hand, may leave their partners dissatisfied because they commonly fear sexual activity. They may shun it altogether lest the excitement lead to another heart attack and death. Many patients can resume sexual activity after a heart attack, so their fears may be out of proportion to the actual risk. Investigators have measured heart rate during sexual intercourse in patients who have had a heart attack, and have found that the average rate (117 beats per minute) approximates that attained when climbing

## PHYSICAL CONDITIONS THAT MAY INTERFERE WITH YOUR PARENTS' SEX LIFE

| Condition | Problems | Approach |
|---|---|---|
| Heart disease | Fear of activity Diminished energy | Monitoring, education, rehabilitation, exercise, counseling, psychotherapy Alternate forms of sexual expression |
| Stroke, cerebral arteriosclerosis | Physical change Loss of desire Impotence Disinhibition | Post-stroke rehabilitation Counseling, psychotherapy, education |
| Arthritis | Pain Stiffness | Careful timing of analgesic medication Sexual counseling on comfortable positions Alternate forms of sexual expression |
| Diabetes | Impotence | Adequate control of diabetes Alternate forms of sexual expression |
| Depression | Loss of desire Impotence | Treatment of depression Psychiatric referral |
| Mastectomy | Altered body image Loss of desire | Education, counseling, psychotherapy |
| Prostatectomy | Impotence Fear of activity Pain | Counseling, psychotherapy, education Alternate forms of sexual expression |

two flights of stairs.[11] In a recent study of male survivors of a first heart attack, about half the patients felt that their sex life was less satisfying following the heart attack, and 39 percent of them cited fear of sexual activity as the cause of this reduced enjoyment.[12]

## DRUGS AND SEX

That heading makes us think of aphrodisiacs—drugs that have been used for centuries to enhance sexual pleasure. The kinds of medication our parents are likely to be taking, how-

### SOME DRUGS THAT MAY IMPAIR SEXUAL ACTIVITY*

| Medication Group† | Presumed Mechanisms | Effect |
| --- | --- | --- |
| Antianxiety drugs: sedatives, hypnotics, alcohol, narcotics | General depression of central nervous system (CNS) | Decreased libido and sexual response |
| Antipsychotic drugs: phenothiazines, butyrophenones | Anticholinergic, antiadrenergic, antidopamine effects; CNS depression | Erectile or ejaculatory difficulties; reduced libido |
| Antidepressant drugs: monoamine oxidase inhibitors, tricyclics | Peripheral autonomic effects | Rare potency or ejaculatory problems |
| Antiandrogens: estrogens (for replacement therapy), cortisone (anti-inflammatory), aldactone, aldactozide (antihypertensives) | Oppose the stimulating effect of androgen in brain and sexual organs | Decreased libido and sexual response |
| Anticholinergic drugs (for glaucoma, ulcers): atropine, banthine | Inhibit acetylcholine | Ejaculatory problems |
| Antiadrenergic drugs: methyldopa | Block autonomic nervous system | Impaired ejaculation; diminished libido and erection |

*If one of these agents is a suspected offender, your parent should seek medical consultation. The physician may decrease the dose, stop the drug, or find a substitute.

†See *Physicians' Desk Reference* (*PDR*) for specific names of drugs.

ever, tend to diminish rather than enhance sexual function. Many drugs have the potential to inhibit sexual performance, and our parents generally take a whole array of drugs for their physical ills. Just because your parent has tolerated a medication for years without side effects does not exonerate that medication as a cause of sexual problems. Physiological changes that accompany aging alter the body's ability to excrete drugs; your parent may, therefore, experience side effects at dosages previously tolerated. The table below lists some of the more common offenders. Be aware that just taking one of the drugs on the list does not necessarily indicate the presence of sexual dysfunction; your parent may be doing just fine despite the drug, or perhaps because of it. Some of these medications can indirectly improve sexual functioning; for example, a depressed parent may regain sexual interest as a result of drug treatment that cured a depression.

## SEX AND YOUR PARENTS

It is true that you may not know the details of your parents' intimate life, and direct questions to them may not only be embarrassing but inappropriate. Usually, your parents' sex life is indeed none of your business. Occasionally, however, they may hint at a problem or even come right out and ask you. Having some understanding of common sexual problems is useful—not only so that you might help them, but one day you may even find yourself profiting from that understanding. Meanwhile, as you help your parents get to their doctor, support them before and after surgery, ask questions about their medications, discuss medical alternatives, or just lend an ear as they air their woes, you may have an opportunity to point out that various medications, illnesses, and surgeries *do* have an effect on the libido as well as on sexual performance. Your parents may not know this and may think their symptoms are results of their specific illness and are therefore irremediable. People in your parents' generation are likely to be more reluctant to talk about such things—or even to think about them. Your knowledge, if conveyed to them, can make them more comfortable and less inhibited. There could be opportunities for you to suggest that they ask their doctors to discuss with them sexual matters relevant to the specific illness. Even if you yourself do not talk to your parents about sex, you may open the door for them to talk to someone else.

## LIFESTYLE CHANGES AND SEX

The lifestyle changes that have revolutionized our generation and that of our children are having an impact on our parents, too. We hear about couples who decide to divorce after marriages of 30 or 40 years. Sometimes the rift is a reflection of the "empty nest syndrome"; when the children have grown up and left the house, the couple cannot tolerate the increased opportunity for intimacy, and conflict heightens. With more healthful lifestyles, people in their sixties, seventies, and beyond may experience a resurgence of earlier sexual desires, and resent the presence of a traditional spouse interfering with life's pleasure. The result is divorce among couples married for three or four decades or more.

Much has been written about the effects of divorce on younger children, but almost nothing about its effects on the adult child—as if the adult child suffered no confusion, shock, bewilderment, or pain. Even adults with few parenting needs and well-developed relationships with their parents are affected by such a breakup. Their confidence in opposite-sex relationships can be undermined, and they may feel that their parents were not honest with them. Then, too, they may be pushed into a parenting role prematurely, as the needier parent turns to them for support and nurturing. They may be forced to take sides, just as younger children are asked to do during divorce battles. This added burden may come at a time when adult children are experiencing their own crises in marriage or other relationships. In the United States today, one out of two marriages ends in divorce. And, of course, children may be forced to face those taboo notions about their parents' sexuality. The realization that *"libido* is perpetual," including their parents' libido, may arouse in the adult child long-buried sexual conflicts.

Marcia's parents divorced after 35 years of marriage and the final payment of their 25-year mortgage. Marcia's mother, Eileen, kept the house, the furniture, and the dog. Her father,

Bert—who left the marriage to live with a 34-year-old woman, her four kids, and a car—kept some money, but not much. Both parents held on to a lot of memories, as well as questions, doubts, and fears about their futures.

Marcia and her mother helped each other through many of the unexpected changes resulting from the divorce—the missing place at the table, the mail that had to be forwarded, the phone calls from friends ignorant of the divorce, and the general adjustment to an "incomplete" family. Eileen had few social contacts at the time—she had not felt the need when her husband was around—and turned to her daughter. Although torn between her two parents, Marcia enjoyed spending more time with her mother. For her, it was important to maintain a close relationship with at least one parent. Marcia reintroduced her mother to activities that she had abandoned since her marriage, such as movies, dining out, and jogging in the park.

After the first year, Eileen became more comfortable with being single. She developed outside contacts, began her first full-time job in over 20 years, and started dating. Besides recovering emotionally from the divorce, Eileen was losing weight and receiving compliments on her "new single look." And then, suddenly, there was the excitement of a potentially intimate relationship with someone besides her husband—after 35 years of fidelity.

Marcia, who had at first been delighted when her mother had "a date," started to become uncomfortable with the role-reversal. It seemed as if her mother would always ask her to drop by on some pretense on nights when she was going out, so that Marcia could "inspect" her date. Eileen would telephone Marcia early the next day and talk about the pros and cons of each man. The first time her mother shyly, but with pride, mentioned that she had had a very nice time with her friend John, who had spent the night, Marcia felt angry and concerned. She wanted to give her mother the same lecture her mother had given her when years ago she had begun dating— "The Hazards of Casual Sex." At that time there had not been AIDS to worry about. And then Marcia became aware of the competitive feelings developing between her mother and herself, which made her uncomfortable. How could she compete with her own mother? Their special, close friendship began to erode. She was beginning to be as jealous of her mother's dates as she was of some of her friends'. Marcia found herself making up excuses so that she would not *have* to meet her mother's latest boyfriend, who seemed uninterested in meeting his date's daughter, anyway. Marcia wished her parents would just get back together. She wanted things the way they were—a mother who acted like a mother, and her father the only man in the house.

When her parents divorced, Marcia was already over 30 and out on her own. But even adult children who live away from the parents' home can be affected by the legal and emotional battles, the holidays spent as an "incomplete family," and the changed relationship with one parent or both.

Marcia's experience is not unique. Sexual activity among older singles, whether divorced or widowed, is not uncommon and is believed to be on the increase. The most extensive studies of the 1950s found that fewer than one out of ten single elderly people (aged 60 to 93 years) were sexually active.[13] By contrast, studies from the 1980s report that at least three out of four men and about half of all women who are more than 60 years of age and single are sexually active.[14] Many more indicate a desire to have sex if only the right partner were available. How do adult children respond to this unexpected sexual activity among their parents? Marcia had her troubles. Though at first she enjoyed the closeness she experienced when she spent more time with her mother, that closeness turned to discomfort when her mother became a sexually active single. True, Marcia's mother was insecure and anxious about her new sexual role, and turned to her daughter for counsel and support. But her mother's sexual activity was in sharp contrast to Marcia's current lack of a sexual relationship, and stirred up feelings of jealousy. Eventually, her mother remarried and mother and daughter again became close, though Marcia continued to miss a fulfilling sexual relationship of her own for several years.

Marcia wanted to change her mother's sexual attitudes and behavior. But what about the reverse situation? What should adult children do if their parents show an interest in their sex lives, or become intrusive and try to meddle? There is no simple answer. In Marcia's case, her mother's interest and concern may have helped her come to terms with her own psychological conflicts. In other situations they take the risk—

one that adult children may also take—of overstepping boundaries. A walk through the six steps of the Commonsense Approach to Problem Solving may point to answers for you.

For some parents, the "empty nest syndrome" brings about a breakup of their marriage and their sexual relationship. Others experience a sense of freedom, relief, and excitement about their renewed privacy. With the children out of the house and fewer work-related worries and aggravations during retirement, couples may rediscover the romance in their relationship and find that many endings are really new beginnings in disguise. For many, though, as their years increase, their sexual activity diminishes and is replaced by other pursuits, as was true for King David and King Solomon, who, as James Bell Taylor wrote in *Ancient Authors,*

> . . . *led merry, merry lives,*
> *With many, many lady friends*
> *And many, many wives;*
> *But when old age crept over them—*
> *With many, many qualms,*
> *King Solomon wrote the Proverbs,*
> *And King David wrote the Psalms.*

Regardless of whether or not "old age has crept over" our own parents, the adult child's efforts to remove the taboos governing frank sexual discussion with parents, could lead to ameliorating the unnecessary pain that so many experience when they can no longer fulfill this basic and important function.

---

### WHAT TO DO ABOUT SEX AND PARENTS

- Know the differences between facts and myths about sex and aging.
- Recognize that your parents really may have sex now.
- Recognize how illnesses and medications may interfere with sexual functioning.
- Do not let your lifestyle or theirs interfere with satisfying sex for you or your parents.

# 7

# HOUSING:
# How Can We Live with
# Them—or without Them?

> *. . . age and youth cannot live together:*
> *Youth is full of pleasure, age is full of care.*
>
> William Shakespeare,
> *The Passionate Pilgrim*

Steve thought about the previous week with a heavy heart. The day he had to drive his mother to a retirement home may have been one of the worst days of his life. Although not bedridden, she was too frail to continue living alone in her apartment. While driving along in the car, it seemed to him like a funeral, as if he were taking her to her last stop after disposing of her furniture and apartment. She had simply run out of money in the two years since his father's death. She could no longer afford the companion/housekeeper. He had learned that his parents had been dipping into their savings even while his father was alive, and that they had sold their sterling silver and jewelry over the years to keep up their standard of living. Their retirement plan had no provision for runaway inflation, and their Social Security benefits barely paid the rent and food bills.

It made him sad to think of his mother—the lady, always prim and proper, with maids, fancy clothes, and jewelry—going from a six-room apartment to half a room in a retirement home. She herself could not face the reality; she had told her friends that she was moving to a resort hotel. Steve wondered if it would not have been easier just to let his mother live with his family. He had considered that, but knew it would be the end of his marriage. His wife had enough trouble getting along with his mother at a distance, let alone under the same roof.

Steve's experience is not unique. Conflicts over a surviving or ailing parent are bound to occur for most adult children. With an illness or a death, questions invariably come up:

*83*

"Where now? Should Mother stay home? Move into our house? Not a nursing home, never!" As long as both parents are living together and in reasonably good health, more or less "looking after" one another, the demands upon children are usually minimal. Even if one of the parents becomes physically disabled or dies, the demands upon children may be limited to the crisis period if the survivor is healthy and has interests, hobbies, friends, and financial security. Often, however, this is not the case, and parents must face the prospect of a more dependent living arrangement. The decision about where an ill or lonely parent can best live often becomes a guilt-provoking and conflict-ridden task for the parent as well as the adult children.

Since women live longer than men, the surviving parent is usually the mother. If they make the adjustment and are in reasonably good health, women seem to be better able to survive by themselves and care for themselves than men. According to the U.S. Census Bureau, in 1982 less than 20 percent of men 75 years of age and older lived alone, but nearly half (45 percent) of the women did. The disparity in marital status of older men and women may partly account for the different living arrangements of these two groups. Most of the more than 7 million elderly persons living alone in 1982 were women. Nearly two out of three men 75 years of age or older lived with a spouse, but only one in five women did. For every man age 75 or older, there were nearly two women of that age![1]

Only a small number of the elderly live in intergenerational homes—homes with children or other relatives—but the percentage increases with advancing age, particularly for older women. Nearly one in four women 75 years of age or older lives in a household with someone else.[2] Having Mother or Father move in may solve some immediate problems, but may create others. When that move is not feasible, we often look to retirement homes or convalescent hospitals (also known as extended care facilities or nursing homes) as an alternative.

And what if Father outlives Mother and is forced to move in with his adult children? He may have expectations of being waited on hand and foot, particularly if Mother set a precedent for such expectations. The result may be disappointment for the father and resentment in the adult child. Or Father may interfere with the household in other ways, perhaps by rearranging the tools in his son's workshop. The delicate balance in family relations is likely to be disrupted whenever a parent moves in.

Usually, adult daughters (and, to some extent, daughters-in-law) become the principal caregivers to elderly parents. In the absence of daughters, a son may assume that role. Added to the ordinary stresses of daily living, the stress of taking care of a disabled or dependent parent can take its toll of the caregiver and family. Psychological symptoms are common; the  caregiver may become depressed, anxious, frustrated, sleepless, and emotionally exhausted. Particularly when a parent moves in, or when long-distance travel is required, the middle-aged child's spouse and children are affected. Their lifestyles are disturbed, their privacy invaded, their plans often disrupted; the family's income is reduced, and, perhaps most important, the mother's time is diverted from the family. While each case is unique in events and circumstances, the emotional reactions are often similar.

How does geography affect our relationships with our parents, and our ability to care for them? Although technological advances have changed our concepts of geographical separation, physical distances have an impact on how we experience emotional closeness. We can fly across the United States in five hours and be almost anywhere in the world in less than twenty-four. Local telephone calls are different from long-distance ones, although the voices may sound the same. Parents who live within a few miles may take a little too much interest in our lives. How much is too much? That varies from family to family. What is too close for some may be too far away for others. Let us examine a few of the possible living arrangements that are available, and how they might help or hinder your lives.

## LONG-DISTANCE PARENTCARE

Most older parents do live near at least one child; three out of four parents live within a half hour's journey.[3] Researchers have only begun to study older people and their children who live at a distance. This limited research does indicate, however,  that children with more education and greater economic resources are likely to live farther away from their parents than those without such advantages.[4] As distance increases, of course, visits decrease. One study suggests that distances over 50 miles seem to make a substantial difference in frequency of visits.[5] About three-fourths of children living more than 50 miles away saw their parents about once a year, as compared to once a week for children living within ten miles of their parents. For most, contact is still maintained; as distance increases, so does the frequency of telephone and mail contact.

Moving some distance away is one way of dealing with smothering closeness. Shelly and Bob left Chicago for Los Angeles shortly after their wedding, to escape Shelly's intrusive, critical, and controlling parents. Shelly's parents would not speak to them for nearly a year—until they finally got over their feelings of rejection. Though Shelly and Bob missed their families and friends, it was the first time the couple felt they had a life of their own. But it didn't last long—two years later, Shelley's parents followed them out to Los Angeles. Trying to solve a conflict involving emotional closeness by creating geographic distance is not always an enduring solution. Bob's parents did not follow the couple to the West Coast. It was Bob who usually initiated and maintained contact with them. He telephoned often and made his calls at times that meant the most—Sundays, holidays, and an occasional unexpected midweek call. And they visited once a year.

Long-distance parentcare, however, gets more complicated when parents become disabled enough to need personal care. If it is an illness, it may mean more long-distance calls—not only to your parents but also to their doctors and to other relatives and friends. It may mean commuting to their city on weekends or whenever necessary, in an emergency.

All things being equal, it is best for our parents to make their own decisions about where to live. Usually, it is wise to avoid moves, particularly for those who have lived in the same neighborhood for years, as the familiarity and network of friends offer emotional stability and social support. Yet for some people, like Bob's father, a move is the only choice. Widowed suddenly, Bob's father needed someone to look after him. Bob helped him move from Chicago to Los Angeles, and found an apartment near his own. His father's physical health, however, declined rapidly; his arthritis made it difficult for him to climb the stairs, get in and out of the bathtub on his own, and even get dressed. For various reasons, Bob could not bring his father into his own home, so he searched long and hard for a nursing home where his dad could get the necessary help. Bob found one, but after his father moved in, he became withdrawn and depressed. Even though the nursing home had the staff to assist him, Bob's father could not tolerate his new dependent role. After several months, Bob finally got his father to consent to see a psychiatrist. With the aid of antidepressant medication and discussion of the losses suffered, he helped Bob's dad to become more accepting of his dependent role. Bob's father did become less depressed, but he never returned to his "old self."

## CARING FOR PARENTS WHO LIVE NEARBY

Bob's solution, of moving his father into his own town, did remove the expense and time that would have been used up in commuting hundreds of miles. Living in the same town eases many of the burdens often associated with parentcare. Searching for a doctor, a supermarket, or a cleaner is easier on our own turf than on someone else's. Nevertheless, geographic closeness brings a different level of interpersonal responsibility, often to the dismay of some family members. Holiday dinners may become a lot less intimate, with the one or two additional place settings. Your own children may become reluctant to spend time with you because Grandpa or Grandma always "tags along." By contrast, if your parents have close ties with you and your children, geographic closeness may strengthen those ties and provide an opportunity for family members to get to know each other better and enjoy one another's company.

The six steps of the Commonsense Approach to Problem Solving can be valuable in resolving many such conflicts. Margery certainly could have used them. With her mother in the hospital and her father in a nursing home, she felt "frantic about her parents most of the time" (Step 1, Mood Meter Reading). Had she used Personal Reflection (Step 2), she might have realized that some of her panicky feelings were triggered by memories of when she had left home to go away to college. At that time, it was a financial burden for her father, and she could not help but feel selfish. Just attending to these first two steps would have allowed her to gain some perspective on her feelings and lessen their burden.

## IS MOM SAFE IN HER APARTMENT ALONE?

Whether your older parent is living down the block or in another state, day-to-day safety is often a major concern. Sylvia, who had divorced her husband on her sixtieth birthday, was an independent, spirited woman who, 15 years later, was still playing golf twice a week. Although her son and daughter lived near her two-bedroom condominium, she kept very busy with her own household and social activities. Their infrequent visits were all she could handle. One day, while shopping, she slipped and badly bruised her left side. Her doctor told her how lucky she was—many people at her age would surely have fractured a bone. He also told her that she had a mild case of Parkinson disease, which explained the tremor that had been bothering her, and had perhaps contributed to her fall.

Sylvia's bruises healed, but her Parkinson disease got worse. She had difficulty holding her morning coffee cup without spilling it. Even with her housekeeper's assistance twice a week, the shopping trips became too difficult for her. Her children wanted her to get live-in help, but Sylvia protested that she had been independent too long and could not stand "tripping over strange people." Her children wanted to respect her independence, but were terrified that she would have another fall. It was reminiscent of the days when they had first left their own children without a baby-sitter.

Sylvia's situation is not unusual. Although at-home help can be obtained, there is a wide range in quality, price, and skills. If help is to be hired, it is best to shop around. A first-hand recommendation from someone you trust can be helpful, but even with such a recommendation, a trial period is usually necessary to see if the person's particular skills and personality traits meet your parent's needs.

Many older people are very reluctant to give anyone access to their homes. Others do not have the financial resources to hire such help. Sometimes there are less costly and relatively simple practical solutions to these problems. For example, handrails can be installed in the hallways for unsteady people. We know of an elderly man who smoked, and whose children were concerned that one day he might set his apartment on fire because he had grown careless and inattentive. Smoke alarms, fireproofing, and a direct emergency line to the manager's apartment provided reassurance. Chapters 10 and 12 provide details on the various people, services, and devices that can make the home relatively safe for a disabled elderly person.

Sometimes, concern about a parent's safety may reflect the adult child's own conflicts, rather than actual danger to the parent. The child's reaction may be exaggerated out of feelings of guilt, anger, or anxiety. In Sylvia's situation, her daughter, particularly, was overreacting because of guilty feelings and the conviction that she had never done enough for her parents. Now she wanted to make up for it by "hiring help," as if she could hire someone to make up for all the years she herself should have been helping.

## THE NURSING HOME: PROS AND CONS

Have you ever heard your kids ask, "Do we have to visit Grandpa?" when you shepherded them into the car for the journey to your father's nursing home? Perhaps you have asked yourself the same question. Nursing homes can be depressing. Yet for too many debilitated, lonely, and senile elderly people, they are the last stop in life's journey. Even if your own parent is fairly competent and not uncomfortably ill, how do you get through the corridors of senile mumblers, the smell of incontinence, the sounds of agonizing distress, the sight of wheelchair-bound invalids? How do you escape the aura of sadness, desperation, and loneliness? And yet you sense their happiness as their faces light up and they smile when they notice younger people like you and your children. Do you feel guilty when you have the urge to pull away as they try to touch you or speak to you? Do you want to run, to put on blinders, to try to escape your peripheral vision and temporarily stop breathing? Or do you want to help them, try to distract them, find something to make them feel better?

Many nursing-home residents have no visitors. Over half of these residents have no living close relatives, and no one ever

comes to see six out of ten.[6] In the last 20 years, the number
of these lonely people living in nursing homes has increased
substantially, from one-half million in the early 1960s to nearly
one and a half million in the late 1970s. Although most people
over 65 years of age are not nursing-home residents, 90 percent of people living in these facilities are in the upper age
groups. If current trends continue, the U.S. Census Bureau
predicts that by the year 2040, nearly 5 million people 65 years
of age or older will reside in nursing homes.[7]

Those who live in institutions are usually there because
they suffer from some disability and are dependent on others
for care. More than 50 percent of older people in nursing
homes have mild to moderate impairment in intellectual abilities; many probably suffer from Alzheimer disease. Ninety
percent have at least one chronic impairment.

Adult children often have extreme misgivings about moving their parents into nursing homes, which are not always safe.
A study published in the *New England Journal of Medicine* in
1981 found that 16 percent of nursing-home residents suffered from some kind of infection, yet programs to control infection were not well developed. Moreover, the researchers
noted that there were relatively few staff members available to
care for the patients, and of those, even fewer had adequate
training. One attempt to improve the quality of nursing homes
has been a movement among some physicians to affiliate them
with medical schools so that they might become teaching institutions with high-quality staffing and care.

Nursing homes come in all shapes and sizes, and vary
widely in the quality and extent of their services. If your parents need such a facility, what should you know? How do you
help them pick the best, as well as the most affordable? There
are certainly many from which to choose. The age and sex ra-
tios of residents in these nursing homes will vary, too, though
the average nursing home resident is over 85 years old. Don't
be surprised if you find most residents to be women, because,
in general, women outnumber men by three to one.[8]

There are different types of long-term care residences;
most fall into one of two categories: skilled nursing facilities
(SNF) and intermediate care facilities (ICF).

### Skilled Nursing Facilities
These facilities provide 24-hour nursing care, as well as

rehabilitative, pharmaceutical, dietetic, laboratory, and radio-
logical services. In addition, they are required to offer social
services and activities for residents. An attending physician
must visit patients every 30 days for the first 90 days. There-
after, visits may be reduced to every 60 days.

There are several questions to ask when choosing an SNF:

1.   Is the facility licensed by the state and certified under federal law to meet Medicare requirements?

2.   Is 24-hour nursing care provided by licensed nurses
who know about medication, special feeding methods, catheterization, and skin care?

3.   Are there emergency policies and services?

4.   Do physicians design a medical care plan? Are there
doctors on call for immediate attention?

5.   Does the pharmacy satisfy federal, state, and local
regulations?

6.   Are there transfer arrangements, by contract or otherwise, with a nearby hospital?

7.   Are special services, such as dental care, available?

8.   Are special diets available? Is the food nutritious and
appetizing? Is there a registered dietitian? Are snacks available? Do the patients seem to enjoy the food? How do the
kitchen facilities look?

9.   What kinds of rehabilitative services are available—
speech, hearing, physical, and occupational therapy? Are the
specialists in these services licensed and Medicare-approved?

10.   What about recreational services: social events, exercise groups, arts and crafts, trips, activities calendar, volunteer programs?

11.   Are there measures for infection control?

12.   What about services for personal grooming: in-house
barbers or beauticians, laundry services?

13.   What is the general atmosphere? Is it homelike,
pleasant, attractive, and comfortable? Are the grounds well
kept? Is there an odor problem? When odors develop, is there
adequate ventilation?

14.   Is the facility safe? Does it meet fire safety codes?

Have you seen the Fire Safety Inspection document? Are the hallways wide enough to allow passage of two wheelchairs? Are there hand-grip rails?

15. What are the qualifications of the administrators? How do people get along with them?

Another important factor to take into account is how the staff treats the residents. Are they friendly, courteous, helpful? How do the residents look and act? Is the location of the facility convenient for you? Personal recommendations from friends, family members, and physicians and other health care professionals can also be helpful in making your choice.

People who experience problems with nursing homes may obtain assistance from the Nursing Home Ombudsman, a person in your state or local office on aging, who is designated to investigate complaints and take corrective action on behalf of nursing home residents.

Other sources of information include the following (adapted from *Age Pages*, published by the National Institute on Aging):

- The Nursing Home Information Service, an information and referral center for consumers of long-term care and their families, friends, and advocates. The service provides information on nursing homes and alternative community and health services, including a free guide on how to select a nursing home. For more information, write to the National Council of Senior Citizens, Nursing Home Information Service, National Senior Citizens Education and Research Center, Inc., 925 15th Street, N.W., Washington, DC 20005, or call (202) 347-8800.

- The National Citizens Coalition for Nursing Home Reform, an organization that helps local organizations work for nursing home reform and improvements in the long-term care system to improve the quality of life for older people. To learn more about the Coalition, write to the national office at 1825 Connecticut Avenue, N.W., Suite 417B, Washington, DC 20009, or call (202) 797-0657.

- A handbook, *How to Select a Nursing Home*, is available for $4.75 from the Consumer Information Center, Department 152-M, Pueblo, CO 81009.

• The American Association of Retired Persons can provide general information on long-term care for consumers. To receive their publications, write to AARP, Health Advocacy Services, 1909 K Street, N.W., Washington, DC 20049.

## Intermediate Care Facilities

This level of care was defined by the Medicaid legislation of the late 1960s as a facility for residents who require less intensive nursing care than that provided by SNFs. They offer medical, nursing, social, and rehabilitative services, as well as room and board for people who are not able to live independently.

## Board and Care

No federal laws regulate this level of care; each state has its own definitions and rules. Essentially, the care is personal and custodial. Usually the requirements include that the facility meet fire and safety codes; that there be a full-time administrator to supervise staff and residents; that nursing staff be on call; and that facilities be available for occasional distribution of medication.

## Adult Day Care

These facilities provide nursing, recreational, and medical services, and meet nutritional needs. By definition, they are nonresidential facilities. Day care often offers families a respite from the unending task of caring for an impaired older person. Day care can also be useful in rehabilitation following hospitalization, or help the patient's transition from dependency following an acute illness or trauma back to a more independent lifestyle.

## Home Health Care

A wide range of agencies provide in-home health care, including home care units of community hospitals, social service departments, public agencies, private nonprofit community agencies (e.g., Associated Catholic Charities, Jewish Family and Children's Services), community health centers, and proprietary agencies. Home health care offers a number of advantages. Well-planned programs allow the individual to remain at home with all the familiar conveniences, both material and personal. A crucial question in determining the extent of such care is who will pay. Medicare and Medicaid pay for some home health-care services, but such services as full-time nursing care, medications, personal comfort items, housekeeping, Meals on Wheels (meals delivered to the home), and blood transfusions generally require payment from other sources. Because Medicare regulations change often, contact your nearest Social Security office (listed in the phone book under "Social Security Administration" in the U.S. Government section) for the most recent information on Medicare benefits.

## HAVING YOUR PARENTS HOME WITH YOU

Living alone with disability may eventually become untenable for your parent. Perhaps you have an extra bedroom in your home, and having Mom move in with you may be the best solution to your parentcare problems. Some families can afford to remodel their homes so that their dependent parent has maximum privacy, such as a separate entrance or kitchen facilities, yet remains close enough to be easily reachable in case of need. Others are not so lucky and must grapple with the conflicts that may surface from living in close quarters. Tricia's story highlights how such moves can have long-lasting effects on a family.

"Right after Dad died, Mom moved in with us—moved her bed right into my daughter Sally's room. Within a week, my ten-year-old daughter began to wet her bed. The doctor ordered all kinds of tests, but while the tests were negative, something was clearly wrong. Our pediatrician said that she was probably traumatized by her grandfather's death. Sally had told him she was afraid that Grandma was going to die in her room.

"I moved Mom to another room, and Sally's bedwetting stopped, but she still kept getting sick, with stomachaches and diarrhea. We went from doctor to doctor, and they X-rayed her from head to toe. They finally diagnosed ulcerative colitis. With all the worrying over Sally's illness, Mother's needs had to take second place. I don't know how I managed to keep my household in balance, to care for my other two kids as well as my husband, Ken. I know at some point I started to resent and secretly blame Mother for all of Sally's problems. The doctors said neither of us had anything to do with Sally's ulcerative colitis, but how could they be so sure, when they didn't know what caused it?

"We finally felt that Mother was strong enough to be in her own place, and she moved out two months ago. But every time Sally gets a bellyache, I go to pieces, even though her colitis is much improved. Every time Mother calls and reports an ache or pain, I feel either guilty, angry, or scared. It's like the two of them have put this cloud over my head."

Tricia's relationships with her mother and daughter were greatly complicated by their living arrangements. Moving into separate quarters was no panacea for their long-term emotional conflicts, but it did relieve much of the acute tension. Her story highlights the fact that living arrangements can affect not only the emotional health of family members, but their physical health, too.

## WHAT TO DO IF MOM OR DAD MOVES IN

For many adult children, the most viable option available is to have their parent move in with them. This option poses a threat to existing family life and routine, but offers the advantages of physical proximity and financial savings, often making it the only option. Sometimes it works very well, especially if personalities are compatible. What should you do if faced with this option? We suggest a few guidelines:

*Prepare emotionally.*   Remember what it was like when you were a child or a teenager and lived in your parents' household? How did you get along with others in your family then? Were your parents strict, giving, caring, or indifferent? Did you enjoy their company or resent their presence? Recalling your previous relationships and feelings will help you to anticipate what you may experience when you and your parent again live under the same roof. If you and your father always argued before, there is a fair chance that you will argue now. Being aware of this possibility allows you to plan ahead, and perhaps anticipate losing some arguments, which may soften the shock of the move.

If your early home life was less than ideal, you may be asking yourself, "Why bother having Mom move in?" Perhaps it will not work out; her move may be too disruptive to your family. Before you decide against it, evaluate the other possibilities: What would it mean to have Mom move into a nursing home, or your sister's mobile home, or whatever other option is available? Being aware of the alternatives may help you persevere and at least seriously attempt to make the move into your home a successful one.

Before you decide for or against the move, go through the six steps of the Commonsense Approach to Problem Solving. Though some parents may be too sick to participate, others may not; and as many family members as possible should participate.

*Prepare practically.* In addition to preparing emotionally, some simple practical changes around the house can make it comfortable and safe for you and your parent (also see chapter 12). If your parent suffers from a physical disability, you may need to invest in handrails or wheelchair ramps. Rearranging items around the house that are used regularly can make a difference if your parent suffers from arthritis and has difficulty reaching for objects. Adding a separate entrance, kitchen, or bathroom facilities, if practical and affordable, may reduce conflicts and increase privacy. Even if your parent suffers from serious memory disorders, such as Alzheimer disease, and gets easily confused and disoriented, anticipating potential problems (e.g., removing the handles from gas stoves, providing portable electric heaters with safety grilles) could readily convert at least portions of your house into "dementia-proof" areas. Prominently displayed clocks and calendars can help a forgetful parent maintain orientation to time, and thus a sense of independence and control.

*Respect their privacy and individuality.* Privacy can be respected in ways besides the practical preparation of the home. If you can, encourage your parents to get out of the house and spend time with friends or other relatives. Make an effort to give them time alone. On other occasions, solicit their help in activities you know they can perform; get them to participate in family enterprises. If your mother enjoys sewing, have her hem your daughter's dress, or perhaps Dad can help out in the toolshed. If your parents help out in these ways, their sense of indebtedness to you and consequent feelings of guilt may diminish.

*Respect your own privacy and individuality.* Perhaps most important in making our environment comfortable for our parents is conveying a sense of love and caring. If we feel resentment that our parents have intruded into our household, most often those feelings are expressed to them one way or another, even if we try to keep them to ourselves. To avoid resentment, make sure that you respect your own privacy and independence. Remember that it is your house and family, and that, as much as possible, your parent's move should not disrupt your established family life. Do not forget your own needs. If your parent cannot be left alone, hired help or assistance from another family member may give you enough time to yourself to recharge your emotional and physical batteries.

## PRESENCE CAN MAKE THE HEART GROW FONDER

Whether your parent is at home with you, in a nursing home, or in a separate residence—regardless of how close or how far away you may be from your parents physically—get the most out of your closeness emotionally. Remember a few do's:

- *Do* call them, even if they have not called you.
- *Do* respect their privacy.
- *Do* try to visit regularly (call ahead).
- *Do* remember the *quality* of time spent is at least as important as the quantity.
- *Do* tell them about your own needs for privacy.
- *Do* tell them about your other needs.
- *Do* remember that they may get as much from the Commonsense Approach as you do.

As Ralph Waldo Emerson once said, "The best of life is conversation, and the greatest success is confidence, or perfect understanding between two people." Perhaps Emerson was too optimistic to expect "perfect understanding," but our ongoing conversations with our parents can be among the satisfying, gratifying, and good parts of our lives.

---

### HOUSING AND YOUR PARENTS

- Remember that physical distance affects emotional closeness.
- Regardless of the distance, prepare emotionally by using the Commonsense Approach to Problem Solving.
- Avoid moves if possible.
- Make use of resources—people, services, and devices—to make the home a safe place (see chapters 10 and 12).
- Choose a nursing home carefully; ask the right questions.
- If parents move into your home:
  - Prepare practically and emotionally
  - Respect their privacy and individuality
  - Respect your own privacy and individuality

# 8

# THREE GENERATIONS:
# They Raised Me, Can't
# They Let Me Raise
# My Own Kids?

*I have found the best way to give advice to
your children is to find out what they want
and then advise them to do it.*

Harry S. Truman

One of the most common complaints adult children have
about parents is that of interference in and criticism of their
child-rearing. It is a source of constant conflict between the
generations. In no other area is the "squeeze" of the "sandwich generation" more evident—feeling like children toward
their parents on the one hand, and wanting to be exemplary
parents to their children, on the other. Tricia and Ken had
these difficulties in their family.

Tricia had been in love with Ken since high school. They
had come a long way since those days of football games and
homecomings. Even after more than 20 years of marriage, Ken
remained his burly, handsome self, except for a little graying
at the temples. He was still the "big man on campus" long after
he left school and joined a prestigious law firm. But inside, he
did not always feel like a big man; around his parents, he still
felt like a child. And it seemed that as his own children grew
older, his parents loomed larger and larger.

Just the other day, minutes after he dropped in to visit his
mother, she began: "What do you mean, Scott pierced one of
his ears and got an earring? I don't care if every single 16-year-
old boy at his high school has one, I won't allow my grandson
to parade around town looking like a gypsy!"

"*She won't allow?* What gives her the right to allow or not
to allow?" Ken's face turned red, his fists clenched, and he began to tremble as he recounted the incident to Tricia. "I felt
like strangling her right then and there. Who does she think

99

she is? Scott is our son, not hers! She can boss me around, but not him. She just doesn't understand what's going on in this world now. Does that stop her? No!" But something had stopped Ken. He had controlled himself in front of his mother, and had been mostly quiet during the rest of his visit. No wonder he dreaded being with her.

Communication between Ken and his father was not much better. Rather than talk directly to him, his father would use the children. He told his 14-year-old grandson, Jonathan, that he was much too young to have karate lessons, and his 8-year-old granddaughter, Sally, that her mother was spoiling her by buying her Calvin Klein jeans. The children never forgot to report all the grandparents' critiques to their parents. That did little to improve relations between the generations.

Far too often, disagreements like those in Ken's family persist over months and years, fester below the surface, and spread their poisons. And these kinds of unresolved, chronic disagreements take on an added complexity when three generations become involved. For example, Jonathan resented his father's insistence on karate lessons. He was angry at his father and welcomed his grandfather's support. The battle lines were drawn, grandson and grandfather allied against father in the middle. Not only did Ken have to do battle with his adolescent son, but he had to contend with his own father as well. His father's intervention clouded the issue. After all, what greater authority could the son have on his side than his father's very own father? And, more than that, why should Jonathan, the son, do Ken's, the father's bidding when Ken himself provided the model example of how *not* to do your father's bidding? So the grandparents' interference in the rearing of their grandchildren undermined the parents' authority.

Ironically, interference from the grandparents reached intolerable proportions just at the time when Ken and Tricia began to appreciate the responsibilities and conflicts of parenthood. They had just begun to understand what their parents must have experienced in raising them, now that they had their own teenagers. Ken's parents put that understanding in jeopardy, without realizing they were doing so. Ken, in turn, failed to tell his parents how he and Tricia resented their interference in the children's upbringing. In other words, they failed to communicate with each other. Some ways of communicating, of course, are not much help. "They are *my* children! You'd think you and Dad would have gotten your child-rearing out of your systems by now." That would not have been an effective way to solve the conflict. Neither would this: "You raised me, didn't you? Now my kids, too? What do you need it for?" Instead, it might have been useful for Ken to have taken a closer look at his thoughts and feelings, and to have used the six steps of the Commonsense Approach to Problem Solving, as follows:

*1. Mood Meter Reading.* Ken's Mood Meter crossed over to the Unpleasant Zone when his mother began complaining about his son's earring. He had tried to shut out all his feelings, but his discomfort continued.

*2. Personal Reflection.* Thinking about why his angry feelings would not go away (Personal Reflection), Ken recalled how, in his pre-teens, he had been enraged when his mother told the barber how to cut his hair. He hated the hairstyle she chose, and he remembered he had had trouble controlling his anger then. Now, when his mother picked on his son's earring, he felt just the way he had felt at the barber's—angry and impotent. His good sense told him that he was not impotent now, but his feelings told him otherwise.

The intense feelings triggered from the past had other roots as well. Ken remembered the humiliation he had felt when some neighborhood kids called him a sissy because he refused to fight them. (His parents had taught him never to fight.) Ken had vowed to himself that no one would ever call his son a sissy because of him. Karate lessons were the answer for his child. How Ken wished he could have had them in his own youth!

Ken knew intellectually what he wanted to say to his parents, but emotionally he could not get himself to do it. His feelings of inadequacy—when confronting the neighborhood children and when faced with the responsibilities of parenthood—stemmed from a general sense of inadequacy as a person. It seemed that his parents' incessant criticism throughout his childhood had always made him feel "not quite good enough." And now they confirmed his feelings of inadequacy as a parent. His mother implied that he could not care for his own son; his father faulted his judgment.

*3. Recollection.* Ken recalled strategies that had *not* worked for him in the past, such as using sarcasm. Wisecracks did not help the situation, and did not touch his rage. He recalled the contrast between his feelings of inadequacy around his parents and his feelings of pride and accomplishment at work. At work, he felt good about himself; he had none of his usual feelings of not quite measuring up—feelings his parents always seemed to elicit. He knew his talents as a litigation lawyer, and recognized his ability to confront and mediate problems with his clients and employees. Why could he not use these same strategies with his parents? Perhaps a soft voice and a positive tone would do the trick, just as they did at work. But when he tried, he just couldn't do it.

*4. Reassessment.* Ken concluded that he had to keep his parents at a more realistic distance when it came to rearing his children—but how? He realized he needed help beyond that which his wife could give him, and he was able to find the right therapist. In psychotherapy he learned that his unresolved conflicts and chronic anger toward his parents had prevented him from setting reasonable boundaries. He let his parents dominate him, his family, and his life. Before he gained this insight, his unconscious fears had made it impossible for him to assess the situation in a rational way. What were these fears? At first, Ken was afraid that confronting his parents could lead to one of them, particularly his father, having a heart attack or stroke. A confrontation could kill them. After all, they were not young anymore. Even if it did not kill them, the rift could cause them immeasurable pain, and would be too cruel. In therapy, Ken also discovered that he was keeping so much anger and hostility under a tight lid that he was afraid that once he opened the lid, even if only a crack, he would no longer be able to control his anger. He might literally hit out at his father, hurt him physically, or say all the nasty, hurtful things he had stored up for years. Once he became aware of the feelings, he knew he could control his rage, and knowing that, he could look at what was going on without having his emotions replace his common sense. He was ready for the next step.

*5. Negotiation.* With his past and present emotions better understood, Ken was finally able to talk to his parents. Rather than accusing them of butting into his affairs, he was able to tell them about his feelings of inadequacy when they interfered. Rather than telling them to mind their own business, he told them how he felt like a child when he was with them. And he told them that he needed their help now. He acknowledged his own problems, instead of blaming his parents. They made their contribution, too, but now, at last, they could talk about the situation, discuss with one another the problems as they saw them, and try to solve them in ways that would be acceptable to all of them. He was surprised and relieved to find out that it was possible to be honest with his parents.

*6. Compromise.* His parents were surprised to learn how Ken felt. They had never suspected or realized what lay behind his obvious anger every time they tried to help, made suggestions, or just visited or went out together. Although they did not understand why Ken felt the way he did, they were satisfied, knowing that they really had never been able to figure out what made him tick. They looked up to him and respected his professional legal judgment, but otherwise they still thought of him as a child. The child they raised, in their eyes, had never really matured into a man. But they could see how the conflicts about the grandchildren were poisoning the family atmosphere, and they were eager to do what they could to clear the air. Once Ken and his parents had worked out some of their previously unspoken conflicts, it seemed as if a time bomb on which all three generations had been sitting had been defused. Of course, Ken's parents did not abruptly stop expressing their divergent opinions, but now they could all openly acknowledge them—and sometimes laugh about them. When the kids conveyed their messages, Ken could say, "Let's talk with Grandpa and Grandma about that the next time they come." Sometimes Ken and Tricia could explain why they did things the way they did. For example, Ken could talk about the karate lessons and why his own memories made him so insistent. It was something he had not been able to talk about before his therapy, but now he could. And he even convinced Jonathan!

Not all issues were easily resolved. Sometimes Ken and Tricia made decisions that were irrational. Sometimes the grandparents were able to be more objective about the children's interests than the parents were, and sometimes the grandparents' views were grounded in outdated concepts or obsolete values. But the important change was that they now talked openly about their differences—at least some of the time. Old habits are hard to break.

Although Ken resolved some of his problems by using the six steps, he did, in fact, need psychotherapy. Sharing his feelings with his wife and gaining understanding at an intellectual level had not been enough. Without psychotherapy, he had been unable to change the way he acted toward his parents, or to talk to them about his feelings. Not everyone, of course, needs psychotherapy, and most three-generational conflicts do not require the intervention of a trained therapist. Sometimes, talking things over with a good friend, spouse, or other relative, or with a priest, minister, or rabbi, can lead to a solution. Sometimes, just the action of airing the feelings, talking about them, can relieve the pressure. Freud called it *catharsis*—the reduction of aggressive impulses through their emotional expression.

## STRUGGLES FOR CONTROL

Ken's struggle with his parents is an example of the struggle for control that goes on over the rearing of many a grandchild. What are some of the reasons? Our parents may feel the need to control our children for the same reasons they felt the need to control us when we were children. There are as many different reasons for this need to control as there are parents. In some families it may be as simple as following tradition. Parental authority is unquestioned and remains with the oldest set of parents. Children do as parents dictate. In some families, struggles for control originate in unresolved adolescent conflicts. Most of us emerge from adolescence having gained increased control over, and increased responsibility for, our lives. But when our own children begin to grow up, we may experience a déjà vu phenomenon. Our partially resolved adolescent conflicts may reemerge—conflicts involving those struggles we all experience in the transition from childhood to adulthood, from being taken care of to caring for ourselves. As our children develop, from the terrible twos to the tumultuous teens and beyond, struggles for control may become pervasive. When our parents get into the act, our authority is badly damaged, our feelings badly hurt.

A typical situation might involve your mother telling you that your children should be cleaning up their own rooms. You take this comment to mean that (a) you and your spouse are lousy parents for not insisting upon it in the first place; (b) you have no control over your children; (c) your children are spoiled rotten; (d) you and your spouse are slobs who don't care about clean rooms; (e) whatever other hurtful explanations come to mind.

Some of the interpretations may be true, or have at least a kernel of truth. Moreover, this kind of situation could make you feel as if you were still in your teens, with your mother nagging you about *your* room. You may be getting mad at her now, just thinking about it. When our parents try to exert control over the rearing of our children, we often interpret the message as "You are doing it wrong." Or, "Without our help, you cannot do it right." The meaning to our parents may be, "We are needed—it is important for the welfare of our grandchildren that we watch and guide their development." It would be more constructive to find some other areas in which our parents can function effectively, and feel needed and appreciated. The federal government has recognized this need for and by grandparents, and supports the Foster Grandparents and Senior Companions program, in which nearly 20,000 older Americans volunteer their services for 20 hours a week to care for needy children.

In some families, the grandparents' help is vital in caring for the grandchildren. An example of such a family was Melanie's. For her, a 34-year-old divorcée, the direct care her parents provided her children helped her survive the fracture of her family. "When my husband left me and went off to Alaska, I don't know what I would have done without my parents. I had a two-year-old and a four-year-old, no money, no job, and no home. They took me in and took care of my children so I could go to beauty school and learn a trade. I couldn't have done without them while I got my life back in order and saved some money to get out on my own. They were wonderful with my kids. The children are in school full-time now, and I have a good job. It's a nice feeling to know that my folks are nearby in case I need them. I think grandparents like to be needed, but I also know that I sure needed *them*."

Melanie was not aware of any conflicts between her parents and herself. Oh yes, they had occasional disagreements, but they were quickly resolved. There were no major struggles for control. Melanie and her parents had decided early on that they would not give the children a chance to play them off against one another—to get from their mother what the grandparents had refused, and vice versa. It worked well. Melanie shared many of her parents' child-rearing values. She had always had a good relationship with her parents, and had been able to discuss problems openly with them, especially with her mother. Others, however, pay a high price when they abdicate—voluntarily or involuntarily—and turn over parental child-rearing responsibilities to grandparents.

In some families, the grandparents, though available in theory because they are geographically close, are unavailable in fact. These grandparents choose to maintain their distance. Norman, for example, found that his parents never offered to help with his baby, nor did they show much interest in the baby's care. Norman and his wife, Joan, did not understand and were deeply hurt. Joan was convinced her in-laws disliked her and for that reason were cold and uninterested in their grandchild. Her own parents, too, were of no help. "I'm furious with my mother," Joan cried. "Here I am with the most adorable little boy, and my parents have seen him twice—and only because I took him to see them. Mom is so busy taking care of her own mother that she has completely abandoned me. She even moved out of the city to be near Grandma's house. Ten years ago, when my older sister had her children, those kids practically lived at my parents' home. And now I have absolutely no one to give me a hand. Norman's working all the time, and his parents don't even know I exist."

Single and working mothers who live away from or are without their parents have similar complaints. They long for some attention. They dream of someone to share their child-rearing problems, someone who might even give advice and support. When they were in their late seventies, Norman's maternal grandparents had come to live with his family, and he remembered many quarrels between his parents and his grandparents. What he did not remember, and in fact never knew, was that his parents had resolved never to interfere in their children's lives; they had never forgiven their parents' intrusive "grandparenting"; they never considered that he and Joan might have welcomed their help instead of regarding it as interference. How could any daughter-in-law possibly welcome their help? It was beyond their conception. Yet they both longed to play with their grandchild. They felt sad and lonely with Norman grown up and married; they felt excluded from his life, never thinking that they had excluded themselves.

What if Norman had invited his parents to discuss these issues? What if he had told them that he and Joan could use their help and suggestions in dealing with the crises that kept cropping up ever since the baby was born? They might have been pleased. Such a discussion might have led to their beginning to contribute time, effort, and know-how as grandparents.

On the other hand, his parents might have responded, "Oh no! We've done our job—we raised you—we're too old to start all over again. Changing diapers is not exactly what we had in mind for our leisure years. Neither you nor Joan consulted us *before* deciding to have the baby—it was your choice, so now it's up to you to take the consequences." Or, "We're used to having our peace and quiet. Finally we have the chance to relax, travel, and enjoy ourselves. We can't take crying babies anymore." Even with these kinds of responses, openly discussing the issues and starting a dialogue often turns out to be helpful. Discussion offers a chance to find out what made the grandparents act the way they did, and thus leads to better understanding and acceptance.

Some grandparents anticipate being used as unpaid baby-sitters and resent what they consider exploitation. Some grandparents are afraid of the responsibility—what if the baby got sick or hurt? Would they be blamed? Would they blame themselves? What if they dropped the baby? Would they ever be forgiven? Would they ever forgive themselves? They feel insecure and anxious. The anxiety may raise their blood pressure. What if they got sick or passed out? What would happen to the baby? What if they just dozed off and didn't hear the baby? If everyone's concerns are acknowledged, it may become possible to work out what is best for all three generations. Few grandparents can resist either the plea that they are wanted and needed or the opportunity to be with and get to know their grandchild. No one is a mind reader, and unless we make our needs known, and ask how others feel, we are likely to act on false assumptions.

There are, of course, parents who refuse to allow grandparents even to get near the children. At times, such refusals reflect a temporary conflict that can be resolved. For some, though, the conflicts are not easily settled. In families disrupted by hostile divorce or death, a daughter-in-law or son-in-law may withhold visitation rights from former in-laws. Increasingly, grandparents are going to court to claim visitation rights for their grandchildren. Nearly every state has some law that gives grandparents the right to sue for visitation privileges.

On the other end of the continuum, Nancy, who had been widowed, always encouraged contact between her children and their paternal grandparents. "My former in-laws are very generous, but now I'm remarried and have two younger children whom they completely ignore. Every Christmas or birthday, when those extravagant gifts are opened, I can't stand the looks on the faces of my two little ones. I suppose they have to face reality. I used to buy gifts for them, but I can't keep up. I'm delighted that my older children have the advantage of special trips and gifts, but it doesn't help the sadness I feel for my younger children."

## WHAT CAN WE DO?

A brick wall often seems to separate the generations. Need the barrier be so formidable? Of course not! But how do we keep it from arising? That is up to our individual ingenuity. Meanwhile, here are a few suggestions to guide adult children through the three-generational maze of problems that invariably arise.

1. *Get acquainted with each generation's values.*   Remembering and reviewing your parents' perspectives, attitudes, and prejudices about the world, and contrasting them with your own, will give you insight into some of the sources of conflict. You may want to list attitudes about life with each generation's values alongside the other, and do not forget your children's values. Having an idea of how the generations in your family feel about life points out not only differences but similar values as well.

2. *Do not try to change their values just so they will conform to yours.*   Your values may not be the best for them. Religious values, for example, often cause conflicts between generations, yet they can be a great source of comfort.

Given that the generations have grown up in such different times, it is important that one generation not attempt to impose its view of the world on others. "That old house is too large for one person—it just doesn't make sense, and costs too much, too. We insist you move." That kind of approach to your

## VALUES OF THE THREE GENERATIONS IN KEN'S FAMILY

|  | Grandparents | Ken and Tricia | Scott, Jonathan, and Sally |
|---|---|---|---|
| Marriage, sex: | People should marry in their early twenties and pick someone from the same religion and culture. Sex before marriage is okay for boys, especially with prostitutes, but not for girls. | Cohabitation may be best before marriage. Intermarriage is acceptable. | Why bother with a piece of paper—it is just a legal document and has nothing to do with romance or love. Teenagers can take birth-control pills. |
| Divorce: | Disgraceful. | A reality of today's society; one of two marriages ends in divorce. | If you don't get married, you don't have to worry about divorce. |
| Education: | Our children should go to college and learn a profession; we never had the chance. | My kids should go to college, but they can study whatever they want to study. | We can learn more in the real world than we can from books. |
| Money: | We grew up in the Depression, so we always save for a rainy day; we do not need luxuries, we'd rather leave the money for our children and grandchildren. | It's all right to enjoy ourselves a little today; we've earned it. | Why worry about retirement? Why save? We will probably see nuclear winter before our IRAs. |
| Religion: | We never miss a Sunday at church. | We are not that religious; when we go to church, we do so out of respect for our parents. | Religion is a personal matter; organized religion is not for us. |

mother—or to your sister, son, or daughter—just does not
work. If you respect their values, they will be inclined to respect yours and you will have taken the first essential step toward intergenerational closeness. When the care of that old
house gets to be an obvious burden to your parents, a better
approach might be to open a dialogue, to inquire how *they* feel
about the situation, what alternatives *they* have considered—if
any. At the right moment you might then say, "How can I help
you? Would you like to look at some smaller places?" Or, "Perhaps you might enjoy the freedom of an apartment. Should we
make a date to go looking and see what's available?"

   *3. Define any alliances and identify control struggles.* Do your
children turn to your parents for support when you attempt
to discipline them? Are struggles for control common among
the generations in your family? If so, try to clarify the reasons
for such struggles. In some families, parental authority is a
firmly respected tradition. In others, unresolved adolescent
conflicts in any of the generations may contribute to conflict.
By defining alliances and identifying motives underlying
struggles for control, you may learn that one generation is
"acting out" unresolved conflicts by trying to control another.
Ken did so when he pressured his son to take karate lessons
because of his own experiences as a child.

   *4. Encourage the generations to help each other rather than use
one another.* Identifying reasons for struggles over control and
intergenerational "acting out" will help dissipate these kinds of
interactions and make way for more constructive and rewarding relationships. Instead of arguing with you about how to
raise your daughter, your mother may then have time to teach
your daughter how to bake that pecan pie from the recipe she
inherited from her mother. Or maybe your daughter could
take your mother to her low-impact aerobics class.

   *5. Keep a comfortable distance.* In Oriental and most European traditional cultures and families, input from grandparents is expected and respected. Sometimes the grandparents'
home is the center of activity and tradition. By contrast, the
eagerly assimilating younger generations in many second- and
third-generation American immigrant families often view their
grandparents' input as intrusive and old-fashioned. These
kinds of cultural differences will in part determine the most
comfortable level of closeness among the generations in your
family. Getting close to others often involves keeping some

distance as well. It is crucial to be clear as to how much, if any, responsibility you can or want to give to your parents. If you allow what you consider meddling and interference to persist, it will only lead to resentment and ill will, and you may feel undermined as a parent. If you give too little responsibility, and family members remain aloof, your parents may feel rejected and cut off from "their own flesh and blood." Your children may lose out, too, not having a chance to experience that special relationship with a grandparent.

*6. Give grandparents and grandchildren time to themselves.* Our parents and children have an opportunity to develop a unique relationship. We can foster its development by allowing them to get to know one another without having us around. If both enjoy such time together, both will gain.

Let us not forget that grandparents have a major share in determining how grandchildren view the old in society—how they will view us when we are old. If we encourage their relationship with their grandparents, they in turn will be more likely to do the same when their time comes. The future is rooted in the past. As the psychoanalyst Erik Erikson noted in his book *Insight and Responsibility*, published in 1966:

"Defenseless as babies are, they have mothers at their command, families to protect the mothers, societies to support the structure of families, and traditions to give a cultural continuity to systems of tending and training."

---

### HOW TO GET ALONG WITH THREE GENERATIONS

- Get acquainted with each generation's values.
- Don't try to change their values just so they will conform to yours.
- Define any alliances and identify struggles over control.
- Encourage the generations to help rather than exploit one another.
- Keep a comfortable distance.
- Give grandparents and grandchildren time to themselves.
- Walk through the six-step Commonsense Approach to Problem Solving.

# 9

# RETIREMENT:
# Is There Life After Work?

*My coals are spent, my iron's gone,*
*My nails are drove, my work is done.*

Anonymous epitaph for a blacksmith

Paul could not believe it—his father had been fired. After disbelief came anger, and then sadness. They had fired his father, yet it almost felt as if they had fired *him*. Those ungrateful wretches. It was his father who had started the practice, not they.

Dr. Steven Brill's practice was as old as Paul himself. As far back as Paul could remember, Dad was always at work in the operating room, in the hospital, in the office. Many family get-togethers were spoiled by his father's being called away. Many vacations came to naught because Dad would not take off—because Dr. Brill could not or would not find someone to monitor his patients while he was on vacation.

When Paul started high school, his father finally took in a partner. Some of the doctors didn't like the new partner's personality, but at least his father now had alternate nights and weekends off, and his parents had some time together. The partners had their differences, but in time the practice grew. The lean years of Paul's childhood were replaced by years of comfort. Finally there was enough money for all the family, enough to help his grandparents and still pay tuition and other college expenses for him and his brother.

Just five years ago, the practice had grown too large for two, and the partners had recruited a third surgeon to join them. Again, the relationships were not always smooth. It seemed to Paul that his father might have done better had he considered personalities as well as competence; but then, surgeons never placed much importance on "interpersonal skills." Nonetheless, Paul's father offered the youngest colleague a full partnership. And on the very day his partners gained control of two-thirds of the practice, they fired Paul's dad. Suddenly they had discovered that his procedures were not "up-to-date." The vote was final—two against one.

Paul's dad was stunned, and he could not help feeling responsible. He himself had set it up, let himself in for it by trusting his partners and not protecting his own interests. All this, just as he was approaching his sixtieth birthday. He thought of an old saying: "At fifty you begin to be tired of the world, and at sixty the world is tired of you."

Paul's relationship with his father changed. No longer did he feel comfortable in sharing his own achievements with him. After all, how much of a success could his father have been, to have gotten himself into this mess? Paul also felt guilty, and he could not help thinking, "If only I had gone into surgery, I would have been one of Dad's partners, and none of this would have happened."

Dr. Brill filed a lawsuit, and that was when the fight really began. There were depositions and arguments; months went by; the possibility of a settlement was brought up.

Paul's father got some part-time work, but most days he had little to do. Though he jogged, played tennis, read novels, and did crossword puzzles, his anger distracted him from his hobbies, friends, and family. Paul's mother was also at home most days, so his parents saw a lot of each other. And the unexpected closeness made them even more tense. It was not easy for his mother to see her husband hanging around the house. Dad's hobbies just were not enough. He had worked for over 30 years. His job had made him feel important and needed; he had been someone of value. Without it, he felt like a nobody, superfluous, antiquated, his value gone.

## LOSS OF WORK: WHAT DOES IT MEAN TO YOUR PARENT?

Getting fired, retiring, being laid off—whatever form it takes—loss of livelihood is one of the most significant losses a man can experience in our culture. And with changing life-styles, the same may become true for many women, too. What we create, what we produce, how much money we make—all play a crucial role in the feelings of others toward us, and in our own feelings toward ourselves. Work ranks among life's highest goals, and our jobs have both personal and social meaning. Freud pointed out that in our attempts to attain psychological well-being, we basically strive "to love and to work."

Throughout life, most of us spend more time at work than we do at any other activity except, perhaps, sleeping. When the job goes, a major source of self-esteem goes as well—along with the money, the friends, the challenges, the stimulations, the frustrations, the fights, the headaches, the drudgery, and the outside life. Paul's father certainly felt the loss of all those sources of self-esteem. Many others, like Dr. Brill, complain about the drudgery, responsibility, and time demands while working, yet when they retire they desperately miss the challenges, people, and rewards that in part drove them to work so hard in the first place. Leisure activities were not enough to sustain his interest, and he felt bored, as do many retirees, even those who plan a retirement filled with their favorite pastimes and hobbies.

As of 1982, more than 80 percent of men 65 years of age or older were not part of the labor force. That is, they were neither gainfully employed nor looking for such employment. By contrast, in 1950, only 30 years earlier, nearly half of all men 65 years old or older were working or seeking work.[1] Thus, the twentieth century has brought dramatic changes in our work and leisure. Retirement, once considered a luxury, is now an expected stage in a person's life trajectory. At the turn of the century, the average life expectancy was 46 years; the average man spent only 3 percent of his time in retirement (1.2 years). For most men, this meant no time in retirement at all. By 1980, the average life span for men had increased to 69 years (a 50-percent gain), and 20 percent of that lifetime was spent in retirement (14 years; more than a 1,000-percent gain).[2] The American Association of Retired Persons had 21 million members in 1985 (perhaps two-thirds of them actually retired). That number exceeds the population of every state, except California!

Retirement can be experienced in different ways. For some people it signifies a transition to old age. It is a time to step down and to settle into a quieter lifestyle. Work is associated with pressure and responsibility. Retirement is a time to relax and give up some responsibilities, to enjoy life as a spectator. Such people are content to sit down and watch; they subscribe to Jane Ellen Harrison's sentiment, "Old age, believe me, is a good and pleasant time." Or they may take up new activities, or continue to work. In fact, up to one-third of retired men and women return to work, and the working retired are generally in better health and have more positive attitudes than the nonworking retired. Working part-time after retirement may allow a person to enjoy the increased leisure as well as the continued employment benefits of income and job satisfaction.

Morton had made up his mind to retire from his engineering job at the age of 62. He had been thinking about it for a long time, especially after his bypass surgery the year before. "I won't have to ride that freeway two hours a day. I'll be able to relax and read, do all those things I never had time for. I'll use the money from my pension plan, have some income from it, and Edna and I will be able to live on that—even travel a little. We'll have enough. Our house is paid for, the girls will be married and finished with school, no more responsibilities."

He talked to everyone about his plans, and thought about them even more. Now it was almost his sixty-fourth birthday, and he still hadn't *done* a thing. His firm had changed the mandatory retirement age to 70. Morton wished they hadn't. Then *he* wouldn't have to make the choice. He felt angry and frustrated, and hated his own ambivalence—he, an engineer, so precise and decisive in his work. Some days he didn't feel like getting out of bed in the morning, and everyone seemed to get on his nerves.

Morton tried to blame everyone else for his inability to retire. "The firm needed me to finish a special project, and then they were short of skilled help. My wife was always telling me how unhappy I'd be without a place to go; I think she really didn't want me around. She said we needed to make up the money we spent on Jane's wedding and my surgery."

But Morton failed to consider that perhaps he needed to make concrete plans for his retirement and investigate some of his options, so that he could feel more secure about his decision. All his life he had had specific daily goals and followed them in an orderly fashion. As much as he longed for freedom from responsibility, the unknown and unstructured life ahead was threatening for someone who had worked diligently for 35 years. This unrecognized anxiety about an unstructured future immobilized him, yet the ambivalence he felt and the impasse he faced were far from a solution.

Morton's story contrasts with that of Donald, who more

realistically explored his future options—things he could do alone, and those he could do with his wife and others. Donald was a 63-year-old building contractor who had always had a desire to help the elderly. He also wanted to learn to play the piano and to paint. He timed his retirement for when his first grandchild was due to arrive. He and his wife took a long-overdue vacation and visited their children. When they returned, it was time to enroll in piano and art classes at the junior college. In the meantime, he began to offer his much-needed services to a local retirement home on Sunday mornings. "I'm busier, it seems, than when I went to work, but I feel as if I'm playing all the time," he reported. He felt appreciated and needed at the retirement home, a reward that offset the loss of his previous monetary ones.

Thus, retirement may be a new beginning, a time to live according to needs, desires, wishes, and whims that had to be set aside during the working life; a time to explore the world around us and the depth of our own inner being. For others, retirement is a time of loss—loss of job, loss of friends, loss of income, loss of status, loss of social role. One of America's foremost psychologists, William James, wrote in 1896 that "the deepest principle of Human Nature is the craving to be appreciated." Retirement can bring a sharp reduction in the opportunity to be appreciated. Even when retirement is anticipated and planned, as in Donald's case, there is usually an accompanying sense of loss and void, as well as a grief reaction and a mourning process. When retirement is forced, unwanted, unexpected, unplanned, then anger and depression often result as well, adversely affecting not only the retiree but also the family, even those family members living outside the home. Several studies of involuntary retirees have indicated that they are at a disadvantage. They tend to have lower income and poorer health before and after retirement. They are less satisfied with retirement, feel less useful, and have fewer interpersonal relations than those who choose to retire.[3]

## LOSS OF YOUR PARENT'S JOB:
## WHAT IT MEANS TO YOU

Parents' retirement, whether planned or unexpected, usually stirs up strong feelings in their adult children. We may feel

## FEELINGS YOU MAY EXPERIENCE
## WHEN YOUR PARENT RETIRES

| Feelings | Questions to Ask |
|---|---|
| Guilt | What did I do? When did I do it? Today? Yesterday? During childhood? |
| Annoyance | Am I angry at my parents for disappointing me? Do I want them to change? |
| Anger | Do I identify with my parents? Is this my problem? Will they expect me to take care of them? Do I feel threatened? |
| Boredom | Am I avoiding anger that I don't want to face? |
| Sadness | Do I feel my parents are deserting me? |
| Anxiety | Am I feeling guilty? How do I think this change will affect me? |
| Fear | Are there real threats? Poor health? Financial crisis? |
| Numbness | Am I avoiding strong feelings that I don't want to face? |
| Pleasure | Did my parents hate their jobs? Do they now have time to play? Or am I now the one with the good job, not my father or mother? |
| Jealousy | Am I thinking, "Dad can go out and have fun, while I have to struggle working two jobs, even though my wife works, too—just to make ends meet! He collects Social Security and I have to pay"? |
| Shame | Do I think less of my parent now for not "producing"? |

anxious or worried about the uncertainty that lies ahead for them—or for us. We may feel sad about our parents' loss, and guilty that we are not doing enough to help. We do not know what to say or do. We have mixed feelings: we are ashamed that we are working and they are not; we are happy because they finally have leisure time for themselves. But it is our parents' retirement, not ours, so why do we react so strongly?

Whether we like it or not, we identify with our parents and have a tendency to experience the same feelings they do (see chapter 14). Moreover, their retirement is another reminder that they will not always be able to care for us. Even a "normal" retirement, one that is anticipated and carefully planned, can stir up feelings of abandonment for adult children.

Whatever feelings you and your parents may be experiencing, they are a signal to each of you to ask yourselves some questions. Feelings do not come out of the blue; they point to conflicts and attitudes about ourselves. Don't ignore them. Your past experiences shape and color what you feel right now. Asking yourself about them can help you to better understand and gain control over them (see chapter 2).

## THE FAMILY: ADJUSTMENT OR DISRUPTION

The way you, your parents, and your brothers and sisters get along with each other may change when your parents retire. Most families maintain a delicate balance in their relationships. One family member may be the worker, another the thinker; one the leader, another the martyr. Someone may be the patient, someone else the achiever. When a parent retires, the familiar roles may change. Thrust together, your parents may become more intimate, or they may have frequent conflicts and collisions as their time together swallows up all their time alone. They may be reminded of the cliché, "I married you for better or for worse, but not for lunch!"

The increasing trend for women to enter the work force can intensify post-retirement conflicts. Father, the career employee, is fired close to retirement age, frequently by employers trying to save on pension payments. Mother, who may have a part-time job or may have resumed full-time work only after the children had grown up, might not be entitled to much by way of pension benefits, if anything at all. She may, however, become a valued employee. For some mothers it is a delight to finally get out of the house. Or she may feel compelled to work, especially with her husband out of a job and with the prospect of financial insecurity that too often haunts retirement. She may or may not be enthusiastic about working; it may even be her first job outside the home. A recent study of middle-aged married women showed that if their husbands retire, the wives are likely to retire soon after.[4]

The well-known gerontologist Bernice Neugarten conducted classic studies of personality changes in middle and later life. She noted that as they grow older, men appear to cope with the environment in increasingly abstract and intellectual terms, while becoming increasingly occupied with their own personal concerns and more receptive of their affiliative and nurturing needs. Other investigators who studied middle-aged and older men also reported that "aging men seem to move from active involvement with the world to more introversive, passive, and self-centered positions."[5] Women, by contrast, appear to become more assertive, active, and outwardly oriented.

Marjorie Fiske, the University of California gerontologist who has spent a lifetime observing the social aspects of age changes, further describes these phenomena. She speaks of the way in which the life trajectories of American men and women approach one another, intersect, cross, and diverge. These diverging trajectories may create marital difficulties around the time of retirement, as men become more oriented toward the home and women toward the outside world. Others suggest that retirement has little effect on marital stability.[6] This lack of agreement applies to traditional families; the studies are over a decade old, and times have changed, family relationships have changed. People get married at increasingly older ages, children are born to older parents, to single parents, and into blended families. Working mothers are becoming more the norm than the exception. The influence of retirement upon these family constellations is largely unknown and will be influenced by numerous other factors—including the individual reasons for retirement.

## WHY DID YOUR PARENT RETIRE?

People stop working for many reasons; often they stop involuntarily. One survey found that poor health was the most common reason for involuntary retirement (43 percent of men, 36 percent of women).[7] This study agrees with several other surveys carried out over the past two decades.[8] In general, about one-third to one-half of retirees stop working voluntarily, while the other half to two-thirds retire because of poor health or other compulsory reasons. Involuntary retirement, therefore, has been a major problem, and although the Age Discrimination Act has largely eliminated compulsory retirement ages, poor health will continue to force people, against their wishes, to stop working.

What about your parents? Are they in a position to choose leisure over work? Do they enjoy financial security and good health, two essential ingredients for contentment during retirement? A recent study showed that 80 percent of people 75 years of age or older could not take part in outdoor recreation because of poor physical health, in contrast to 25 percent of those between 44 and 50.[9] With limited funds, your parents will have to budget and put off, perhaps forever, all those dreams they had during their working lives. Usually, you can neither cure their sicknesses nor make them rich, though there are things you *can* do to mitigate their suffering and make the most of whatever money they do have (see chapters 4 and 11).

When your parents have time to anticipate and prepare for their retirement it can help financially as well as emotionally, as it did in Donald's case. Unfortunately, like Paul's father, your parents may not have a say in whether their retirement will be "on" time or "off" time. Too frequently, someone who is not ready for retirement is fired because it makes good business sense to hire a younger person who, although less experienced, is willing and anxious to perform a similar service at a much lower cost.

## AGEISM AND FORCED RETIREMENT

Dr. Brill's partners accused him of not performing the up-to-date procedures that younger surgeons were doing, and in part they were right. He always referred patients who needed the latest procedures, such as gastric stapling for uncontrollable obesity, to his younger colleagues. But the procedures he did know, he performed extremely well—in fact, often better than the younger surgeons who lacked his years of experience. So why should they fire him? Aside from greed, his firing may have reflected ageism—prejudice against older people.

Until recently, people were forced to stop working at 65, an age chosen arbitrarily for Social Security benefits. Our government now admits that forced retirement represents a form of age discrimination. In 1978, Congress raised the age cap for mandatory retirement from 65 to 70. As of January 1, 1987, a law passed unanimously by both the House and Senate amended the Age Discrimination Act and banned forced retirement at any age. The law also prohibits age discrimination in hiring, firing, and salary scales. But as the baby-boom generation grows into its fifth and sixth decade and beyond, job competition will escalate. Age discrimination causing forced retirement may be outlawed, but professional ruthlessness, like that which Dr. Brill experienced, can still flourish unchecked.

## WHAT CAN WE DO?

Some parents just do not believe in retirement. In the words of one parent we know, "Retirement? Not for me! I'm not retiring, I'm just changing priorities." Is that an attitude we should all have to emulate? The question is still open. Although social scientists have looked at the effect of retirement on morbidity (sickness) and mortality, the results of these studies are inconclusive. Are people more likely to get sick or die after retiring than if they keep on working? Some do, some do not. Thus far, we cannot predict who will suffer and who will flourish in retirement. What we can do is follow a few general guidelines to help ease the pain of this critical transition period:

*1. Get an idea of what retirement means to your parent.* One way to get a perspective on retirement is to take a look at our long-term priorities. The American Association of Retired Persons suggests that people facing retirement construct a lifeline to review past accomplishments and formulate future goals. Here is an example of one person's lifeline.

---

## DR. BRILL'S LIFELINE

**Birth**

**Past Accomplishments**

—started school

—first job, selling newspapers

—finalist in eighth-grade photography contest

—won high school debate contest

—graduated from medical school

—got married

—became father of son and started surgical residency

—drafted into army as captain, chief of surgery

—started private practice, second son born

—built "dream house"

—elected president of local medical/surgical society

—appointed chief of staff at the hospital

—won 50-plus tennis championship

**Now**

—forced to retire at 60

—got job teaching part-time

**Future Goals**

—learn to paint and sculpt

—enjoy being a grandfather

—garden

—teach children tennis

—write autobiography

**Death**

---

How about *your* lifeline? You might try filling in the sample. Where is "now" for you? If you are in your late forties, you may have come more than halfway already. If you are near 60, you may have used up two-thirds and have only one-third left. That in itself is a sobering discovery. Once you have gotten over that shock, look again. Try having your retiring parent fill in a lifeline. It may help your parent gain perspective on past achievements and the meaning of retirement. Does retirement represent a time of relief, dread, excitement, boredom? What are the expectations?

*2. Know what your parent's retirement means to you.* Don't be alarmed if you become anxious, worried, or distressed when one of your parents retires. It is a time when your feelings about being protected and parented by them may resurface. Filling out your own lifeline will help you gain perspective on your sense of identification with them and your feelings about your own retirement.

*3. Keep an eye on your Mood Meter.* Review the kinds of questions to ask when you experience intense feelings (see table on page 117). This may also be a time to review the six steps of the Commonsense Approach to Problem Solving.

*4. Keep on the lookout for depression.* For your parent, depression can come before or after retirement. Depression resulting from anticipating retirement can interfere with your parent's ability to work, thus contributing to the job loss. We know of a 60-year-old executive who began to dwell on his company's early-retirement program, under which he would leave in five years. His worries, however, shifted to physical illness when he began to lose weight and could not sleep. He became absent-minded at work and began to misplace documents. His internist did a thorough checkup, including X rays and blood tests. Medical illness did not cause the symptoms; depression did. Referral to a psychiatrist was successful; the executive recovered with psychiatric treatment and was able to return to work, where he performed productively for five more years (for a discussion of depression and its treatment, see chapter 13).

*5. Expect changes in family relationships.* With your parents no longer "in the driver's seat," at least symbolically, someone else in your family may take over that role. Anticipation of such changes can help you adjust.

*6. Do not hesitate to spend time with them.* Nearly everyone who retires gains some free time. This may be an opportunity for you to spend more time with your parents and help them with some of the losses they may be experiencing.

*7. Anticipate financially.* One way of categorizing[10] the typical means for financing retirement is to consider the following four types of resources:

- Private savings
- Employer pensions (both public and private)

- Old-age survivor's and disability benefits (i.e., Social Security)
- Other public-assistance programs (e.g., Supplemental Security Income).

How much money will be available from each category for your parents? Part-time employment or pursuit of a second career provide additional options.

*8. Know your other resources.* You alone cannot fill in for the losses your parents suffer upon retirement. Probably no one can, but help is available. Take inventory of the social and emotional resources available to people who retire.

One example is a national nonprofit organization, the American Association of Retired Persons (AARP). The organization aims to help older Americans achieve lives of independence, purpose, and dignity. AARP provides a wide range of member benefits, service programs, and activities. They publish a number of helpful pamphlets and booklets, such as the following:

- *Money Matters: How to Talk to and Select Lawyers, Financial Planners, Tax Preparers, Real Estate Brokers*
- *Learning Opportunities for Older Persons*
- *A Fitness Book for Seniors*
- *Community Program Idea Book*

In addition, AARP publishes a magazine, *Modern Maturity* (it comes out every other month), covering the spectrum of interests pertinent to retired persons.

For more information, write to the American Association of Retired Persons, 1909 K Street, N.W., Washington, DC 20049.

Retirement *can* be fun. As long as their health is maintained, many of our parents welcome retirement, especially if they are financially secure. They have the time to pursue their hobbies, travel, and avoid the pressures of the clock and many of the responsibilities of their earlier years. Some *do* get the chance to live out their dreams and love it.

Others pursue second careers. Grandma Moses had been a farmer and housewife before producing her first painting at 78 years of age. Somerset Maugham retired from the practice

# YOUR PARENT'S LIFELINE

# YOUR LIFELINE

BIRTH

PAST ACCOMPLISHMENTS

NOW

FUTURE GOALS

DEATH

BIRTH

PAST ACCOMPLISHMENTS

NOW

FUTURE GOALS

DEATH

of medicine at an early age to become a successful writer. And, of course, Ronald Reagan is a most famous example of a late-life career shift—from acting to politics, and ultimately to the presidency. As the twentieth century draws to a close, we may expect many career shifts late in life. How will that affect the adult children? We shall have to wait for time to teach us, for the world to teach us.

As Montesquieu so aptly wrote: "We receive three educations, one from our parents, one from our teachers, and one from the world. The third contradicts all that the first two teach us."

---

### WHAT YOU CAN DO WHEN YOUR PARENT RETIRES

- Get an idea of what retirement means to your parent. Have your parent fill in a lifeline.
- Know what your parent's retirement means to *you*. Fill in your own lifeline.
- Keep an eye on your Mood Meter. Ask questions when you experience feelings.
- Keep on the lookout for depression in your parent.
- Expect changes in family relationships.
- Spend time with your parent.
- Anticipate financially.
- Know your other resources.

# 10

# HEALTH ENHANCEMENT:
## How Can We Reduce the
## Risk of Illness?

> *Look to your health . . . for health is the second blessing that we mortals are capable of; a blessing that money cannot buy.*
>
> Izaak Walton, *Life of Donne*

Our parents may be getting older; they may have arrived at "old age" and may suffer from physical illness. They do, however, have some control over some illnesses and, if they still enjoy reasonably good health, may, with attention to their lifestyle, even prevent some diseases. The following information is based on *Age Pages*, a handbook published by the National Institute on Aging. Sections have been reprinted verbatim; some were altered and others added. It may help adult children assist their parents in enhancing health and preventing illness. This kind of information is often requested by adult children caring for their parents. To their surprise, they find that much of what they learn applies to their own lives as well. You too may find useful information for yourself, your family, and your friends, and may wish to give this chapter to your parents to read for themselves.

## CAN LIFE BE EXTENDED?

Why do people grow old and die? Can anything be done to slow aging or extend life? These questions have no simple answers. Each day, scientists learn more about changes in the human body as it ages, but why these changes occur remains a mystery. Most scientists believe that aging is a complex process involving many body systems.

### What Causes Aging?
Theories about why aging and death occur focus on what

happens in the body's cells as time goes by. Changes occur that alter the cell's ability to function. When enough cells are altered, aging—and finally death—results. Some theories of aging suggest that such changes are due to a built-in genetic program. Just as early growth and development follow a set timetable, so do maturity, aging, and death. Other theories assume that aging is caused by damage to the body throughout life. Such damage could be caused by "wear and tear," harmful substances that we breathe and eat, or natural processes within the body. The "damage" theories hold promise that such changes might be corrected someday or avoided, and life expectancy extended. However, they have also opened the way for so-called anti-aging treatments that scientists do not endorse.

## Proposed "Anti-Aging" Treatments

One damage theory says that aging is caused by free radicals, chemicals produced naturally in all animals that use oxygen. They bounce around inside body cells, often damaging their membranes and the vital proteins, fats, and DNA (deoxyribonucleic acid—the holder of the genetic code) within them. To protect itself, the body uses antioxidants, compounds that block much of this free radical damage. Some antioxidants, such as SOD (superoxide dismutase), are produced in the body. Others (vitamins A, C, and E and the minerals zinc and selenium, for example) are derived from food.

Based on this theory, some people suggest that we can extend our lives by taking large amounts of antioxidant supplements, although there is little evidence that antioxidants will extend life span. However, a few studies suggest they may reduce the risk of some age-associated diseases, including some types of cancer. Most nutritionists believe that the body's needs for antioxidants can be met by eating a variety of nutritious foods. Furthermore, taking large doses of some of these vitamins and minerals can be harmful.

Other people believe that aging results from a slow buildup of damage to the DNA in body cells. DNA directs the machinery of every cell. Eventually, DNA damage would cause cells, then body tissues and organs, to break down or die. Supplements containing DNA and RNA (ribonucleic acid, which works with DNA in the cell) are being sold to slow aging, cure senility, and treat skin and hair changes. Again, there is little scientific evidence to support such claims.

According to another theory, changes in body hormones are responsible for aging. At some point, a gland such as the pituitary releases a hormone (or fails to produce one), and aging changes begin. For example, scientists have shown that a hormone called DHEA (dehydroepiandrosterone), which is produced in the adrenal gland, may play a role in aging. Young people have higher levels of DHEA in their blood than do older ones. Tests on laboratory rats suggest that DHEA supplements help them stay healthy and live longer. Pharmaceutical companies are exploring the potential usefulness of these types of substances.

Another theory of aging focuses on the immune system, which is the body's weapon for fighting disease. As people grow older, this system becomes less effective, opening the way for infection by viruses, bacteria, and other disease-producing organisms. As the immune system ages, it also tends to lose the ability to tell the difference between the body's own tissues and foreign substances. As a result, cells of the immune system that once would fight invading organisms now attack the body itself, producing diseases.

A way was proposed recently to extend life by delaying aging changes in the immune system. The technique involves reducing the amount of food eaten, so that a large percentage of the body weight is lost over a period of years. Dietary restriction is known to extend the lives of laboratory mice and rats, but its effect in humans awaits definition (see chapter 5).

Scientists are studying the aging theories described above. Even if they discover the correct one (or ones), there is no guarantee that a way to extend life will result quickly or at all. Meanwhile, check with a doctor before buying a supplement or making a dietary change. Be suspicious of any product that promises to slow aging, extend life, or produce major changes in appearance or vigor—and before taking it, make sure it will not hurt you.

## DON'T TAKE IT EASY— EXERCISE!

*If exercise could be packed into a pill, it would be the single most widely prescribed, and beneficial medicine in the nation.*

Robert N. Butler, M.D., former director of
the National Institute on Aging

Each year, more scientific evidence reinforces the truth of this statement. Regular physical activity can help the human body maintain, repair, and improve itself to an amazing degree. And most older people—even those with illnesses or disabilities—can take part in moderate exercise programs.

Anyone planning to start a fitness program should see a doctor first. Those with medical problems may have to avoid some kinds of exercise, or adjust their level of activity. But even people who are confined to wheelchairs can do some exercises to improve their strength and sense of well-being.

Many older people enjoy such exercises as walking, swimming, and bicycle riding. But there are other possibilities: modified aerobic dancing, calisthenics, and yoga, to name a few. People who have kept in good condition may be able to participate in a wider range of activities. It is important that your parents tailor exercise to their own level of ability and special needs. For example, jogging may be dangerous for those who have unsuspected heart disease or joint problems.

## The Benefits of Exercise

Although more research is needed, there is evidence that exercise may strengthen the heart and lungs, lower blood pressure, and protect against the start of adult-onset diabetes. Exercise can strengthen bones, slowing down the progress of osteoporosis, a bone-thinning disorder common in elderly women (see chapter 5). It can also strengthen and tone muscles and help a person move about more easily by keeping joints, tendons, and ligaments more flexible.

When combined with good eating habits, exercise can help people lose weight or maintain ideal weight by burning excess calories and helping control appetite. Exercise may also increase energy, improve sleep, reduce tension, and contribute to mental health by keeping people socially active.

## Designing an Exercise Program

A useful maxim in designing an exercise program is, "Don't do too much too soon." Your parents should start by seeing a physician, especially if they are over 60, have a disease or disability, or take medications. The doctor can evaluate your parents' physical condition, help decide which activities will suit them best, and check progress after the exercise program is under way.

It is important they choose an activity they like, and decide whether they want to join a group or exercise with a friend or alone. If they exercise alone, they ought to tell someone of their schedule and plans in case they need assistance. They need to decide on the best time of day and whether they prefer outdoor or indoor activity. They may have to try different activities and times before making an exercise period a routine part of their schedule.

It is best to begin by exercising slowly, starting with short periods of about five to ten minutes twice a week, then build up slowly, adding no more than a few minutes each week. If all goes well, your parents can gradually increase their exercise periods to fifteen to thirty minutes, three or four times a week. Their doctor may advise stretching as well as warm-up and cool-down periods of five to fifteen minutes to tune up the body before exercise and to help wind down afterwards. Although most people will have no problems if they start exercising slowly, your parents ought to be alert to symptoms such as chest pain, breathlessness, joint discomfort, or muscle cramps, and call the doctor if any of these occurs.

### Finding an Exercise Program

Most communities have centers where older people can join exercise classes and other recreational programs. Find out about fitness programs at a local church or synagogue, civic center, community college, park or recreation association, senior citizens' center, or service organization (such as an area agency on aging). YMCAs, YWCAs, and Jewish community centers usually offer a variety of programs. Organized activities designed for older adults provide many benefits to people who have been inactive, or to those with health problems. If your parents work, they should ask about programs there. Knowing that fitness improves performance on the job, many companies provide opportunities for their employees to exercise regularly.

If your parents are convinced that regular exercise is not for them, they should try to stay active in other ways. Bowling, square dancing, fishing, nature walks, arts and crafts, card and table games, gardening, and community projects do not offer all the benefits of regular, moderate exercise, but they can help a person remain actively involved in life, possibly adding years. For a list of information sources and free or low-cost publications that describe exercise programs, write to the National Institute on Aging/Exercise, Bethesda, MD 20892.

## SMOKING: IT'S NEVER TOO LATE TO STOP

"I've smoked two packs of cigarettes a day for 40 years—what's the use of quitting now?"

Stopping at any age will improve health. Some of the benefits for older people include reduced risk of cancer and lung disease, healthier heart and lungs, improved blood circulation, and better health for nonsmoking family members, particularly children. Smoking does not just cut a few years off the end of each smoker's life—it prematurely kills hundreds of thousands of people and seriously disables millions of others.

### What Smoking Does

Cigarette smoke affects the air passages in a smoker's lungs, causing irritation, inflammation, and excess production of mucus. These smoking effects often result in a chronic cough and, in more severe cases, can cause the lung disease known as chronic obstructive bronchitis. Cigarette smoke can also damage the tiny air sacs deep within the lungs, leading to emphysema. Both chronic obstructive bronchitis and emphysema interfere with normal breathing, leading to shortness of breath.

Smoking, high blood pressure, and high blood cholesterol (a fatty substance in the blood) all contribute to coronary heart disease (see chapter 5). A person with high blood pressure or high cholesterol who also smokes has a greater risk of heart attack than a person who has only one of these risk factors. When a person stops smoking, the benefits to the heart and circulatory system are believed to begin right away. The risk of heart attack, stroke, and other circulatory diseases drops. Circulation of blood to the hands and feet improves. Although quitting smoking will not reverse chronic lung damage, such as emphysema, it may slow the disease and help retain existing lung function.

Smoking causes several types of cancer, including those of the lungs, mouth, larynx, and esophagus. It also plays a role in cancers of the pancreas, kidney, and bladder. A smoker's risk of cancer depends in part on the number of cigarettes smoked, the number of years smoking, and how deeply the smoke is inhaled. After a smoker quits, the risk of smoking-related cancer begins to decline and eventually may be reduced to that of the nonsmoker.

Smokers have a higher risk than nonsmokers of getting influenza, pneumonia, and other respiratory conditions, including colds. Even today, with modern antibiotics, influenza and pneumonia can be life-threatening in older people. Finally, cigarette smoking has been associated with an increased risk of osteoporosis, the disabling bone-thinning disorder developed by one woman in four over age 60.

### Involuntary Smoking

Nonsmokers have become concerned about the effects of secondhand tobacco smoke on their health. This should be an especially important concern if the husband or wife of a smoker has asthma, another lung condition, or heart disease. Involuntary smoking (exposure to another's smoke) by nonsmokers has been linked to a higher incidence of bronchitis, pneumonia, asthma, and middle-ear infections in children. This is a good reason for a parent or grandparent to consider quitting or to avoid smoking while in the presence of young children and infants. Several studies even suggest that involuntary smoking increases the nonsmoker's risk of cancer.

### How to Stop Smoking

Of the many ways to stop smoking, no single method works for everyone, so each person must try to find what works best for him or her. Most people stop on their own, but others need help from doctors, clinics, or organized groups. Some studies have found that older people who take part in programs to stop smoking have higher success rates than younger ones do.

Withdrawal symptoms reported by some people who quit smoking include anxiety, restlessness, drowsiness, difficulty concentrating, and digestive problems. Many people have no withdrawal symptoms at all. Chewing gum containing nicotine can be prescribed by a physician to help people who are dependent on nicotine overcome withdrawal symptoms. When prescribing the gum, many doctors also recommend joining an organized support group or using self-help materials to assist the patient in quitting smoking. Nicotine chewing gum is not recommended for people who have certain forms of heart disease. Denture wearers may find it difficult to chew.

### Where to Get Help

Organizations, doctors, and clinics offering stop-smoking programs are listed in telephone books under "Smokers' Treatment and Information Centers." Further information can be obtained from the following organizations:

| | |
|---|---|
| American Cancer Society* <br> 90 Park Avenue <br> New York, NY 10016 | Office on Smoking and Health <br> National Institute of Mental <br>   Health <br> 5600 Fishers Lane <br> Rockville, MD 20852 |
| American Heart Association* <br> 7320 Greenville Avenue <br> Dallas, TX 75231 | |
| American Lung Association* <br> 1740 Broadway <br> New York, NY 10019 | Office of Cancer <br>   Communications <br> National Cancer Institute <br> 9000 Rockville Pike <br> Bethesda, MD 20892 |

* Consult your local telephone directory for listings of local chapters.

Or call the Cancer Information Service (see Appendix 1 for phone numbers in your area).

More than 30 million Americans have been able to quit smoking, and recent surveys suggest that this decline in smoking is continuing. By giving up cigarettes, your parents can be healthier and feel healthier, regardless of how many years they have been smoking or how many cigarettes they have smoked.

## TAKING CARE OF TEETH

Preventive health care also includes regular dental care, both in the home and in the dentist's office. Too often, older people—especially those who wear dentures—feel they no longer need dental checkups. And because the idea of preventive dental care dates back only to the 1950s, many people over 65 were not trained at an early age to be concerned with preventive care of the teeth. Others have astounded hospital personnel with their own healthy teeth when admitted for unrelated surgery in their ninth and tenth decades of life.

## Cleaning Teeth

The most important part of good dental care is knowing how to clean teeth. They should be brushed on all sides with short strokes, using a soft-bristle brush. The gum line needs special attention. Brushing the tongue and roof of the mouth will help remove germs and prevent bad breath. It is best to brush after every meal, but brushing thoroughly at least once a day, preferably at bedtime, is a must. If brushing results in repeated bleeding or pain, your parents should see a dentist.

Some people with arthritis or other conditions that limit motion may find it hard to hold a toothbrush. To overcome this, the brush handle can be attached to the hand with a wide elastic band or may be enlarged by attaching it to a sponge, Styrofoam ball, or similar object. Those with limited shoulder movement might find brushing easier if the handle of the brush is lengthened by attaching a long piece of wood or plastic. Electric toothbrushes are of benefit to many.

Careful daily brushing can help remove plaque, a sticky, colorless film that forms on the teeth and contains harmful germs. If the plaque is not removed every day, it hardens into calculus (tartar), a substance that can be removed only by a dentist or dental hygienist. The buildup of plaque and calculus can lead to periodontal (gum) disease, in which the normally pink gums redden, swell, and occasionally bleed. If untreated, periodontal disease worsens, and pockets of infection form between the teeth and gums. As the infection spreads, the gums recede. Eventually, the structures that hold the teeth in place are destroyed, the bone socket enlarges, and the tooth loosens and is lost. A regular program of complete oral hygiene can prevent gum disease and tooth decay in most people. Special toothpastes and mouthwash preparations with anti-plaque ingredients have been sold abroad for years and have recently become available in the United States.

Even though brushing is the most important means of removing film and food particles from the mouth, a toothbrush cannot reach many places. To remove germs and pieces of food from between the teeth and near the gum line, dentists recommend daily flossing with dental floss. A dentist or dental hygienist can instruct your parents in its proper use.

## Caring for Dentures

If your parents have dentures, they should keep them

clean and free from deposits that can cause permanent staining, bad breath, and gum irritation. Once a day, all surfaces of the dentures should be brushed with a denture-care product. When dentures are removed from the mouth, they should be placed in water or a denture-cleansing solution. It is also helpful to rinse the mouth with a warm saltwater solution in the morning, after meals, and at bedtime. Partial dentures should be cared for in the same way as full dentures. Because germs tend to collect under the clasps of partial dentures, it is especially important that this area be cleaned thoroughly.

### Adjusting to Dentures

Dentures will seem awkward at first. When learning to eat with dentures, your parents should select soft, nonsticky food. Cutting food into small pieces and chewing slowly, using both sides of the mouth, may help. Dentures tend to make the mouth less sensitive to hot foods and liquids, and less able to detect the presence of harmful objects such as bones. If problems in eating, talking, or simply wearing dentures continue after the first few weeks, the dentist can make adjustments.

At some point, dentures might have to be relined or even replaced. They should not be repaired at home, as this can damage the dentures and be harmful to the tissues of the mouth.

### Professional Care

Even with good home oral hygiene, it is important to have dental checkups at least twice a year. Dental checkups not only help maintain a healthy mouth, but are necessary for the early discovery of oral cancer and other diseases. Mouth cancer often goes unnoticed in its early and curable stages. This is true in part because many older people do not visit their dentists often enough, and because pain is not an early symptom of the disease. If your parents notice any red or white spots, or sores in the mouth that bleed or do not go away within two weeks, they should have them checked by a dentist.

It is essential to take care of dental problems before undergoing major surgery. The results of a complicated and successful heart operation, for example, could be endangered if bacteria from an untreated dental infection got into the bloodstream and lodged on heart valves.

For information on dental research, write to the National

Institute of Dental Research, 9000 Rockville Pike, Bethesda, MD 20892.

Information on general dental care can be obtained from the American Dental Association, 211 East Chicago Avenue, Chicago, IL 60611.

## SKIN CARE

Consumers spend hundreds of millions of dollars each year on wrinkle creams, skin bleaches to fade "age spots," oils, and other cosmetics in order to keep their skin looking young. At the same time, they spend not only money but countless hours trying to tan their skin, in the belief that a tan will make them look healthy and more attractive. Many changes in the skin that are considered age-related are actually due to chronic sun exposure. Signs of aging rarely appear in protected skin until sometime after age 50, and even then aging may progress very slowly.

### Sun-Damaged Skin

Ultraviolet (UV) radiation from the sun causes long-term damage to the skin, even if the skin does not appear to burn. A suntan may prevent further sunburn, but it does not protect the skin from sun damage, which may not be visible for many years. The sun's rays damage the elastic fibers beneath the skin's surface. With age, dark patches ("age spots" or "liver spots"), dilated blood vessels, and blackheads may appear on sun-exposed skin. In addition to thickened, leathery-looking skin, lines and wrinkles around the eyes, on the upper lip, and on the neck and hands usually result from prolonged sun exposure.

Sunlamps also deliver a strong dose of UV radiation. Dermatologists agree that sunlamps and tanning salons produce skin damage, and are not recommended.

An estimated 500,000 cases of skin cancer each year result from exposure to the sun over a period of years. Skin cancer is easily cured in most cases when detected early. However, new cancers can occur if prolonged sun exposure continues.

The best way to guard against the harmful effects of exposure to the sun's rays is to avoid the sun altogether. For those exposed to the sun, early morning or late afternoon sun (before 9 A.M. or after 3 P.M.) is less damaging to the skin than sun in the middle of the day. People whose work requires them to be outside all day, such as farmers and sailors, should be especially careful to protect their skin from the sun.

The scalp can be protected by hats, and the brim of a hat can partially protect the face. The best protection is to apply a sunscreen to all skin that is not covered by clothing.

Sunscreens are oils, creams, gels, or lotions that absorb or scatter UV light. It is important to note the rating, called the sun protection factor (SPF), that appears on the label of a sunscreen product. The higher the number, the more protection the sunscreen provides. An SPF of 15 or greater is recommended for maximum protection, although even a product with a 15 rating will allow some tanning. To be effective, sunscreens should be applied at least a half hour before sun exposure, and they must be reapplied after swimming or perspiring.

People often believe that a tanned person is healthier. While this is not true as far as the skin itself is concerned, limited sun exposure is one way to provide the body with vitamin D, which is necessary for maintaining and repairing bone. Although sun is necessary to convert vitamin D to its active form, minimal exposure is necessary for this conversion.

### Dry Skin

Mild to severe itching resulting from dryness is one of the most common and uncomfortable characteristics of aging skin. Dry skin can appear after exposure to soaps, irritating cleaning products (disinfectants, cleansers, etc.), and dry air in overheated rooms (often called "winter itch"). It is important for an older person to use lotions to prevent severe itching, because the scratching that often follows can lead to infection or long-term skin irritation.

Many different kinds of moisturizers are available, ranging from heavy creams to light, nongreasy lotions. Although they vary greatly in price, the most expensive product is not necessarily the best. Many dermatologists recommend moisturizers that contain petrolatum and are hypoallergenic and fragrance-free.

The skin becomes more fragile, wounds more easily, and is more prone to infection with age. Because the skin reacts more slowly to irritants, an older person may not realize that the skin can be damaged by a strong chemical or a hot substance. Care must be taken to prevent injury by not using water that is too hot, by wearing gloves when cleaning, and by avoiding the use of harsh products, even if no reaction appears on the skin immediately.

---

### TIPS FOR MAINTAINING HEALTHY SKIN

---

- Wear sunscreens when skin is exposed to the sun. Once skin shows signs of aging, the damage may not be reversed, but further damage can be prevented.
- To prevent dryness, wear latex gloves when washing dishes and when using strong cleaning agents or other chemicals; use mild soaps; use petroleum jelly or other moisturizers as often as necessary, especially after bathing.
- Wear soft clothing and avoid strong washing detergents. Some fabric softeners can also cause skin irritation and itching.
- Abrupt onset of generalized itching can be a sign of certain diseases. If it persists after taking preventive measures to avoid dry skin, check with the doctor.
- Many age-related skin changes as well as most skin cancers are surgically correctable. People over age 65 would benefit from an annual skin exam performed by a dermatologist.

---

## HEALTH QUACKERY

We hear a great deal today about the rising cost of health care. But seldom do health-care costs reflect the money wasted on medical quackery. Each year, American consumers pay roughly $10 billion for ineffective, expensive, scientifically unproven, and sometimes harmful remedies and devices. Also staggering are the indirect costs of health quackery—medical expenses resulting from a delay in legitimate treatment or from injury by a quack "treatment." In 1983, the indirect cost for arthritis fraud alone was estimated at $25 million.

Quacks—those who sell unproven remedies—have been around for years. In the past it was the "snake-oil salesman" who traveled from town to town making outrageous claims about a doubtful product. Today's quack uses more sophisticated means. He or she sells products through advertisements, bogus sales corporations, foundations, and clinics.

## Who Are the Victims?

To the quack, people of all ages are fair game, but older people form the largest group of victims. So serious is the impact of fraud on the elderly that the Subcommittee on Health and Long-Term Care of the U.S. House of Representatives conducted a four-year investigation on quackery. The committee issued its findings in the report *Quackery: A $10 Billion Scandal,* concluding that 60 percent of all victims of health-care fraud are older persons, although this group makes up only 11 percent of the U.S. population.

Most people who succumb to the quack's worthless and sometimes dangerous "treatments" are desperate for some offer of hope. Because older people as a group have more chronic illnesses (arthritis, high blood pressure, diabetes, and cancer) compared to younger people, they are likely targets for medical fraud.

## Major Targets of Quackery

In addition to the aging process, arthritis and cancer are the largest areas for health quackery. It is especially easy to fall for arthritis "remedies" because symptoms of arthritis tend to recede or disappear for a period of time for unknown reasons; persons with arthritis then associate the remedy they happen to be using with relief from symptoms. Arthritis sufferers have paid good money for bottled sea water, "extracts" from New Zealand green-lipped mussels, and purported Chinese herbal medicines (which often have no herbs but do contain drugs that may be dangerous).

Most forms of arthritis have no cure at present, but treatments are available through qualified medical sources that can help reduce pain and enable greater movement. These include drugs, heat and cold treatments, a balance of rest and exercise, and in some cases surgical implants.

Cancer is currently responsible for one-fifth of all deaths

in the United States, and, as with arthritis, it occurs more often in older people. Quacks prey on the older person's fear of cancer by offering "treatments" that have no proven value—for example, a vegetarian diet dangerously low in protein.

Nonetheless, by staying alert to signs of quackery, your parents can protect themselves and help stop the spread of medical fraud. One way of doing this is to encourage your parents to question carefully what they see or hear in advertisements. With some exceptions, the editors of newspapers and magazines and the management of radio and TV networks and stations do not regularly screen their ads for truth or accuracy. Your parents should be aware that ads for cosmetics and health aids are not necessarily true just because they are presented by what may otherwise be a reputable source. They need to find out about a product before buying it. Health products sold door-to-door should be checked out first through a local agency, always keeping in mind the common ploys listed below.

---

**COMMON PLOYS USED BY DISHONEST PROMOTERS**

---

- Promising a quick or painless cure.
- Promoting a product made from a "special" or "secret" formula, usually available only through the mail and only from a single source.
- Presenting testimonials or case histories from satisfied patients.
- Advertising a product as effective for a wide variety of ailments.
- Claiming to understand the cause of, or cure for, a disease (such as arthritis or cancer) not yet understood by medical science.

## For More Information

In addition to a physician, the following agencies can tell your parents about a particular product and can offer further advice on steps to take:

- Council of Better Business Bureaus: The CBBB offers general advice on products and has published, in collaboration with the Food and Drug Administration, *Tips on Medical Quackery and Arthritis: Quackery and Unproven Remedies*. For a free copy, send one self-addressed, stamped envelope to the Council of Better Business Bureaus, 1515 Wilson Boulevard, Arlington, VA 22209 (Attention: Standards and Practices).

• Food and Drug Administration: The FDA can answer questions about medical devices, medicines, and food supplements that are mislabeled, misrepresented, or in some way harmful. The FDA also oversees federal regulations concerning these products. Write to the Food and Drug Administration, 5600 Fishers Lane, Rockville, MD 20852.

• U.S. Postal Service: The USPS monitors quack products purchased by mail. Write to the U.S. Postal Inspection Service, Office of Criminal Investigation, Washington, DC 20260-2166.

• Federal Trade Commission: The FTC looks into charges of false or deceptive advertising in publications or on the radio and TV. Write to the Federal Trade Commission, Sixth Street and Pennsylvania Avenue, N.W., Washington, DC 20580.

When questioning a medical device used for a specific disease, contact the professional association concerned with the disease—for example, a local office of the American Cancer Society, the Arthritis Foundation, or the Alzheimer's Disease and Related Disorders Association.

## ACCIDENTS AND YOUR PARENTS

Accidents seldom "just happen," and many can be prevented. Accidental injuries become more frequent and serious in later life. Thus, attention to safety is especially important for older persons.

Several factors make older people prone to accidents. Poor eyesight and hearing can decrease their awareness of hazards. Arthritis, neurological diseases, and impaired coordination and balance can make them unsteady. Various diseases, medications, alcohol, and preoccupation with personal problems can result in drowsiness or distraction. Often, mishaps are expressions of mental depression or of poor physical conditioning.

When accidents occur, older persons are especially vulnerable to severe injury and tend to heal slowly. Particularly in women, the bones often become thin and brittle with age, causing seemingly minor falls to result in broken bones. Many accidents can be prevented by maintaining mental and physical health and conditioning, and by cultivating good safety habits.

Falls are the most common cause of fatal injury in the aged. Proper lighting can help prevent them. Here are some tips for your parents:

- Illuminate all stairways and provide light switches at both the bottom and the top.
- Provide night lights or bedside remote-control light switches.
- Be sure both sides of stairways have sturdy handrails.
- Tack down carpeting on stairs, and use nonskid treads.
- Remove throw rugs that tend to slide.
- Arrange furniture and other objects so they are not obstacles.
- Install grab bars on bathroom walls and nonskid mats or strips in the bathtub.
- Keep outdoor steps and walkways in good repair.

Personal health practices are also important in preventing falls. Because many older persons tend to become faint or dizzy when standing too quickly, experts recommend rising slowly from sitting or lying positions. Both illness and the side effects of drugs increase the risk of falls.

Burns are especially disabling in the aged, who recover from such injuries very slowly. The following are some good practices to follow:

- Never smoke in bed or when drowsy.
- When cooking, do not wear loose-fitting, flammable clothing. Bathrobes, nightgowns, and pajamas can easily catch fire.
- Set water heater thermostats or faucets so that water does not scald the skin.

- Plan which emergency exits to use in case of fire. Many older people trap themselves behind multiple door locks, which are hard to open during an emergency. Install one good lock that can be opened from the inside quickly, rather than many inexpensive, flimsy locks.

An older person's ability to drive may be impaired by such age-related changes as increased sensitivity to glare, poorer adaptation to darkness, diminished coordination, and slower reaction time. People can compensate for these changes by driving fewer miles, driving less often and more slowly, and driving less at night, during rush hours, and in the winter.

If your parents ride on public transportation, they should take the following precautions:

- Remain alert and brace themselves when a bus is slowing down or turning.
- Watch for slippery pavement and other hazards when entering or leaving a vehicle.
- Have their fare ready to prevent losing balance while fumbling for change.
- Not carry too many packages, and leave one hand free to grasp railings.
- Allow extra time to cross streets, especially in bad weather.
- At night wear light-colored or fluorescent clothing and carry a flashlight.

The National Safety Council reports that each year about 24,000 persons over age 65 die from accidental injuries and at least 800,000 others sustain injuries severe enough to disable them for at least one day. Thus, attention to safety, especially in later life, can prevent much untimely death and disability.

### Home Safety Checklist

Each year, many older Americans are injured in and around their homes. In 1981, over 622,000 people over age 65 were treated in hospital emergency rooms for injuries associated with products they use every day.

Many of these injuries result from hazards that are easy to

overlook, but also easy to fix. By spotting these hazards and taking some simple steps to correct them, many injuries can be prevented.

The U.S. Consumer Product Safety Commission publishes a home safety checklist to help spot possible safety problems that may be present in the home. Call their toll-free numbers, 1-800-638-2772 or 1-800-638-8270 (including Alaska and Hawaii), or 1-800-492-8104 (Maryland only). Or write, U.S. Consumer Product Safety Commission, Washington, DC 20207.

---

### WHAT YOUR PARENTS CAN DO TO REDUCE RISK OF ILLNESS AND ENHANCE QUALITY OF LIFE

- Don't smoke.
- Eat a balanced diet and maintain a desirable weight.
- Exercise regularly.
- Have regular health checkups, see a doctor when a problem appears, and follow a doctor's advice when taking medications.
- Stay involved with family and friends.
- Allow time for rest and relaxation.
- Get enough sleep.
- Stay active through work, recreation, and community activities.
- Drink alcoholic beverages in moderation, if at all, and never drive after drinking.
- Use seatbelts.
- Avoid overexposure to the sun and cold.
- Take care of your body.
- Practice good safety habits at home to prevent accidents such as fires and falls.
- Have a positive attitude toward life.

# 11

# HEALTH CARE:
# Surgery at 85?

*Beneath the bleeding hands we feel*
*The sharp compassion of the healer's art*
*Resolving the enigma of the fever chart.*

T. S. Eliot, *"East Coker"*

Surgery at 85? "Oh no!" That was Mildred's response when her widowed father-in-law, Frank, told her that he was considering a coronary bypass operation. She recalled visiting her cousin, John, in the hospital when he had his bypass surgery, and all the pain and suffering he had had to endure. For a whole week, every time the nurses made him cough, he felt his chest was going to burst open. Her experience as the chief laboratory technician had not helped her much in trying to cope with her favorite cousin's suffering. He was only 55 then, and he recovered. He was doing well now, often went swimming and jogging, and enjoyed climbing in the Sierra Nevadas. Before the operation he had not even been able to get up the flight of stairs to his bedroom without severe chest pains.

But at the time of his surgery, John had been 30 years younger than Frank, and wished desperately to watch his kids grow up and start their own families. Frank was a great-grandfather already. Why should he go through the pain and agony of the surgery? He did not swim or jog or play ball or tennis, anyhow. What he liked to do was read, watch a movie, or play a game of cards once in a while. How many years did he have left? What kind of years would they be?

The problems went beyond the medical ones. Who would take care of Frank after his surgery? Would he come to live with Mildred? Would she have to take care of him? Was that why she had reacted the way she did? Was she more afraid of what the surgery would do to her than to him? What kind of an ogre was she? She had always thought of herself as a caring person. She took care of her kids, and looked after her ailing aunt, and still had time for her career. She looked forward to going to work each morning, and now, would she have to give it up?

Mildred had been lost in her thoughts when suddenly she realized that Frank was talking. "You haven't been listening, have you, Mildred?" He smiled and said, "I've been doing a lot of thinking since the doctor talked to me last week." Frank had memorized most of the statistics relevant to bypass surgery, and could not wait to tell them to Mildred. He had learned that there were 191,000 bypass operations in the United States in 1983—that is more than 500 every day of the year. Most of the patients who had the bypass surgery were men (145,000 men; 46,000 women). He knew about the complications, too. Bypass patients had strokes, bleeding troubles, heart attacks, all kinds of infections, and more than 5 percent of patients who were 65 years or older at the time of surgery died within a month of the operation, according to a major study that had been going on for ten years.[1]

"I've been thinking that if I have surgery and I die, that's okay; but what if I'm one of those others who gets a stroke? What if I can't get around at all by myself anymore? And what if my mind goes? I know my mind is as clear as a bell, but it could happen. It may be the anesthetic, or having your blood pumped through a bunch of tubes outside your body. Did you know that the longer you're on the pump, the more chance you have of losing your marbles, and that for us old folks it's an especially high risk? Now, I know we take chances all our lives, and you know that I like to gamble, but I also like to know the odds and the payoff. And here I don't have a clear idea of either of them. Even if the odds aren't too bad, what about the payoff? Let's say I come through this surgery okay. Will I be better off afterwards than I am now?"

That conversation took place nearly four years ago, and last Christmas had been their big family reunion. Ultimately, Frank had decided against having surgery. He was the center of the party, with all the grandchildren and great-grandchildren, and they kidded about having to wait another year for his ninetieth birthday. He dug into the honey-baked ham dinner with the best of them. After dinner, he said he felt his stomach complaining; he wasn't used to all that food. He went to lie down for a little nap. He never woke up. That wasn't such a bad way to die.

Surgery at 85—how different is it from surgery at 65, or 45? Mortality is different. With coronary bypass, the death rate is more than twice as high for those over 65 years of age as compared to those under 65 (5 percent against 2 percent). Also, nine out of ten patients under age 65 survive five years, compared to seven out of ten patients age 75 and older.[2] When it comes to medical problems, chronological age is an important factor, particularly when the age of the patient is high. Many of our parents have already reached 75 years of age; many others soon will.

## BODIES HAVE LIMITED WARRANTIES

As our parents age, they face a high probability of developing one or more chronic diseases. Their generation has reaped the benefits of the medical technology explosion, and the last decade has brought the most significant increases in life expectancy for older age groups. A greater number of people are living longer lives, but medical technology has failed to increase the life span (the highest age to which anyone survives) or to control chronic illness. Diseases relatively rare in younger people become common as we grow older. Most likely our parents are suffering, or will suffer, from more than one physical illness—high blood pressure, arthritis, heart conditions, hearing impairment, or poor vision. Poor health and the disabilities that often accompany illness have a tremendous impact on the quality of our parents' lives and on our relationships with them.

Chronic illness is the leading cause of disability among older adults. The severity of a particular disease varies from person to person, with marked differences in degrees of disability and limitation in activities. For example, chronic arthritis may cause such severe pain and stiffness as to render one person housebound, while another may experience only occasional flare-ups and maintain a full schedule of activities. The degree of disability, moreover, increases with age. Compared to those under 65, a significantly higher proportion of people 65 or older are limited by a chronic condition. For people 75 years of age and older, more than half are limited in carrying out activities of daily living, which include preparing food, doing laundry, shopping, and maintaining personal hygiene. Such a disability and limitation of activity may have a profound effect on an individual's feeling of self-worth and independence (see chapter 12).

What can we do to help? Can our parents adjust to their chronic illnesses and disabilities? When are we being helpful? When are we intrusive and infantilizing? When are we selfish and concerned primarily with our own needs? Mildred, for example, had been confused by her father-in-law's decision not to have surgery. It raised questions in her mind about the reasons for her relief at his decision. Was she being selfish in thinking about her own life? Did she really want what was best for him, or for herself? Financial considerations had not entered Mildred's thoughts, but for most of us they do, or will. Medical care in the United States is expensive and becoming more so. Medical complications are costly, and severely disabled patients can survive for years with the aid of high technology. But someone has to pay for it, and pay dearly. High-tech means high cost.

## THE WORLD OF MEDICINE IS CHANGING

Rising health-care costs have had a tremendous impact on the practice of medicine. Aside from West Germany and Sweden, the United States spends more on health care than does any other country in the world. In 1950, only about 4 percent of the gross national product went to health care, as compared to over 10 percent in the 1980s.[3] The amounts of actual dollars spent were $12.7 billion in 1950 and $355 billion in 1983—an increase of over 2,500 percent[4]—much more than any inflationary change. The government has a considerable investment in health care. Forty-two percent of all health-care expenditures come from public sources.

Why is health care so expensive today? The reasons are complicated, but can be understood as a response to the basic economic rules of supply and demand. One of the most important changes affecting the demand for health care is the rapidly increasing proportion of people 65 years of age or older, the very segment of the population into which our parents are most likely to fit. Our successes at prolonging individuals' lives have increased our health-care expenses. Other factors influencing demand include the new technologies for sustaining life (e.g., organ transplantation, dialysis) and the availability of health-care insurance. If the government or our insurance companies will pay for the services, instead of our bank accounts, we are more likely to seek those services. In 1983, third parties (government or private health insurance) paid for 73 percent of all personal health-care expenditures.[5]

Costly medical procedures are used more often in the United States than in any other country. The frequency of coronary artery surgery (a procedure costing approximately $25,000 in the United States) varies throughout the world—the per capita rate in the United States is about 25 times the rate in France.[6] The increasing demand and cost of health-care services has led to increasing competition for patients among health-care providers. It has also led to the growth of health maintenance organizations (HMOs), the evolution of medicine from a profession into a business, and a shift of emphasis from a primary concern of serving the patient to that of marketing a "product." Large corporate chains are taking over hospitals throughout the country. Profit-making institutions are replacing nonprofit hospitals. And doctors, too, are being forced to pay attention to the commercial aspects of medicine. Health care has entered the marketplace; it is being packaged, cost-accounted, and sold and bought in DRGs (diagnosis-related groups). Marketing approaches never before used in medicine have become commonplace. The increasing demand for medical services, together with pressure on physicians to see more patients per hour (in order to make ends meet with Medicare payments), has resulted in longer waits at the doctor's office and less time with the doctor at each visit.

## AN APPLE A DAY KEEPS THE PHARMACIST AWAY

Medications, too, have multiplied in an unprecedented fashion. In 1947, the *Physicians' Desk Reference* described approximately 1,500 medications; the 1986 *PDR* lists more than 2,500 prescription drugs. In addition, there are more than 1,500 separate listings of nonprescription drugs, which are available from the druggist on request, or "over the counter." These nonprescription medications represent 40 percent of all drugs used by the elderly.[7] The *PDR* of prescription drugs, which contained jealously guarded information until 1979, can now be bought by anyone in bookstores for under $20. It contains, for each drug, information on chemical composition, properties, actions (what it does and how it does it), indications, contraindications, precautions, instructions for administration, dosages, and symptoms and treatment of overdose. It also provides color pictures of many drugs, showing the specific tablet, capsule, or spansule.

Most medications are used by persons over the age of 65. In the United States, people 65 years of age or older spend $3 billion per year on prescription and nonprescription drugs, which represents nearly 25 percent of the national total; yet this age group comprises only about 11 percent of the population.[8] Surveys indicate that in the United States, 90 percent of the elderly take at least one drug. One survey of elderly community residents in New York State found that they used more than 300 different kinds of medications (60 percent by prescription), and more than 80 percent of people over age 65 were taking between two and six drugs each. About 15 percent of them were taking seven to fifteen drugs each, and nearly 15 percent of them misused their medications because they did not understand the directions on how to take the drug.[9]

To complicate matters, drugs are more likely to cause side effects in older people than in younger adults, because of age-related changes in physiology. For example, drugs may be absorbed from the stomach and intestines more erratically, and they tend to be eliminated through the kidneys and liver more slowly. As a result, they tend to remain active in the body for longer periods. Also, because so many older people tend to take drugs more or less routinely—digitalis preparations for heart disease, for instance, or any number of preparations to bring down high blood pressure (antihypertensives)—any newly prescribed medication may interact with the drugs the older person is already taking.

It is essential, therefore, that all patients tell their physicians about *all* the drugs they are taking, whether prescribed by another doctor, recently or long ago, locally or far away; whether obtained from a friend, relative, dentist, druggist—no matter from whom or when. The taking of thyroid pills, to restore thyroid function to normal, or antidiabetic medication, to regulate sugar metabolism, may have become a routine, and our parents may be so used to taking these compounds that they forget to tell their doctors about them. The only way doctors can anticipate untoward consequences of what are called drug-drug interactions is through knowing what drugs a patient is already taking before they prescribe a new one. Similarly, doctors need to be informed of chronic diseases and disabilities in order to anticipate drug-disease interactions. For example, your father's physician may not have known about his history of hepatitis. If he had, he would not have prescribed a medication that is metabolized (deactivated) by the liver. Or he might have prescribed it, but in lower doses, carefully watching for side effects.

Sometimes a patient innocently contributes to the problem. Not long ago, a 75-year-old man was rushed to the emergency room of a local hospital because of sudden onset of weakness and dizziness. His wife had called the paramedics; she thought her husband was having a heart attack because he had a long history of heart trouble. After his doctor had been summoned and the immediate emergency was over, the patient was admitted to the hospital for laboratory tests, X rays, an electrocardiogram, and observation. All the tests were negative, and the doctor could not account for the patient's sudden drop in blood pressure. He asked his patient if he had taken anything other than his usual medications. "No, Doc, I swear," was the response. But the patient's wife remembered that her husband had used some new over-the-counter nose drops the morning he got so sick. Once the doctor heard the name of the nose drops, he knew that one of its ingredients, in combination with the patient's antihypertensive drug, was the source of the trouble. He warned his patient never to take any over-the-counter drugs without first consulting him. The nose drops could have killed him. Who would think that nose drops could be deadly?

Medications come in many forms. Today we are seeing battles and lawsuits about whether physicians should prescribe the generic drug, the less expensive form not identified with any particular pharmaceutical company, or the brand produced by a specific company. In 1984, Congress passed the Hatch-Waxman Act, which made it easier for generic copies of original drugs to receive Food and Drug Administration approval. The law has not, however, resolved the controversy about the so-called bioequivalence or relative efficacy of generic and brand-name drugs. The answer may vary from drug to drug. Many physicians have definite reasons for not prescribing generic drugs for some treatments, but find them perfectly acceptable for others. It is best to consult the doctor; patients should not make that choice on their own—at least not without hearing the doctor's reasons.

## HOW TO USE MEDICINES SAFELY

- Take exactly the amount of drug prescribed by the doctor, and follow the dosage schedule as closely as possible. (Call your doctor or pharmacist if you have questions.)

- Never take drugs prescribed for a friend or relative, even though your symptoms may be the same.

- Always tell the doctor about past problems you have had with drugs. When the doctor prescribes a new drug, be sure to mention all other medicines you are taking currently. It is best to bring a list.

- Keep a daily record of the drugs you are taking.

- If childproof containers are hard to handle, ask the pharmacist for easy-to-open containers. Always be sure, however, that they are out of the reach of children.

- Make sure directions printed on a drug container are understandable and that the name of the medicine is clearly printed on the label.

- Discard old medicines; many drugs lose their effectiveness over time.

- When starting a new drug, ask the doctor or pharmacist about side effects, about special rules for storage, and about foods or beverages, if any, to avoid, or if they should be taken before or after the medication.

- Avoid discontinuing a medicine until the doctor says so. If you do have to stop or forget to take a dose, check with your doctor on how to start again.

- Always call the doctor promptly if you notice unusual reactions.

## GETTING SICK? CAN YOUR PARENTS AFFORD IT?

Today, the average hospital bed in most large cities in the United States costs about $400 per day. This is just the cost for the bed, the food, and the service. Everything else is extra—the charge for just two aspirin tablets can be $5! Then there are the charges for doctors' visits, procedures, laboratory tests, X rays, operating room, nurses, anesthesia, and so on (and on and on). Even outside the hospital, the costs are high; an average visit to the doctor is in the $100 range. What's more, medical insurance premiums are rising. No wonder some people in our society can't afford to buy insurance, even though they can't afford to be without it. They take a chance. Even with insurance, usually coverage is only partial. If your parents are 65 or older, they will have Medicare, which helps some, but it isn't enough, and it would be to your advantage and theirs to make sure they have supplemental insurance coverage.

At the beginning of the 1980s, public programs for medical care (Medicare, Medicaid) paid for up to 80 percent of hospital expenses for people 65 years of age and older.[10] Since October of 1983, however, Medicare payments have been determined on a case-based formula, using diagnosis-related groups (DRGs). This means that hospitals are reimbursed a predetermined amount of money based on the cost for the *average*, not the *individual*, patient with a particular diagnosis. If your mother's diagnosis is myocardial infarction, for example, the hospital is entitled to $8,014.40 if she survives the heart attack, no matter how long she stays there. If she can be sent home or to some other facility after three days in the intensive-care unit and one day on the regular floor, the hospital may make a good profit. The longer she stays, the lower the profit and the greater the losses to the hospital. As a result, hospitals are trying to discharge patients as soon as possible. If she is readmitted within one month with the same diagnosis, the hospital gets no more money at all. To maximize profits, hospitals may be reluctant to readmit sick patients. Since this is a new system, the individual citizens and their families could pay a heavy price, not only in terms of inadequate health care and suffering, but in dollars as well.

How can you save some money? One way is to shop around. Prices vary from community to community, and even within communities. Another way to save is to use a Health Maintenance Organization (HMO) or one of the other professional organizations instead of a private hospital or physician. Rather than charging on a fee-for-service basis, these are prepaid practice plans wherein a group of physicians offers patients a plan that looks like an insurance policy. If they join, your parents will know in advance what their medical expenses will be for the entire year. That is especially important to those on a fixed income. In these plans, a set monthly amount is paid, regardless of whether the medical facility is used a lot or a little or not at all. When your parent needs to see a doctor, there is little or no additional expense. Such prepayment plans also give your doctor incentive to minimize the services and thereby save money. Of course, this could work against you, and you may feel in some HMOs that your doctor is undertreating you. One way to avoid this feeling is to be an active consumer. Another complaint about these organizations is that there are long waits. But the same complaint is also heard about private physicians. A final complaint is that people are passed from physician to physician in these large organizations, that the physician is too impersonal, and that the patient feels like a number. Many of the new organizations have it worked out so that the patient can see the same physician each time. Moreover, having a private physician does not guarantee the service your parents want. It has become increasingly difficult to find physicians who make house calls or meet patients at the emergency room during an emergency.

## SOME TIPS ON GETTING THE MOST AND BEST FROM DOCTORS

Given the complexity of the health-care system and the likelihood of your parents' suffering from several illnesses simultaneously, it is crucial that they make the most out of what time they do spend with the doctor. The following tips may make it easier for you and your parents to maximize communication with the doctor and minimize confusion.

Depending on the situation, either you or your parent or both can take the following steps:

- Keep a written record of the medical history. If you have not done so, consider helping your parent prepare one or do so yourself before going to the doctor. A written record will help you and your parent organize your thoughts beforehand and will simplify and clarify the information conveyed. Most physicians organize their patient information in a standardized format as shown below. Try a similar format.

---

### DOCTOR'S FORMAT FOR RECORDING INFORMATION ABOUT PATIENTS

---

*Identifying data.*   Age, sex, address.

*Chief complaint.*   Main problem(s) that brought the patient to the doctor.

*History of present illness.*   Chronological account of events that led to the chief complaint.

*Past medical history.*   Previous serious illnesses, surgeries, hospitalizations, allergies, other doctors seen, medications.

*Social history.*   Pertinent information about where and with whom you live, what you do, and other personal data.

*Family history.*   Pertinent information about illnesses affecting family members, including psychiatric illnesses and hospitalizations.

*Review of systems.*   Checklist of other complaints or symptoms, organized by organ systems (i.e., heart, lungs, eyes, etc.).

*Physical examination.*   What the doctor records, based on his or her observations and exam.

*Laboratory tests.*   Results of blood tests, X rays, etc.

*Impression.*   The doctor's diagnosis or list of possible diagnoses, based on all the information obtained.

*Plan.*   The treatment(s) or strategies recommended, based on the impression.

---

- Arrange your parent's pertinent medical records and have them sent to the doctor before the visit, or bring them in at the time of the visit. Keep a copy of everything; often, papers are misplaced or lost in the mail, or just disappear without a trace.

- Do not hesitate to ask the doctor for further explanations. The doctor should be able to make clear how he or she understands the problem and the alternative treatments available, so that the patient can make an informed decision.
- Write down the doctor's instructions, and include all the details.
- Be sure to carefully review potential side effects of medications prescribed or treatments recommended.

## SURGERY AT 85

Even if adult children follow the tips above on getting the most and best from their parents' physicians, they are not always successful. The medical and emotional complications they must face have no simple solutions. Mildred, whose father-in-law had refused surgery at 85, was confronted with a similar decision for her 85-year-old mother.

Mildred brought herself back to the present; she had not thought about her conversation with her father-in-law for a long time. It had been nearly six years since they went over the pros and cons of his bypass surgery. Once more it was a question of surgery at 85, but this time it was for her mother, Sarah. After six months of numerous medical consultations, differences of opinion, and painstaking ambivalence, the decision was finally in favor of the operation. They had all agreed, and were anxious for Sarah to have her surgery. Even though the risks were many, the alternative to surgery was a greater risk.

As she sat in the hospital waiting room during Sarah's surgery, Mildred couldn't help recalling the previous months with mounting anger and fear. She thought of how that pleasant holiday with Mother was shattered when, following a lovely dinner, Sarah whispered with embarrassment that she must have wet herself. That was the beginning!

She had wet herself, all right, but not with urine. She was soaked in blood. They summoned the local doctor, who assured them it was only a bladder infection. He prescribed some antibiotics and recommended that Sarah see a urologist when she got home.

Over the next two weeks, Sarah's bleeding went down to a trickle. She was feeling better physically, but was very worried. Whenever she picked up the newspaper, she saw something about cancer; bleeding without pain was near the top of the list of danger signals. Her urologist was sure it was not cancer, but just a prolapse of her bladder, a common condition in older women. (The tissues supporting the uterus weaken, and the uterus protrudes into the vaginal canal.) He assured them that minor surgery could correct the problem, but, while it should be done, there was no rush or emergency.

Mildred discussed her mother's symptoms with her doctor friends, including some geriatricians, doctors who specialize in treating older patients. All of them were concerned and puzzled about the diagnosis; and none of them believed the diagnosis fit the history. They advised against the proposed surgery and suggested a second opinion, this time from a gynecologist.

Sarah readily agreed to such a consultation, and Mildred began to go down her list of highly recommended doctors in that specialty. Dr. Tillman was one of the few available within a reasonable time—and Sarah liked him on first sight. He was sure the bleeding was from the uterus and not the bladder. He suggested a "minor" operation: a D-and-C, or dilation and curettage, which is a scraping out of the inside of the uterus. A pathologist would test the scrapings for malignant cells, which, if the tests were positive, could be removed easily at a later time. Since he was going on vacation, he wanted her to have ultrasound pictures in the meantime. The radiologist who performed this procedure reported that the ultrasound showed something that looked like a growth, but that the films were inconclusive. He could recommend some colleagues if they didn't want to wait for Dr. Tillman to return.

They passed an anxious few weeks until they finally got in to see Dr. Baker—another recommended specialist on Mildred's list. Upon completion of his examination of Sarah, he "whispered" to Mildred that he thought her mother had a malignant growth. His plan was to take a biopsy of the cervix, another "minor" surgical procedure, two weeks hence (his first available appointment). When Mildred told him of her concern about the delay, he assured her that it was a slow-growing tumor, and that, at Sarah's age, it was not dangerous. Then, the week after the biopsy in his office, Dr. Baker would put Sarah in the hospital to do a D-and-C under anesthesia. That would give him the opportunity to get a good look at the tissue and know exactly what to expect during a later surgery.

Mildred felt her heart sink to her stomach. That sounded like an awful lot was going to be done to her mother and it would take a long time. Would they not spread around the cancer by scraping the uterus? Sarah and Mildred drove back to Mildred's home without saying a word. This bleeding had been going on for nearly six months, during which time the cancer could have been growing inside. What had they done wrong—especially Mildred, with all her friends in the medical profession?

Sarah had said all along that she thought it was cancer. Now was not the time for regrets and recriminations; now was the time to get some action. Mildred did not want her mother to have three procedures instead of just one operation. After more talks with her friends, Mildred learned that others with greater knowledge were equally doubtful about Dr. Baker's methods.

So they consulted a third doctor. Though abrupt and matter-of-fact, Dr. Burton seemed to know his business. He examined Sarah quickly and efficiently, and then told them both that he had taken a biopsy inside the uterus—Sarah had hardly felt it—and that he would send it off to the pathology lab. He was fairly sure it was a cancer, though, and would book her at the hospital for the first open date. If the lab confirmed his impression, and he was pretty sure it would, he would take out the uterus, ovaries, and appendix, and dissect out the lymph nodes. After surgery, she would have radiation.

Mildred couldn't bear to think of the harrowing weeks that followed: her mother having to be persuaded to go through with such major surgery; finally consenting; being booked into the hospital; the seemingly interminable wait (even though it was really only three weeks). She recalled the phone call two nights before the scheduled admission, canceling the operation because the internist, upon review of her mother's records, had decided that her large goiter, together with her asthma, made her "too poor a surgical risk"; the soul-searching before trying to convince her mother once more that surgery was the best approach; the efforts to find another hospital with an internist willing to "clear" her for surgery, and a surgeon willing to perform the operation. It had been unreal; she had functioned like a programmed robot, doing what needed to be done in a mechanical way. When Mildred finally checked Sarah into the hospital, neither of them minded the long wait, the complicated admission procedures, the mix-up about the room, or the examinations by the intern and the resident.

Now it was the morning of the surgery, and it was a relief to have the past months behind them. Could that surgical nurse be beckoning her? Mildred's heart began to pound. It seemed hardly any time at all since they had taken her mother into the operating room. The surgery was over. No complications, everything had gone well, and she was in the recovery room. Sarah was doing so well that they did not send her to intensive care. The surgeon had been able to remove everything. They did want to do some postoperative radiation, but the doctor was very optimistic. The pathology report came back. All was well; no spread. Sarah recovered so quickly that nobody could believe it. They decided to take her home on the fifth day after surgery.

## JUDGING THE RISKS OF SURGERY

The choice for surgery depends on the illness and not the age. It depends on the patient's condition and wishes and, in the final analysis, on personal ethics and judgment. Rarely can a decision to operate be based totally on scientific facts. Of course, the patient and the family need to know the medical facts, but rarely do hard facts tell us how a given patient will fare as a result of a given operation—or without it.

Can the doctors tell us the risks of surgery, and help us judge them in light of the potential benefits? Do they know? By and large, doctors are quite willing to tell us all they know about the benefits and the risks of a particular procedure, and most of them did so long before there were regulations requiring them to get informed consent. But all they can tell us are statistics. For example, in Great Britain, general anesthesia is partly or totally responsible for the deaths of two out of 10,000 patients.[11] Patients over the age of 65 are at even higher risk. There are statistics by age, sex, type of operation, and hospital. But the statistics cannot tell us what individual chances really are. For many conditions, we have few statistics about what happens to those who do not have surgery for whatever reason, and fewer statistics yet about what happens to those who specifically refuse surgery.

We no longer have to take the doctor's word for it, but if we do want to make our own decision, we are in for a difficult time. We need to get from the doctors the facts as they see them, and their expert opinions and advice. We need to listen to their opinions and advice, but we also know that we need not heed them.

We are then left with the job of getting opinions from several experts, going through the difficult and emotionally trying recounting of symptoms, reexperiencing physical examinations—especially objectionable when they involve the most intimate parts of our anatomy—and having blood drawn anew for lab tests each time. But at the end we will be able to compare the expert opinions; we will know when there is unanimity and when there is not. We will know the risks of the various procedures as best as they can be assessed, and we will know the consequences of inaction as best as they can be ascertained. In a way, we must become mini-experts in order to help our parents decide, help them choose one of the available options.

## SHOPPING FOR A DOCTOR

How should your parents choose a doctor if they don't have one already, or if they want a second opinion or are new to the community? Personal recommendation is often helpful. If there are people you or they know, friends or relatives, they may provide good leads. Probably the best referral source is a physician you know and trust, and who knows someone in your community. Physicians are likely to know the best qualified and most reputable doctors in a given area. But ask them if they know the new doctor personally, so that you get a thorough picture.

If you have no leads, contact the nearest university hospital. Physicians at a university usually have to keep up with research and new clinical techniques, and their colleagues provide at least a minimum of quality control. If there is no university in your area, try the county medical society, where a list of specialists or generalists can be obtained.

The most appropriate type of physician for your parents may be a geriatrician, especially if they belong to the "old-old" or the "frail old" group—i.e., those over the age of 80—or those with debilitating, multiple disorders. Geriatricians are physicians, usually specialists in internal medicine (internists) who have particular skills in dealing with the diseases of old age. Many geriatricians in the United States are self-trained, although some have taken special training in the United Kingdom, where geriatric medicine and psychiatry have been established for many years.

In the United States, most of the formal training programs in geriatric medicine were not set up until 1980. As of 1985, only 48 such programs had been established nationwide, with a total of 176 training positions available.[12] By 1985, these programs had graduated only 51 geriatricians, not enough even to teach the future physicians in our own medical schools about the diseases of the aged, their treatments, and their effects on the older person. Before the end of the decade, both the American Board of Internal Medicine and the American Academy of Family Practice will have given examinations and certification of special competence in geriatric medicine. It will then be easy for you to find out which physicians have such special competence.

Psychiatrists, too, are taking special training in geriatric programs. Psychiatrists? Your first reaction may be, "Who cares about that? My parents aren't crazy." Geriatric psychiatrists actually see relatively few "crazy" people or psychotic patients. They can help older people who become depressed, sad, down, anxious, withdrawn, or unduly paranoid. Psychiatrists who specialize in treating the aged know how to treat many of the symptoms associated with Alzheimer disease and similar disorders. They know about drugs that affect the mind—and psychiatrists can help people cope.

A list of the current formal specialty training programs in geriatrics can be found in Appendix 7. They may help you and your parents to locate a geriatric psychiatrist or internist in your area. Also be sure to review the questions.

## SOME QUESTIONS TO ASK WHEN
## YOUR PARENTS CHOOSE A PHYSICIAN

- Do they have a personal recommendation from someone they trust?
- Do they have a referral or recommendation from another physician they trust?
- Is the physician affiliated with a university medical center?
- Does the physician have special training or experience in geriatrics?
- Do you and your parents feel comfortable discussing delicate subjects with this physician?
- Does the physician listen and answer questions?
- Does the physician explain things so that your parents can understand him?
- Does the physician have adequate coverage by an associate during vacations?
- What about response to emergencies? Is it speedy and effective?
- Have they checked the listing in Appendix 7 for contacts in their area?

## HOSPITALS AND HOW TO DEAL WITH THEM

Hospital environments can be very uncomfortable. Early awakenings and noisy surroundings, as well as frequent blood samplings and other tests, make the hospital unsuitable for those who need a place for restful recovery. A young woman, for example, hospitalized for bed rest to relieve back pain, counted from 34 to 75 people entering her room on any given day (7:00 A.M. to 10:00 P.M.).[13] Hospitals are designed for the treatment of acutely ill patients; a resort hotel may be a better place for someone who needs rest and relaxation.

It is likely, however, that after the age of 65 our parents will need to spend some time in the hospital. People 65 years of age and older use hospitals at nearly three times the rate of those under 65.[14] That may change with the new reimbursement policies, but the average length of hospital stay will probably remain longer for the older patient than the younger patient. According to a 1982 report, the average length of hospital stay was 10.4 days for people older than 65, compared to 5.9 days for those under age 65.[15] Nonetheless, some people live into their nineties without ever having been hospitalized. They are very rare.

There are ways to minimize the number of hospitalizations, if not to avoid the hospital altogether. If the service can be performed outside the hospital, use the doctor's office or clinic instead. Laboratory tests and X-ray procedures, for example, can often be done on an outpatient basis. Even some surgery is done that way now. Having a good relationship and direct communication with the doctor is another essential ingredient in staying out of the hospital. Follow his or her directions, and if you or your parents do not understand the directions, ask about them. If the doctor knows your parents well, an emergency phone call may be enough to keep them out of the hospital and get them into the office the next day.

Arranging for visiting nurses (RNs, LVNs, or LPNs) may help your parents avoid hospitalization. Many procedures can be done in the home, including intravenous treatments, colostomy care, and use of oxygen for people with lung disease. The advantages of home treatment by specialists are many: the $300 to $400 basic daily hospital cost is avoided, the patient remains in familiar surroundings, and the family has control over nurses, aides, and other personnel. If there are people they do not like, they need not hire them or they may fire them. A disadvantage is that insurance companies often do not reimburse for home health-care services. And having a parent in the hospital may also bring enormous relief to children; they may feel more secure knowing that the parent will have immediate attention in case of an emergency.

If your parents do have to go to the hospital, how can you help them? Above all, encourage them to take an active role in their medical care, to ask questions about diagnosis and alternative treatments, to make decisions with their physician based on all the information available. Tell them not to hesitate to request a second opinion if you or they are dissatisfied with the first. Many people fear that such a request will insult the first doctor and somehow jeopardize their care. A competent and secure physician will welcome a second opinion or consultation. Medicine today has become so specialized that well-trained physicians know they cannot know everything, and they know where to turn for help.

What do you do if your parents do not want to ask any questions, if they just want to "follow the doctor's orders"? You may want to explain to them why you believe certain questions are indicated. If your parents agree, you may ask the questions yourself. Or you may feel as your parents do, and decide to leave well enough alone. As long as you know the options, the choice is yours.

Suppose one of your parents does need surgery. How will you be affected? Will you want to go to the hospital once a day or more? How far away is it? How long will it take you to get back and forth? How will you squeeze it into your schedule? Does your father or mother need transportation? Will other relatives be available to help out? Who will be the one to talk to the doctors, the nurses, the social worker? Is it major, high-risk surgery? Not only will you want to be with your parent, but you will worry, too. You will have to arrange for someone to look after the kids, your job, and all the uncountable little tasks that fill what is left of your day. What about the time you feel you ought to be with your other parent, your husband, or your kids? And your hospitalized parent may not be in the best of spirits when you come; you may feel superfluous, frustrated, angry. Be sure to check your Mood Meter (see chapter 2).

And think of your parent, now the patient. Have you ever spent a week in bed? It is one of the more stressful experiences in life. One study reported that five days of bed rest significantly increased blood pressure and heart rate for a group of healthy men between 55 and 65 years of age.[16] Add to that stress the fact that your parent is not in his or her own home, but in unfamiliar surroundings. Your parent may also have an illness of uncertain outcome, perhaps even an unknown diagnosis; he or she may be facing uncomfortable, often painful procedures, feeling weak and debilitated from being sick in the first place, and may well be frightened, anxious, or depressed. Recent studies have shown that at least one-fourth to one-third of hospitalized elderly patients have significant depression.[17]

If we let our parents choose the wrong course and see them suffer, will we forever afterward blame ourselves for not having chosen a different course? If only Frank had had that bypass surgery, he might still be alive; how proud he would

have been to know his grandson was going to be a doctor. . . .
We cannot avoid this kind of thinking, but we can usually avoid
being the sole decision-maker. If a number of options are
available and carefully considered, if we have been able to share
our mini-expertise with all those concerned in making the decision, if relevant questions have been raised and motives examined, then consenus can usually be reached. Then we can
minimize, if not avoid, the smoldering guilt of "if only."

We must hope that decisions, once made, can be imple-
mented, and not changed as in the case of Mildred's mother.
We must hope that the course of action developed by physician, patient, and family can be carried out, whether for or
against surgery at an advanced age.

---

### HELPING YOUR PARENTS WHEN THEY GET SICK

- Review the tips on getting the most and best from doctors.
- Help your parents write out their medical history using a
  doctor's standard format.
- Ask the right questions when choosing a physician.
- Avoid hospitalization, if possible.
- If your parent is hospitalized, help him or her take an
  active role.
- Follow the guidelines for safe use of medicines.

# 12

# DISABILITY:
# How Can We Help?

*The music in my heart I bore*
*Long after it was heard no more.*

William Wordsworth, *"Rob Roy's Grave"*

Janet couldn't stop asking herself the question, over and over again: Father didn't die, or did he? It haunted her day and night. She thought of her vibrant, active father with his love of life, always on the go, ready for adventure, eager to try new things, from climbing mountains to exploring caves. At the age of 56, her father, Ronald Barton, M.D., had given up his home and his long-established practice to move 3,000 miles to a strange city, just to be close to Janet and her sister. At the age of 65, he still drove his car as if he were a teenager—whether zipping around curves in the Swiss Alps to compete with racing car drivers, or transferring this habit to city streets and accumulating an unprecedented stack of speeding tickets. Janet's father, who loved to play rough-and-tumble just as much as his grandchildren did, had had a stroke. He was now unable to travel, to explore, to romp and play; unable to drive or even walk; unable to stand, or go to the bathroom alone.

How helpless he looked in the hospital bed, immobile and speechless, emitting that horrible sound whenever he tried to talk—like the howling of a wounded animal. She could not get the sound out of her ears, or the picture out of her mind. She stood there by the bedside and felt utterly helpless. Janet tried to think of him before he got sick, and to clear her mind of the sight of him in his hospital bed. She tried instead to picture her father as he used to be—tall, dark, and so handsome, with a full head of hair and always a twinkle in his eyes. His eyes were open now, but there was no light.

Her father's eyes did talk to her, though, and Janet could tell when he was listening and knew when he understood. But often she could also see that he was not there. She wondered where he was, what he was thinking. She wondered what it was like for him to be imprisoned in his own body, in a living tomb. Imprisoned not only for a day or a week or a month, but for nearly five years now.

Janet would never forget the day her mother, Martha, had called at 6:30 A.M. Although she had been distressed, Martha had remained calm as she reported how Ron had awakened, probably to go to the bathroom, and had fallen down and could not get up. Hearing the thump, Martha had rushed to him. Leaning over close to him, she heard him mumble, but could not make out what he said. Immediately she called the doctor. When Martha returned, Ron was lying where he had fallen. Finally she understood that he was mumbling the name of one of his colleagues, a neurologist. He was desperately trying to make her understand, and was relieved when she did.

Janet remembered that frantic call, the ride to the hospital, how it seemed to take forever—the hopes, the fears, the tests, the doctor's words: "It's too early to tell. We'll have to wait and see." And then, "It doesn't look too good." "Don't be too hopeful." "Of course, you should never give up hope." But he was not getting any better—the tests were finished. A large artery in the back of the head had been closed off by a clot. Nothing could be done. He would be discharged from the general hospital to a rehabilitation hospital, where the staff would try to teach him to walk and talk. Ron understood when they told him about the transfer; he had worked at that rehab hospital himself. On the day of his transfer, he howled that unearthly howl. Janet left the hospital as soon as he was settled in. She could not bear to hear him howl. But her mother stayed and talked to him for hours at a time, until Ron calmed down. She told him she would be there every day to watch over him; that he had a chance if he would cooperate with them.

Cooperate he did. He was exhausted by his efforts to exercise his arms, to strengthen his muscles, and by his attempts to walk, with help, between parallel bars. He did learn to move the wheels of his wheelchair, but not for too long. He knew the way, and would direct others by nodding his head, pointing his arm, but he could not control his movements. His arms and legs would flail, his head would drop. The speech therapist tried to help him formulate sounds, but succeeded only in controlling his howls. Although he had been a fine swimmer, all he could do in the therapy pool now was to splash about a bit, with the help of a life preserver. Janet cried when she thought of it—cried in anguish, sorrow, anger, and fury.

When Janet was alone, she often wondered if her father would have been better off if he had not survived the stroke. Such thoughts first came to her after she heard one of the other patients' visitors commenting, "Too bad about Dr. Barton. Too bad he couldn't have died. He's practically dead now—a vegetable that just keeps on breathing." When she first heard the comment, she held her breath and ran outside. She had to, or she would have hit that woman; she wanted to kill her. It had taken days before Janet could think of the incident in a reasonable manner, but then she did start asking herself if her father's life was worth living. He was totally dependent on others, but he was not in pain. He loved the outings in the park when they would push him in the wheelchair. He loved the weekend visits to her house, especially when they would listen to records. He laughed at jokes. How dare that stupid woman call her father a vegetable? If that woman could be there when her mother arrived every morning, she would see her father light up. It was a joy to look at his face when Martha read him the letters from his grandchildren. Janet knew he understood every word. When she finally had the courage to ask him outright, "Do you want to keep on living?" she could not mistake his smile or his attempt to nod his head. Her father did love life, and he was willing to accept any terms.

From the rehab hospital he went to a nursing home. All efforts had failed to teach him to walk, talk, write, or use a typewriter, even with a special large keyboard and giant letters. They tried to communicate by having him blink, once for yes, twice for no. At times he could do it, but most of the time he could not. Yet he could play dominoes by showing others how he wanted his pieces moved, and he continued to show his love for music. Throughout those long five years, her mother never missed one single day. She fed him, she washed him, she talked to him, she read to him, she made sure the children and grandchildren came to see him. She kept his spirits up and sustained his will to live.

How many families could have done what Ron's family did? His wife was at his bedside as many as ten hours a day, seven days a week, 52 weeks a year, and at least one other relative came to see him every day. How many parents have such a rich testimony of being loved, even when they can express so little themselves? How many children and grandchildren can give so much in return for so little beyond the knowledge that they are filling a vast void and the satisfaction gained from helping a loved one in such dire need?

But what kind of life was it for Martha? She seemed fulfilled. She refused to listen to suggestions that she might want to take some time off. It was as if she had found a mission in life, to keep her husband alive as long as possible, as happy and contented as possible. Ron was in Martha's thoughts every waking minute, displacing all else. Of course, no one else was devoted enough to please her. No one could approach, much less equal, Martha's devotion. Though she acknowledged that for other people even occasional visits from grandchildren were unusual, she was dissatisfied with her own grandchildren when they came to visit "only" once or twice a week. Even daily visits from the children were subject to criticism for not being long enough, for not having begun on time: "How could you make him wait for you? He kept looking at the clock. He has so little else in life." Who could live up to her standard of perfection? Who could avoid feeling guilty, ashamed, or unworthy for failing to do so?

Martha, in her long vigils at the nursing home, got to know every patient on the floor—their illnesses, how many visitors they had, when they got worse or better, or died. She often told Janet how lucky Mrs. Weber was to have a wonderful, devoted daughter who tended to her every need, every day. Mrs. Weber did not even know her daughter was there, because she was always full of morphine to relieve the pain of her cancer. Janet had always perceived the daughter, in their brief encounters, as rather frail herself—sad and withdrawn, not capable of such energy.

And then there was poor Mr. Nelson, diagnosed as having Alzheimer disease, whose children did not come to see him more than once a month. "Those ungrateful cads!" Martha called them, and Janet would remind her mother that even she complained about Mr. Nelson barging into Ron's room in his aimless wanderings, yelling at everyone, never even recalling his own name or room number. Janet wondered what his children's accounts of their visits might be. The reports about the other patients always had some moral, as told by Martha. And they always left Janet with the vague feeling that she was not doing enough.

How could she fail to accumulate resentment against her

mother, consciously or unconsciously? How could she fail to wish, selfishly, for limited visiting hours that would provide an excuse for pursuing her own existence? Where should the line be drawn—somewhere between her mother's total commitment at one extreme and the desertion by her father's many "friends" at the other? Nearly all of his friends disappeared within the first few weeks or months—waiting, it seemed, to reappear at the funeral. And how would Martha react when Ron died? Would she be overwhelmed by the unfilled void, or would she feel relieved of the burden, satisfied that she had done all she could—or both?

Many adult children today ask themselves these same questions. Many others dare not even think of them. What answers are there? There is neither a single answer nor an ideal solution that will fit everyone. Illness and death are tragedies, and prolonged, debilitating illness ranks high among the adversities that try human endurance, test human compassion, and scar human souls. Such tragedy cannot be undone. We must accept, adapt, and adjust.

More than six out of ten people over the age of 85 years report that a chronic health problem limits their activity.[1]

## RATES OF TOP CHRONIC CONDITIONS
## FOR PEOPLE AGE 65 AND OLDER

| Condition | Frequency |
|---|---|
| Arthritis | 46% |
| High blood pressure | 38% |
| Hearing impairments | 28% |
| Heart conditions | 28% |
| Chronic sinusitis | 18% |
| Visual impairments | 14% |
| Orthopedic impairments (back, extremities, etc.) | 13% |
| Atherosclerosis | 10% |
| Diabetes | 9% |

*Source: National Center for Health Statistics*

Among those between 75 and 84 years of age, nearly one-half report such limitation in activity.² It has been estimated that more than 2 million older Americans living in the community (not including those in institutions) need assistance with bathing, dressing, or walking—and close to another half-million with shopping, household chores, and other daily activities. One-third of those over the age of 85 are restricted in mobility to their own neighborhoods, and more than one in ten cannot move freely even within their own homes. If your parents are over the age of 85, it is probable that they will need help at some time.

## QUESTIONS TO CONSIDER

What are the ways of rendering help? They depend on the individuals and their family relationships, their particular needs, and the special resources available to them. The following five questions suggest some of the crucial issues:

### 1. How Did You Get Along Before the Disability?

How would you describe your relationship? Was it loving or hateful? Was it somewhere in between? Did you confide in one another, consult each other, make plans jointly? Did your parents make plans for your family, or vice versa? How often did you see each other, communicate with one another? When you did, was it amicable, laden with strife, neutral, or indifferent? Whatever your answer, you are not alone. The degree to which children and parents get along varies greatly. Some are close; other families exist in name only. Some family members avoid contact for months, years, or decades, unaware of each other's whereabouts. Some children hear about the death of a parent by accident, long after the event. In other families, one or more children are in daily contact with their parents.

If you are faced with a parent's illness and disability, it is a time to examine your relationship. Previous ways of getting along may be satisfactory, or the situation may require that you change. Reminding yourself of how things went before the illness and disability may help you cope with its consequences.

### 2. How Has Your Family Handled Past Crises?

Who can be counted on to help whom? Some parents almost always come to the aid of their adult children; in other cases, the reverse is true. In some families, it is traditional for family members to help one another. In other families, members rely on their own friends. Still others refuse aid, needing to be self-reliant. Recalling how the family handled past crises will better prepare you for the current one. You will anticipate some of their reactions and have more realistic expectations.

### 3. What Are Your Parent's Needs?

---

**WITH WHAT KINDS OF ACTIVITIES
DOES YOUR PARENT NEED HELP?
ACTIVITIES OF DAILY LIVING (ADLs)**

---

**"Basic" ADLs**

---

Eating
Dressing
Getting into or out of bed/chair
Bathing
Toileting
Maintaining continence

---

**"Instrumental" ADLs**

---

Preparing meals
Performing household tasks
Going shopping
Handling money

---

Physicians often assess the degree of a person's disability by assessing activities of daily living, or ADLs. It might be helpful for you to do the same. The ADL scales usually measure six basic areas of activities: eating, dressing, transferring to and from a chair or bed (walking), bathing, toileting, and maintaining continence. In addition to these "basic" ADLs, there are measures of "instrumental" ADLs that include preparing meals, performing housework, going shopping, and handling money. Of the 26 million people over age 65 living in the community in 1983, nearly 2½ million needed help in performing such basic ADLs as bathing, dressing, and toileting. Nearly 3 million needed help with such activities as housework and shopping (instrumental ADLs). Your parent may well be in the group that requires help with ADLs. (See the example later in this chapter.) The nature and severity of the particular illness will determine the degree of impairment. Alzheimer disease, for example, attacks nearly every aspect of mental ability and results in eventual impairment in nearly all areas of social and occupational functioning (see Appendix 2).

Try completing this list of your parents' needs before you embark on seeking help. Then check the appropriate section of the appendix for some suggestions as to where to find help.

---

### COPING WITH YOUR PARENT'S DISABILITY

| Parent's needs | Potential resources |
| --- | --- |
| 1. | 1. |
| 2. | 2. |
| 3. | 3. |

---

It is important to remember that it is not enough just to identify your parents' needs and match them to the available resources. Their disabilities and limitations will have a profound effect on their sense of self-worth and well-being, and you too will be affected. If you really do want to help, you will have to identify your own needs in the face of their disability and requirements for increased care.

### 4. What Are Your Needs?

Are you in mid-career? Is it crucial that you devote ten or more hours a day to your work? Do you have to travel extensively? Must you entertain often? Have you been elected to office by the Elks, the Knights of Columbus, Hadassah, the Masons, your neighborhood association, your union, or your professional organization? Are you between jobs, frantically seeking one? Or are you solidly established in your career, so that you can take time off? If your answer to the last question is yes, this may be a period in your life when you can spend time with your parent and reestablish or cement your relationship, the time when you can face unresolved conflicts, or even prepare to say good-bye.

Janet had never pursued much of a career beyond her homemaking, but did help with secretarial work at her husband's office three days a week. When her father first became ill, she neglected many of her duties at home and at the office. Later, she found herself working even more than usual; there was no one else to do the work that had piled up when she was busy with her father. Even though she curtailed visits to her father, his illness affected her own family life. Her children complained when she was not around, and balked at her frequent visits to see Grandpa—visits that Janet's mother thought were too few and too short. Ultimately, she had to reexamine her priorities.

You too may be at the stage of life when you need to spend more time with your children and your spouse. Is it a time when they want you, and you want them? Or have your kids finally reached independence? This may be the time you and your spouse planned to travel, to go out regularly, or just to relax. Someone else in your family—sibling, in-law, other relative, or even spouse or child—may be in ill health or financial need. Your parent may have become disabled just when you became widowed, divorced, or separated. Did it happen just when it seemed as though this was the last time you would have a chance to find a companion for yourself? Overtaxing yourself, providing energy-consuming parentcare while neglecting your own needs, may well diminish your ability to provide that care. Remember how Janet could not help noticing how frail Mrs. Weber's daughter appeared? Was that devoted daughter neglecting her own health to care for her mother? We suggest that you list your personal and professional needs, whatever they are, and assign some reasonable priorities to them.

### 5. How Long Will the Illness Last?

What are the prospects for recovery or improvement? Will the disability increase, decrease, or remain stable? Most of us can mobilize ourselves and our families, friends, and neighbors in a crisis. We can go from one crisis to another, but there is no such thing as a chronic crisis. We can tolerate a lot in the short run. We can take time off from work; arrange for caregivers for the kids; sacrifice all leisure time; skip meals; deprive ourselves of sleep, of exercise, of relaxation; forgo all entertaining; live only in and for the crisis. But we can endure a crisis for only a few days, perhaps a few weeks, rarely as long as a few months. We cannot go on for an unlimited time. Yet chronic illness and disabilities last for years, if not decades. It took only weeks for Janet's father's friends to stop visiting. After months, her children's protests over visiting Grandpa escalated. Eventually, Janet herself felt relief when she could work at the office and avoid the nursing home. Only Janet's mother remained at the bedside. Was the family realistic about the prognosis? Could they have paced their visits to avoid "early burnout"? It is vital to try to get an idea about the prognosis.


## POTENTIAL SOLUTIONS

Asking these questions about relationships and needs will point you to a variety of possible solutions. Answering these critical questions often helps to identify the least burdensome, most tolerable solutions. The key elements underlying them are not only relationships and needs, but also resources. Here are sample answers.

### Leave Well Enough Alone—I Don't Want to Change My Relationship with My Parents

Relationships with parents may be satisfactory or unsatisfactory. But even if their relationships are unsatisfactory, people may not want to make any changes. Brad's point of view is an example: "I haven't seen my parents for 30 years, since the day I dropped out of college and took a job as a gas station attendant. We live 3,000 miles apart, and except for sending them pictures of the kids every few years, we've had no contact. They haven't helped me one bit; they weren't there when I needed them. Now they need me—too bad. I don't want to change our relationship. I got along more than half my life without them—that's the way I like it."

You may have a similar reaction, or have ambivalent feelings. Many people feel that they have a filial obligation to help, regardless of how bad the relationship has been. They secretly wish that their children could know their grandparents. They regret the bitterness and hurt, yet know it is too late to change things. Even if you feel that way, you can still attempt to change; it may not be too late. Consider another walk through the six-step Commonsense Approach to Problem Solving (see chapter 2).

Contradictory as it may sound, a crisis may actually be a good time to try to change the relationship. Under stress, old conflicts reemerge, motivation is heightened, and we often communicate more freely than under ordinary social conditions. If you are using all your energy to keep yourself together during the acute crisis, then try as soon as life normalizes. If you do not succeed in changing the relationship after trying, consider seeking professional help.

On the other hand, you may feel like Holly: "Our relationship is not great, but we get along. We've learned to live with each other. We respect one another and tolerate each other's ways. I'll help as best I can." Sometimes change is not imperative, and things are better left as they are.

## Know About Available Resources

It can be helpful to make a detailed list specifying your parent's needs, and another list detailing resources available to fill these needs. Look not only at your own resources, but at your family's, friends', neighbors', and community's as well. Think how they might be organized to meet your parent's needs and to protect individual family members from burdens beyond their capacities.

## WHAT ARE YOUR POTENTIAL RESOURCES?

### People

Family members
Friends
Neighbors
People at work
People in religious group
People in social group
Hired help—maid, visiting nurse, sitter
Physicians and other health-care professionals, e.g., physical therapists, speech therapists, social workers, nutritionists
Attorneys (help with wills, conservatorships)
Accountants

### Services

Grocery delivery
Meals on Wheels
Laundry/cleaner's services and delivery
Milkman
Newspaper
Bottled water delivery
Gardener
Cleaning service
Taxi service
Car pooling
Vans for the handicapped
Security service

### Devices, aids

Walkers
Handrails
Rug tapes
Medical alert system
Microwave, frozen dinners
Taxi vouchers
Dentures
Telephone devices (automatic dialers, amplifiers)
Remote-control TV
Large-print reading matter
Medication boxes
Whirlpool bath, Jacuzzi
Safe-deposit box

| Strategies |
|---|
| Do not neglect your own needs.<br>Turn to others for help. |

For example, grandchildren can help fill the need for companionship. They can read to the grandparent, listen to the grandparent, or tell the news of the day and the events in their own lives. Janet's children visited regularly during her father's illness, and helped ease the burden. Sometimes a rotation can be set up so that each grandchild gives a couple of hours once or twice a week—after school, after work, on weekends and evenings. If the grandchildren are unavailable, friends, neighbors, or more distant relatives might be enlisted, either as volunteers or paid helpers.

The following questions need to be considered when hiring help: Who can afford to pay for help? Are they willing to assume that burden? Can more than one person share the expense? Does your parent need to be persuaded to accept paid help? Often, parents will object to spending money on help, even if they can afford it. The parents' objections might reflect their feelings of having been rejected, abandoned by family to "strangers" whose only interest is monetary, whose only loyalty is to the dollar. It is a strange paradox, since many parents who can afford it entrust their young children to paid help and have done so for a long time in our society.

Other practical considerations can prove helpful. Does your parent have a television set? Does someone else need to operate it? If your parent is bedridden, will a remote control help? What about a radio or a cassette player? Does your parent hear well enough for them? If not, a special amplification system or a hearing aid might help. It has been estimated that approximately 30 percent of people over the age of 75 have difficulty hearing, and only one-third of that group have any type of hearing aid.[3]

What about your parent's eyesight? Is it so poor that television is frustrating instead of entertaining? What aids for the blind might help? People 65 years of age or older represent half the population of blind Americans. Fifty-five percent of new cases of blindness reported each year afflict the elderly.[4] Knowing about eye care and eye disease in the upper age groups may prevent a potentially profound disability (see Appendix 1).

A variety of modern or high-tech devices are available to help parents cope with the many disabilities and discomforts that accompany chronic illness in old age. Some of the most

---

## FINDING HIGH-TECH DEVICES

For information on high-tech devices, write to:
AT&T Consumer Sales and Service
AT&T National Special Needs Center
2001 Route 46
Parsippany, NJ 07054
Telephone 1-800-233-1222

Examples of mail-order catalogues that might be useful include the two following:

The Sharper Image
680 Davis Street
San Francisco, CA 94111
Telephone 1-800-344-4444

Although the Sharper Image catalogue is geared toward personalized, high-tech gift items, many products can be adapted for those with disabilities. For example, a bathroom scale with a voice and a memory would be suited for someone with a visual impairment.

Comfortably Yours
Aids for Easier Living
61 West Hunter Avenue
Maywood, NJ 07607
Telephone 1-201-368-0400

This is a general catalogue with items ranging from low-back cushion supports to a device designed to grab boxes and bottles that are out of reach.

---

common and potentially life-saving devices are products linking our parents by telecommunications in emergency situations. Emergency call systems, signaling devices, speakers, and automatic dialing and cordless telephones are available through mail-order catalogues. Other helpful devices include electronic artificial voice boxes for people who have lost their larynxes; hearing and speech amplification systems; enlarged face plates for telephone buttons; and even a special device sensitive to a person's breath, designed for those with motion impairment.

What about meals? Often a relative can bring a cooked meal once a day. Or a rotation can be set up between local relatives, friends, and neighbors. Sometimes meals can be catered or provided by Meals on Wheels. Precooked meals can be stored in the freezer, and the parent may be able to warm them in the microwave or toaster oven. Small microwave ovens can be purchased for $150 or less. Some families may be able to afford to hire a cook for a few hours a week.

Does your parent need help shopping? If so, it can be an opportunity for a family member to spend some time with your parent while doing the errands together. If your parent is incapable of going along, it may be possible to have groceries, laundry, and milk delivered. Or someone can be hired to do the job, and to transport the parent to doctors' offices and other appointments as well.

Financial matters also need consideration. Preventive measures can save a great deal of future pain. Although few of us, parents and children alike, want to face the inevitable issue of death, it is crucial for adult children to discuss it with their parents, in a frank yet caring way. Do not hesitate to ask pertinent questions. Do they have a will? Who are their legal, financial, and religious advisers? Have they made provisions for a trustee and power of attorney in case of disability or incompetence? (See chapter 4 and Appendix 5.) Have they provided for their burial? What are *their* expectations and wishes? Where do they keep such valuables as insurance policies, stocks, income tax records, bank books, and jewelry? How can we be of help?

If these matters have not been arranged before death, someone will be called upon to make the decisions afterwards, and all of the above questions, as well as others, will need to be answered. If one parent is well and capable, he or she can help and may even choose to take complete charge; but these questions need to be answered for the future by the well or surviving parent. If it is the surviving parent who is ill or disabled and cannot function, who assumes the job? Who is to be trusted? Is your parent's judgment reliable? If not, is there a living trust? Should a financial conservator be appointed? If so, who has the parent's best interests at heart? Which family member will put the parent's interests above his or her own? Will children agree, or work at cross-purposes? Which friends can be trusted? Who should make the decision? Can your parent participate in the decision-making? How can your parent's assets be protected from rapacious relatives, friends, professionals, service providers, and financial and other institutions?

The answers to these questions will determine what needs to be done, and the answers may vary from state to state, according to local laws. Parents who are physically impaired but mentally competent and able to communicate are likely to at least participate in the decision-making, if not make the decisions. Janet's father, unfortunately, was unable to participate when Janet finally persuaded her mother to seek legal advice on financial matters. Her mother was eventually appointed conservator, but much heartache, legal maneuvering, and financial expense could have been avoided had the family been prepared to answer the relevant questions in advance.

## Match Needs and Resources

Identifying needs and potential resources is one thing; matching the needs to the resources is another. Often, ingenuity, patience, and a willingness to turn to others are required. Let us look briefly at how Erica tried to manage.

Erica, an only child, was in her late forties when her mother died of cancer and her father suffered a stroke that left him partially paralyzed physically and completely paralyzed mentally. He became depressed, almost totally dependent upon her, and she felt torn in every direction—her father, her children, and her husband. Her husband, in his late fifties, had cut back on his work hours after his own scary brush with cancer. But as a result of his illness, he decided he was going to enjoy life to the fullest while he still could. He wanted Erica to join him; she was part of what made his life enjoyable. She decided to sit down and take inventory, and came up with her survival list—a way for her father to survive without her, thereby enabling her to survive.

| ERICA'S SURVIVAL LIST: COPING WITH FATHER'S DISABILITY | |
| --- | --- |
| **Parent's needs** | **Potential resources\*** |
| 1. Help to cope with depression | 1. Professional consultation and treatment |
| 2. Post-stroke rehabilitation | 2. Companion, physical therapy, speech therapy |
| 3. Help with walking | 3. Grab bars, handrails, rug tapes, walkers |
| 4. Help with hearing problem | 4. Hearing aid, phone amplifiers |
| 5. Provision for potential medical emergency because of poorly controlled hypertension | 5. Medical alert system, life safety device |
| 6. Help with housekeeping, meals, and cooking | 6. Housekeeper, Meals on Wheels, frozen dinners |
| 7. Social activity | 7. "Cronies" at the park and other activities |

\* Medicare will help pay for some of these resources under certain conditions.

## Make Use of Your Resources

There are manifold opportunities among adult children and their parents for closeness and mutual support—as well as for family fights. Most people 65 years of age or older live near their children. One study found that nearly one out of five persons over the age of 65 lived in the same household as one of his or her children. Another one out of three lived within a ten-minute journey. And these parents saw their children either daily or every other day.[5] Given such close proximity, there are many possible scenarios. For example, the parent who is mentally competent, and makes decisions with which the child disagrees, can create an arena for battle. It may be as trivial as the daughter being expected to wash the laundry in a specific way, for example, by watching the machine fill up with water, adding detergent and other ingredients, letting it mix, and then adding the laundry, rather than putting laundry, detergent, and additives in all together, and forgetting about it until completion. Or it may concern decisions, such as investing in real estate or blue-chip stocks; whether to buy tan or dark blue trousers; whether to hire a 22-year-old gorgeous blonde without references, or a 54-year-old experienced housekeeper with excellent recommendations.

Regardless of the specific issues of disagreement, parent and child may have had lifelong divergences of opinion that both parties were able to tolerate, but now the child may not be able to implement decisions when the parents have wishes that contradict the adult child's own best judgment. The point is that having to do things against your better judgment because your parents want them done that way breeds frustration, anger, and ill will. And you cannot say to your impaired parent, "Do it yourself, if you don't like the way I do it." The sad reality is that these parents cannot do it themselves, and our only solution may be to compromise.

What about the parent who is mentally incompetent? There are greedy children, angry children, vengeful children who scheme to acquire their parents' money. There are children who abuse alcohol and drugs, or suffer from mental illness and abuse their parents physically as well as mentally, who want to put them away, to deprive them of happiness, liberty, and life itself. But for every one of these kinds of children there are a multitude of children whose only motive is to make decisions that are in their parents' best interests; who agonize over whether they have made the right decision, whether they have done what their parent would have wanted them to do. There are children who neglect themselves, their own health, and their own families while trying to preserve and enhance their parents' well-being.

There comes a time when children who ignore their own needs have to take stock. How long can they keep it up? What are the costs to their personal lives, their family lives, their careers, and their health? Experts have begun to talk about the burden of caregiving, and the frequency of physical illness and depression among caregivers; but so far, there are no hard facts. Even without enough data, common sense combined with some observations tells us that the stress of caregiving takes its toll and places the caregiving spouse, child, or sibling at increased risk of illness. Whether or not you are among those at risk, remember to make an inventory—to list *your* needs in order of priority. Then list the time and the resources available and allocate them realistically—to yourself as well as others.

One of the most trying aspects of the human condition is accepting losses that keep mounting over a prolonged period. When someone dies, the emotional work tends to be straightforward. There is a finality to the death; we mourn and eventually go on with our own lives. By contrast, the incomplete losses of prolonged disability, especially those owing to progressive illness, bring with them uncertainties, complexities, and fears. Yet herein is the crux of the human condition. We may view life, from birth to death, as a prolonged period of repeated losses. But herein, too, lies the challenge to human existence: to replace the losses whenever we can; to substitute for them when we cannot replace them; to cherish the memories in all their richness.

---

### COPING WITH YOUR PARENTS' DISABILITY

- Review the six-step Commonsense Approach to Problem Solving.
- Ask these questions:
    1. How did you and your parents get along before the disability?
    2. How has your family handled past crises?
    3. What are your parents' needs?
    4. What are *your* needs?
    5. How long will the illness last?
- Consider these answers and approaches:
    1. Leave well enough alone.
    2. Know about available resources.
    3. Match needs and resources.
    4. Make use of your resources.

# 13

# DEATH:
# How Do We Say Good-bye?

*Like pilgrims to the appointed place we tend,*
*The world's an inn, and death the journey's*
*end.*

John Dryden, *"Palamon and Arcite"*

Donna pressed her friend Tricia's number and waited for
the ring—a busy signal. She tapped the eraser end of the pen-
cil on her chin, shuffled the papers in her hand, and thought
about how many times over the years she had called Tricia.
Donna pressed the numbers again. She often called her friend
just to gossip or to set a date, to ask for advice or help with a
car pool, to complain, to brag, and now . . .

"Hello?"

"Trish, I know it's late, but I had to talk to you. I just can't
believe my father's dead. I know you've been through this. How
did you feel? He went so fast. I never thought he was going to
die—they said it was 'just routine' when they admitted him to
the hospital, some medicines and tests. I just . . . " The rest of
the sentence was lost in tears.

"It's difficult to accept," Trish said, "and it's never the right
time. At least he lived a full life and didn't have a long, painful
illness at the end."

Donna continued, "My brothers arrived from the East, and
Mom's let them make all the arrangements and decisions about
the funeral. At first I thought it was great, but then I felt left
out until I began to write down a few thoughts about Dad for
the eulogy. That's what I've been doing all evening. You knew
Daddy pretty well—from way back before we all moved to California. Could I read to you what I've written?" Not even
hearing Tricia say, "Of course," she began to read.

Tricia listened intently. Her eyes began to well with tears;
at one point she chuckled. When Donna finished, they were
both silent for several seconds. "That was beautiful, Donna; I
could just see your father as you spoke. And don't worry about
tomorrow. I've organized our friends, and we'll be bringing all

the food when you come back to the house after the funeral. Just put out any trays or linens you might want us to use. And now, why don't you get some rest?"

Donna looked around the kitchen and felt exhausted. She had not slept much, and decided to follow her friend's advice. Jim and the children were long asleep. She checked the children's rooms and laid out their clothes for the morning. She then looked in her own closet to make sure her black dress was pressed; she undressed, brushed her teeth, and flopped into bed.

She was up at the crack of dawn. She put her best tablecloth on the dining room table, set out her silver trays, puffed up the sofa pillows, and set out paper towels in the guest bathroom. She thought, How can I worry about these stupid things on the day of my father's funeral? It's like I'm preparing for a party. She moved as if in a trance, waking Jim and the children and asking them what they wanted for breakfast. No one was hungry; they would settle for some juice and help themselves. Donna went to dress. The rest of the family would be arriving within the hour, to wait for the limousine to go to the funeral. As she reached for her black dress, Donna called to Jim, "I don't feel like wearing black. Daddy had a wonderful life, and he hated me in black." Jim was at her side and embraced her tenderly. Donna chose instead her brown tweed suit and ivory blouse.

Her brothers arrived with their families and her mother. They all embraced and decided on the order of the funeral procession. Just as they were about to leave, Donna's mother announced, "I'm not going. I'd rather wait for all of you here!" She took her jacket off and sat down, crossing her legs and arms defiantly. They all looked at her, dumbfounded. "Please leave me here. I want to keep my memory of your father as he was." From past experience, they knew it was hopeless to argue. Florence had made a final decision. And so the family departed.

Riding in the limousine, Donna felt as if she were in a dream. She had attended many funerals, but they had never been for anyone this close to her. When they got to the mortuary, she and her brothers went into a private chamber together. This could not be Dad, lying in a coffin. He looked so peaceful, as if he were sleeping, clean-shaven, almost a smile on his face. She was grateful that her brothers had insisted that the morticians not put any makeup on him. "Rest well, Daddy," she whispered as she blew him a kiss.

The service seemed unreal, but despite the recurring tears, she felt peaceful. There was a definiteness about seeing her father's coffin being lowered into the ground. She was glad that she had been able to say good-bye.

Saying good-bye, emotionally as well as verbally, is a crucial part of grieving. Donna's writing down her thoughts about her father allowed her to remember the good times and helped ease her pain. In the expectable course of our lifetimes, our parents will die. The mourning, grief, and sadness we will experience when they go is as inevitable as are their deaths. Someone once said, "You never really feel alone in the world until you stand over your parents' graves." Perhaps that is the time when we must all finally grow up—when the child in us is forced to become the adult. To help ease the intense feelings that accompany such loss, we have rituals pertaining to death, burial, and mourning. The history of civilization is rich in details about the agonies of the bereaved, and the ceremonies and manners regarding burial. Each religion and culture has its own rituals, from the Western tradition of viewing the embalmed body to the extravagant funeral processions and cremations still performed in India.

Instinctively, for us, death is frightening. Unconsciously, it is inconceivable. We live our lives from day to day as if we were immortal. Death is taboo. Our society considers discussions of death morbid, and we use euphemisms to describe it. People do not die; they "pass away," or are "gone," or are "not with us any more." We may tell our children that "Grandpa has gone on a long trip." The destination of his trip remains a mystery, and death becomes an elusive enigma.

Professionals have long described the common emotional reactions people experience when someone dies. In 1917, Freud pointed out that normal grief was time-limited, but that on occasion it progressed to the more severe depression known as melancholia. Some 30 years later, the Boston psychiatrist Erich Lindemann wrote about the varied symptoms of normal grief: physical complaints, preoccupation with the deceased, guilt feelings involving the deceased, hostility toward others, restlessness, and social awkwardness. He also described abnormal grief reactions, in which the mourner displays symptoms of the deceased person's last illness, becomes extremely hostile or apathetic, or shows poor judgment, for example, by making foolish business deals or by giving away the deceased person's valuable possessions.

Depression and grief reactions are common in terminally ill patients, and Elisabeth Kübler-Ross, in her book *On Death and Dying*, tells how she observed that not only the terminally ill but also their families go through a grieving and mourning process. She described the following five stages of grief: (1) Denial and Isolation; (2) Anger; (3) Bargaining; (4) Depression; and (5) Acceptance. According to Dr. Kübler-Ross, until the mourner passes through all five stages—not necessarily in that order, and sometimes through more than one stage simultaneously—the mourning process is not complete.

The old saying "Time heals all wounds" is true only in part. The stages of grief represent coping mechanisms we use to deal with extremely difficult situations. While they last different lengths of time for different people—weeks for some, months for others—they can also coexist or replace each other. Some people, for example, may be depressed while they simultaneously deny the reality of death. Some may not go through the bargaining phase. Although the sense of loss is generally greater when the relationship has been longer and closer, the duration and intensity of grief have much to do with the individual's strengths, interests, and work, and help obtained from others.

The funeral per se offers closure—has a finality to it, and serves as a buffer between the past and the future. Sometimes, however, the process is not completed; sometimes the mourner cannot move on beyond the first or second stage of grieving. For example, Donna was able to experience the various stages of the grief process, while her mother could not do it without professional help.

*Denial and isolation (push it away).*   Florence's refusal to go to the funeral was an example of denial and isolation. Unconsciously, she may have felt, "If I don't go, he really isn't dead. I'll show them." Donna's decision not to wear her black dress because "Daddy never liked me in black"—as if he were still alive—also expressed denial of his death. The fact that Donna's father "went quickly" may have facilitated the denial. Although he had been suffering from hypertension for many years, and had survived two mild heart attacks, he had never "acted sick" (*his* denial). The last time he was ill, it was only for one day, and no one expected him to die.

Many people first react to news of a death the way Donna and her mother did: "No—it can't be true. It's impossible!" These reactions are not based on the reality of the loss. Usually they are a temporary defense, acting as a cushion, giving us time to prepare for the full impact of the loss.

*Anger.*   Rage and resentment often replace denial, or coexist with it. "Why him? It's not fair." "How dare Martin leave me! I'll show him and not go to his funeral!" (Perhaps Florence's unspoken feelings). Such anger is often displaced; that is, we blame others. "Those doctors are no good. They didn't recommend the right treatment." When anger is directed toward us, it is difficult not to take it personally. Trying to think of the real reasons why the mourner may be angry often helps lessen the hurt for us.

*Bargaining.*   "If getting angry doesn't help, then maybe if I'm extra nice, that will change things." Although this kind of "magical thinking" is common during childhood, we do not have to be children to have such thoughts. Under stress or when confronted with loss, it is a common strategy. Florence may have been bargaining as well as isolating herself: "If I sit in this chair and don't move, maybe I can get God to bring him back to me."

Martin's long-term illness was not debilitating. Other elderly parents, however, suffer chronic illnesses that do cause prolonged debility, and the family begins the mourning process long before the actual death. The bargaining stage is often extended, and sometimes precedes the other stages. We have all heard of heroic attempts of families who try to find the "magic" cure for a family member with terminal cancer. Hospital vigils by devoted spouses and children, in addition to expressing a desire to be with and comfort the sick family member, sometimes represent attempts at bargaining—hoping to induce a miracle by some action or promise. Often families are relieved when death comes, but they then feel guilt.

*Depression.*   Eventually, mourners become down, depressed, sad. The actual loss, the feelings of having been abandoned and deserted, and the anger aroused by these feelings must be acknowledged before the depth of the sadness can be felt. Activities, overworking, caring for others, or taking sedatives, alcohol, and tranquilizers can postpone these feelings and prolong the mourning process. When we survive parents or children—"our own flesh and blood"—we symbolically lose a part of ourselves.

*Acceptance.* With time, most people are able to go on with their lives despite their losses. When we lose someone close to us, however, we may never fully accept the loss. You may think, for example, about your mother every day for months after her death, or for years; for the rest of your life you will remember her—on an anniversary, holiday, or birthday, when you hear a song she hummed, or smell a batch of cookies baking in the oven that reminds you of your mother's recipe. Sometimes you may mistake someone else for your deceased parents, or hear voices that sound like theirs. These experiences can all be within the realm of normal grieving.

The week following the funeral was a busy one for Donna and her family. Her mother stayed at her house for the first week, where every evening friends and family gathered, bearing food and sweets, talking about Martin. It helped the family grieve. There were even moments of laughter and joyful reminiscences. Donna's mother, however, felt worse and worse. Florence often asked for her nitroglycerin pills as she clutched her heart. She talked about Martin in the present tense. Uncontrollably, she would burst into tears every time a new visitor greeted her. She barely picked at her food and had difficulty breathing. When her physician dropped by to pay a condolence call, he listened to some of her complaints and prescribed tranquilizers during the day, as well as a sleeping pill for the night; it seemed that he was trying to keep Florence quiet, to keep her from feeling her pain.

Donna was glad when the week following the funeral had ended. She dreaded going into her parents' apartment for the first time since her father's death. Her mother looked so tiny and frail—dragged her feet and spoke in monosyllables, and that only in response to direct questions. Aunt Betty, her father's widowed sister, had offered to stay on after the funeral to help out for a few weeks.

Donna and Betty entered Florence's apartment cautiously. "I can't go on. I don't want to live without him. Martin, Martin, why didn't you take me with you?" Florence sobbed. The three women embraced in a circle, all of them crying, and then Betty straightened up, took Florence's chin gently in her hand,

and said sternly, "Your daughter has a family to take care of, and I'm sending her home to do that. You have a right to feel terrible now, but it will get better in time. *I know*. Donna, that's enough for today—go home. I'll look after your mother." As Donna drove the short distance to her home, the tears flowed without stopping.

The next few weeks were filled with countless details. After getting her own home and family routine in order, Donna spent every extra hour with her mother and aunt. There were endless forms to fill out and papers to sign for Social Security, insurance companies, stockbrokers, banks, and accountants. Although Florence's eyes would brighten every time she received a condolence card or letter from a friend, she wanted no part in acknowledging them. Donna and Betty addressed all the envelopes, but insisted that Florence sign them. She only seemed interested in talking about the past—her early years with Martin, when the children were young, how they had met—no talk of his death. Donna knew there was one thing she had to do before her aunt left. "Mom, I want you to help me gather Daddy's clothes together to give away. I think it's time to do that." She did not anticipate Florence's reaction. "Give away? Give away? After the way he criticized me for spending too much money, that last night? You'll sell those for a good price, or they'll not leave this house!" Was this her mother, the one who used to give away her nearly new clothes the minute her waist grew a quarter of an inch, so that "the poor can have clothing to wear?" She saw Florence put a pill under her tongue, medicine to treat another of the many recent angina attacks. That ended the conversation for now. "I'll put them in this carton, and you can decide later." Donna felt a shiver up her spine. Her mother had changed so much—would Florence ever return to her old self? Had her father's death deprived her as well of the mother she knew?

Three months after her father's death, Donna found herself rushing to the hospital once more. Florence had been brought to the emergency room with symptoms of a heart attack. Donna arrived just as Dr. Miller finished his examination. He was fairly confident that Florence was going to be all right, but he wanted to talk to both of them. "Florence," he said, "you've lost a lot of weight, about 12 pounds in the last two months; you seem exhausted, not surprising since you've been sleeping only three or four hours a night. You're preoccupied with your grief, so much so that you've neglected yourself and your family; you hardly notice what goes on around you. Today you hyperventilated [breathed too fast], got scared, had a panic attack, and couldn't catch your breath. I'm concerned that you haven't recovered as quickly from Martin's death as you should have. I'm going to ask you to see Dr. Winter. He's a psychiatrist, and I think that right now he may be able to help you more than I can." Florence nodded her head and began to cry.

## RECOGNIZING ABNORMAL GRIEF OR DEPRESSION IN YOUR PARENT

Florence had symptoms of anxiety and depression, which became debilitating before she was able to get help. Usually the depression following a death passes with the help of family, friends, work, or school. Sometimes professional intervention is needed.

The symptoms of normal grief are indistinguishable from those of abnormal grief or depression; it is a matter of degree. Grief and depression are considered abnormal when they are unusually intense, profound, or prolonged. If this occurs, it is time to get professional help.

The following symptoms, when intense and/or prolonged, signal the presence of abnormal grief or depression and are likely to benefit from professional (e.g., psychiatric or psychological) treatment:

*Interrupted sleep.* Depressed people usually have difficulty getting through the night. They will wake up in the middle of the night and have trouble falling asleep again. They may awaken early in the morning, perhaps 5:00 A.M. or earlier. Sometimes, however, depressed people sleep too much—12, 14, or more hours a day. They may not get out of bed at all. They have *hypersomnia*, rather than insomnia.

*Lack of interest.* Depressed people become preoccupied with their loss, feel blue, and tend to lose interest in day-to-day events, in everything that goes on around them. Seriously depressed people have such a pervasive loss of interest that they often have no capacity to experience pleasure at all.

*Guilt.* Depressed people are likely to blame themselves. In more serious depressions, distorted guilt feelings may become extreme. They may believe that some action they took, or failed to take, caused the death of the loved one, or that the loss was a punishment for some past sin.

*Loss of energy.* Fatigue, weakness, and listlessness are common complaints during a depression. Often the symptoms are worse in the morning (after several hours of sleep) than in the afternoon or evening, which may have something to do with the body's internal clock, or energy metabolism.

*Concentration and memory problems.* Depressed people complain of difficulties focusing their thoughts and concentrating. They are thus easily distracted and may even have problems reading a newspaper or watching television. In older people, this symptom may confuse us and cause us to think the person is senile or demented rather than depressed.

*Change in appetite.* Typically, loss of appetite accompanies depression. Loss of weight may be so severe that a physical illness, such as cancer, may be suspected. Atypically, people experience an increase in appetite that results in weight gain.

*Agitation/retardation.* Often, depressed persons will pace, wring their hands, or fidget. On the other hand, sometimes the reverse occurs and their movements, thoughts, and speech become agonizingly slow.

*Thoughts of suicide.* Thoughts of death are common when people are seriously depressed. As people age, the risk of suicide increases, particularly for white males. Sometimes people who do not actually want to kill themselves, for religious or other reasons, may wish they were dead.

Your parent may experience the above symptoms in different degrees or in a variety of ways, but no one may suspect a depression. Serious depressions may be more difficult to recognize in older adults than in younger ones. Their inability to concentrate may be mistaken for illnesses such as Alzheimer disease. Such a mistake is even more common when they experience memory loss, as older people often do, especially depressed older people. Also, depressed older people sometimes complain excessively about physical symptoms, which have been termed "depressive equivalents." Often such patients do not actually feel sad, blue, or depressed; they have no crying spells, no suicidal ideas, and if you ask them if they feel sad, they will answer no, not at all. They would be just fine and enjoy life, they say, if only their back pain or their abdominal pain or their

## CHECKLIST FOR IDENTIFYING DEPRESSION
## IN YOUR PARENT OR YOURSELF*

1. Mood: sad _____
   life not pleasurable _____

2. Altered sleep: decreased _____
   increased _____

3. Lack of interest: uninterested, apathetic _____
   reclusive _____

4. Guilt: let people down _____
   self-blame _____

5. Loss of energy: fatigue _____
   weakness _____

6. Concentration and memory problems:
   cannot focus _____
   mind wanders _____

7. Change in appetite:
   decreased _____ weight loss _____
   increased _____ weight gain _____

8. Agitation/retardation: pacing _____
   wringing hands _____
   behavior slowed down _____

9. Thoughts of suicide: better off dead _____
   wants to kill self _____

10. Future: looks hopeless _____
    no enjoyment _____

*All of us have some of these feelings, thoughts, and behaviors some of the time; and not all of them are present in any one depressed person. If you place checks in 3 or more of the 10 categories, your parent (or you) should seek professional attention. Anyone suicidal needs immediate attention.

shortness of breath or their sleep or memory problems could be relieved. In those cases, all efforts may be focused on physical symptoms and the diagnosis of depression overlooked. How can you say someone is depressed if that person denies it? The answer often lies in the treatment. The physical symptoms of many patients with depressive equivalents or "masked depression," that is, a depression disguised or masked as some other illness, improve with antidepressant drugs. In retrospect, these patients will agree that they had been depressed. But trying an antidepressant drug is not a sure test either. Not every depressed patient, clearly suffering from a major depression, recovers on antidepressant medication. Drugs are not always successful against depression.

To further complicate the diagnosis, sometimes people who appear depressed, or appear to have a masked depression, do have an underlying physical illness. Some physical illnesses have depression as a symptom, sometimes the first symptom. Since physical illness occurs frequently among the elderly, with or without depression, it is not surprising that it is often difficult to recognize depression in an older patient.

## COPING WITH ABNORMAL GRIEF OR DEPRESSION IN THE FAMILY

When it comes to family, it is the adult child who generally provides much of the help and bears the brunt of the burden. What can we do?

*1. Recognize the symptoms of depression and acknowledge that there is a problem.*   Most of us would, like Donna, ascribe Florence's behavior to her grief and tell ourselves that she needed more time to get over Martin's death. Most likely, we would fail to recognize and give due importance to the fact that Florence was getting worse, not better. Not everyone suffers a serious depression following the death of a spouse, but it is important for us to recognize the symptoms when they do occur. Be sure to review the checklist for identifying depression in your parents. Remember also that other family members may experience these symptoms.

*2. Recognize that it is difficult to spend time with depressed people.*   Sadly, the more depressed parents get, the harder it becomes to spend time with them. Some complain monotonously about the same symptoms, or ruminate about the deceased, about what they could have done, or should not have done, to prevent the illness and death. Characteristically, people who are depressed tend to turn others off. They have only a perfunctory interest, if that, in what is going on in the world or the community. They have no interest in the news, they do not enjoy anything at all. They often lose interest in the family. They may spend their time crying and bemoaning their fate and actions, or they may display morose silence. It is depressing to be around depressed people. When we are with someone who wallows in misery, we tend to feel down, sad, and blue ourselves. Recognizing this fact helps relieve the guilt many adult children experience because they wish to avoid a depressed parent.

*3. Remember that your parent's depression is not your fault.* The more depressed our parent gets, the less time we want to spend with him or her, and we find excuses not to be around. Then we feel guilty for not being readily available and supportive— for not *wanting* to spend more time with the parent.

Many adult children feel that if they were present to see that their depressed parent had proper meals, then the parent would eat more and feel stronger. If they were available to go for walks or do the shopping with them, the parent might sleep better because of the exercise and reduced worry about transportation to get to the cleaner, the shoemaker, the supermarket. Then the parent would be less fatigued and might have fewer physical complaints. If only we had the patience to talk to them about their symptoms, their losses, and their feelings, they might not be so sad, dejected, or hopeless. Sometimes we *can* help a depressed parent feel less sad and alone, but rarely do we have the power or ability to alleviate their depression entirely.

*4. Recognize that you cannot replace the deceased parent.* You can spend more time with your surviving parent, as Donna did with her mother—at least for the initial few weeks—but you cannot reorganize your life to devote it exclusively to the widowed parent. Even if you could, it would not bring back the lost spouse or create long-term happiness.

*5. Remember that you have to go on with your own life.* The more depressed the parents get, the guiltier we tend to feel going about our own activities while they are suffering. Cruel though it may sound, we have our own lives to lead, our own families, careers, and interests to consider. We are not going to live forever, either. We are getting older too; "This is not a dress rehearsal, this is it." We only have one chance, one life. Nonetheless, we can help.

6. *Try to help your parent make the transition from married to widowed life.* Aside from the emotional meaning of the personal loss, your parent may have suffered loss of the financial manager or homemaker, sexual partner, and social companion, and may have suffered loss of income as well. The surviving parent is usually the mother, because women usually live longer than men. Every so often we hear talk of the survival gap between the sexes narrowing, but women have, in fact, gained more than men have from the increased life expectancy between 1950 and 1980.[1]

The changes in social status that accompany a death often go unrecognized. The surviving parent is no longer part of a couple, and no one wants—or wants to be—a "fifth wheel." Widows are often not invited out, and may find it awkward to host even simple dinners. By contrast, widowers may find themselves much in demand—they have joined the ever-shrinking group of eligible men—but their social circles will change, which can be stressful. For both, the accustomed social network becomes strained, if it does not disintegrate altogether.

Children often feel guilty for not inviting a widowed parent to their parties, dinners, and other affairs. Sometimes they try, but it does not work out because the generational difference is too great, and the widowed parent feels out of place. Surviving parents usually have to find their own new social network. It does not happen by itself, but requires effort and planning. Children can help in this effort. Bringing the changes to the parent's awareness is the first step, and some extra attention in the beginning can help their transition.

7. *Do not hesitate to get professional help when it is needed.* When, despite the efforts of relatives, friends, ministers, priests, or rabbis, the parent's grief remains unremitting; when social and personal activities continue to suffer; when the surviving parent has little or no interest in making a new life— it is time to consult a mental health professional, such as a psychiatrist or psychologist. In addition to using the checklist for identifying depression in your parent, a medical checkup may

also be needed. As mentioned previously, not only depressive illness but physical illness as well can be a consequence of loss, and the frequency of physical illness increases with age. More than that, depression and physical illness seem to be intricately interrelated. The death of a spouse has been related to both increased likelihood of illness in the spouse and even increased risk of death, with widowers at especially high risk.

8. *Recognize depression when it strikes you.* Remember that you, the adult child, are not immune to stress and depression. Not only do you have to cope with the stress of having lost a parent, but you may also have to cope with physical or mental illness in your surviving parent. Even if your parent remains healthy, you may have to deal with many of the other problems your surviving parent faces. As a result, you may experience undue stress and depression. Remember, you have to cope with your own grief and face your own problems. You may find it helpful to complete the depression checklist on page 195 for yourself, too. If you get a high score, follow through and see your physician first. Remember, you can reduce stress through relaxation techniques, exercise, changes in lifestyle, and personal relationships, as well as through psychotherapy.

If you get a clean bill of health physically from your physician, but still suffer from serious depression or anxiety, your physician may wish to prescribe drugs, or may recommend that you see a psychiatrist, clinical psychologist, psychiatric social worker, or other health professional trained in psychotherapy. Only a physician can use drug treatment, and among psychotherapists, only psychiatrists are physicians. By and large, drugs seem to produce results more quickly than do various forms of psychotherapy, but they do have undesirable side effects. See Appendix 4 for a list of some of the more commonly used antidepressant drugs and their side effects.


## TREATING DEPRESSION IN YOUR PARENT

Despite long-held beliefs that elderly depressed people do not get better, most physicians dealing with older patients are able to diagnose and treat depression effectively. Unfortunately, not all doctors are successful. If you or your parent feels that no progress has been made after several weeks of treatment, consider consulting an expert in geriatric medicine or geriatric psychiatry. Geriatric psychiatrists are physicians with expertise in both psychiatry and geriatrics, so they know about psychiatric illnesses in general, as well as how these illnesses manifest themselves differently in older patients. Geriatric psychiatrists have experience in treating patients with the many medical problems common in older people who also experience depression, dementia, and other mental disorders. In the United States, unfortunately, geriatric psychiatry is a relatively young field, so only a limited number of adequately trained specialists are available. Appendix 7 contains a list of geriatric psychiatry fellowship training programs and their administrators at some of the major universities throughout the United States, which will help you find a specialist in your area.

While psychiatric consultation may be needed or potentially helpful, the idea of psychiatry may be totally unacceptable to some parents. It may raise the specter of insanity. It may confirm their worst fears, that you think they have gone "round the bend," are "out of it," are "ready for the looney bin"—that you want to "put them away." In their generation, psychiatrists were "for crazies only." Be aware of this attitude. Some parents will understand your explanation and accept your suggestion to seek psychiatric consultation. Others will not be convinced, and you may need to insist that they get help.

A variety of treatments are available to your parent, including individual, group, and family psychotherapy, as well as antidepressant medication. The few controlled studies that have been carried out in the elderly, as well as the experience of practitioners, suggest that psychotherapy can be an effective treatment for depression in older adults. This is contrary to the long-held myth that because older people are more rigid than younger people that, when depressed, older people are unlikely to respond to psychotherapy.

Other studies indicate that, when given the appropriate doses of antidepressants, at least half of depressed older patients improve so much as to be considered recovered.[2] These were people with a psychiatric diagnosis of major depression, not a simple grief reaction, and not mild, lifelong depressive moods or normal existential sadness, both of which are part of the human condition. By first admitting to ourselves that there is a problem, we can then help our depressed parent seek the proper treatment.

Some parents may require hospitalization. But usually they can remain at home and see the doctor or other treating professional in the office. In general, outpatient treatment is preferable because a move into the hospital is bound to be disruptive in that it removes the parent from the familiar environment and can lead to anxiety and increased stress and confusion, especially if memory problems are also present. If your parent is suicidal, rapidly losing weight, or suffering from a medical illness that may increase the risk of taking antidepressant medication, hospitalization may be required.

Saying good-bye is painful—for the adult child as well as for the surviving parent. There is comfort, though, in knowing that we have done our best. Death is part of living; we cannot avoid it.

> *Some natural sorrow, loss, or pain*
> *That has been, and may be again.*

William Wordsworth, *"Rob Roy's Grave"*

---

### HOW TO COPE WITH DEATH OR DEPRESSION IN YOUR FAMILY

- Expect that you and your surviving parent may experience various stages of grief, including denial, anger, bargaining, depression, and acceptance.
- Acknowledge the presence of a problem. Review the checklist on page 195 for identifying depression in your parent.
- Remember that:
  It is difficult to spend time with depressed people.
  Your parent's depression is not your fault.
  You cannot replace a deceased parent.
  You have to go on with your own life.
- Help your parent make the transition from married to widowed life.
- Get professional help when needed.
- Recognize depression when it strikes you—you're not immune to it.

# 14

# FOR BETTER OR WORSE, OUR PARENTS ARE PART OF US

*People will not look forward to posterity, who never look backward to their ancestors.*

Edmund Burke

Thanksgiving had arrived once again. This year Alex invited Phil, a South American business colleague, to the family dinner. Alex's parents were looking forward to seeing Phil again. They had just returned from their first trip to South America, where they had met Phil's parents, and they were eager to deliver their greetings in person. Alex and Phil were delighted to hear that their fathers had gotten along so well. It was uncanny how easily they had taken to each other, just like long-lost friends, though they had never met before and had spent only one evening together in Buenos Aires. They had developed an immediate closeness and understanding. It didn't seem to matter that they lived on two separate continents and could barely speak a couple of words in each other's language. Both had parents who had escaped religious persecution by fleeing from Europe to the Americas. Both were children of these first-generation immigrants who had worked their way up the ladder of success. Both had experienced major business losses in the past few years, yet had managed to bounce back. Both were generous and loving toward their families, but had a way of attempting to influence and control those who were close to them. Alex was amazed by the similarities when he listened to Phil's description of his father.

"My father's a great guy, a wonderful and caring person; I love him dearly. Too often, though, he cares too much. It wasn't easy growing up with him, and it still isn't easy spending a lot of time with him. He's the kind of person who wants the best for you, but he's always telling you what that is. And if you disagree, he takes it personally. Whether we're ordering dinner at a restaurant, deciding where my kids ought to go to college, or discussing political candidates, he'll try to influence me to live my life his way. And if you have a topic, he has an opinion; he seems to be an expert on just about everything. I must admit that at times I do agree with his way of seeing things, but too often he just doesn't know what he's talking about. I feel close to him, but having him five thousand miles away sure makes life easier."

As Alex listened, he couldn't help thinking that was an exact description of his own father. No wonder those two had gotten along so well. Perhaps that was why he and Phil were also friends. Then it occurred to Alex that the description also fit Phil. Phil, too, was generous and family-oriented, but he was also opinionated and liked to be the one in control. Alex wondered how much he himself was like his own father. He had never given it much thought before. Was he generous and caring toward his family? Did he try to control and influence them? Alex didn't mind thinking of himself as generous and caring, but he wasn't sure he wanted to be described as stubborn and opinionated like his father.

Those attributes that we disdain are much easier to recognize in others than in ourselves. Alex could clearly see the stubbornness in his friend but not in himself. The same principle applies to our relationships with our parents. We can see their faults much more readily than our own. Whether we like it or not, we identify with our parents. Consider those "little" things your mother does that annoy you so much—how she is always late, or how she is nosy about your social life. Look at yourself for a moment. Do you have those same tendencies to be late or nosy? What about your father's moodiness, his compassion for the less fortunate, or your mother's sensitivity and warmth? Usually, that which we love or hate most about our parents, we also share with them—often without conscious awareness.

We identify with our parents, both consciously and unconsciously, and at the same time we depend upon them. We even take their presence for granted—until they become physically ill, disabled, depressed, or senile. Then the writing on the wall reads, "They won't be around forever." It reminds us of the unwelcome reality that they are not immortal. They may have seemed so when we were young—life without our parents was unthinkable. They fed us, clothed us, protected us, and made the world a safe place. They were all-powerful to us. But one day we found out that they were not omnipotent, that they too had weaknesses. Maybe it was that day you discovered your mother cheated at cards. Maybe it was when you found out your father had had an affair. Whatever you discovered was painful. We all, at some point, observe our parents' imperfections; as the process continues, we separate from them, and accept that they are vulnerable and real human beings. This process is part of our growing into adulthood. Eventually, if we have not done so already, we will have to confront their ultimate imperfection—their mortality.

The child in us fears abandonment. For most of us, that fear presages reality; in the normal course of our lifetimes, most of us will bury our parents. Coping with this realization is painful, but most of us are prepared to do so unless our parents die prematurely. Generally, however, we have not been prepared for drawn-out periods of a parent's disease, debility, and dependency. Generations preceding ours rarely had to deal with protracted illness in the old. Without modern medicine, the frailties of old age, when combined with disease, precluded prolonged survival. Even patients with Alzheimer disease generally succumbed in two to five years, whereas today the average is close to eight years, and some patients are known to have survived for 20 years or more. Long-term chronic illness, then, is becoming the rule, and in the absence of a healthy parent, it is usually the adult child—especially the daughter— who cares for the infirm older parent. Parenting our parents is a role for which we are ill-prepared.

We know what it means to be our parents' children—we have experienced it. We know what it means to be our children's parents—most of us have experienced it. We do not know what it means to become our parents' parents—we have yet to learn it. This book has been an attempt to help us in that learning.

Familiarity with the many psychological strategies, potentially destructive as well as potentially constructive, together with the six steps of the Commonsense Approach to Problem Solving, facilitates the task of parentcare. But different families face different problems. Some families, for example, struggle with housing. Long-distance and in-house parentcare have their own respective advantages and drawbacks; each suits a particular family at a certain time in a specific situation. For many families, a nursing home becomes the best option. If so, there are questions to ask about basic characteristics such as staff-to-resident ratio, licensing status, and, for example, presence or absence of handrails. And there are questions to ask, too, when a parent moves in with you.

---

## WHEN A PARENT MOVES IN

### Think About Common Sources of Conflict

---

Time            Money

Children

Housing         Health

---

### Try the Commonsense Approach

---

1. Mood Meter Reading: What am I feeling?
2. Personal Reflection: Why do I feel this way?
3. Recollection: How did I deal with the feeling before?
4. Reassessment: What am I willing to give and to give up?
5. Negotiation: It is time to talk and actively listen.
6. Compromise: Prepare to give up something, to give in.

---

Particularly with a parent in residence, but at almost any time, children can be the pawns in intergenerational conflicts. If your parents tell you that it is unforgivable how you neglect your children, and how little time you spend with your children, they may really be telling you that it is unforgivable how you neglect *them*, and how little time you spend with *them*. When your parents tell you that they cannot bear to see how you let your children go their own way, disrespecting your opinion, they may really be telling you that they cannot bear to see how you fail to respect *their* opinions and advice. A struggle between you and your parents long ago, when you

were a child, may be at the root of their complaints about your
children now. Differentiating current issues from your "closet
skeletons," and taking into consideration your parents' and
your children's values as well as your own, are essential in solving three-generational conflicts.

Our "sandwich generation" has been caught between the
demands of our growing children and those of our declining
parents, tyrannized by the clock, our archenemy. The culprits
that eat up our time and commonly initiate the most insistent
and persistent needs for parentcare are disease, disability, debility, and death. They pose difficult questions: How much
should we intervene? How should our parents go about choosing a doctor? Which illnesses are they likely to get? How will
their illnesses affect us and our relationships with them and the
rest of the family? Some answers are offered in this book.

Our intention has been to help you help your parents effectively and humanely, enhancing their autonomy without
losing your own. As you thumb through the chapters, you will
find guidelines, checklists, questions, answers, more questions,
tips, suggestions, and approaches that spell out the seemingly
endless details that arise in tackling the sometimes overwhelming job of parentcare. But the job need not be overwhelming;
the details need not be endless. With the recognition that we
and our parents are as similar as we are different, the job becomes easier because we are less disappointed in them and
more understanding of their weaknesses. To ease the burden
of parentcare, we need to know about ourselves, our parents,
and our world. With that knowledge we can identify our needs
and those of our parents, our potential resources as well as
theirs. We can then match needs to available resources.

Our parents' aging brings about the likelihood of illness
and disability for them and a developmental crisis for many of
us. We are forced into growing up and entering a new phase
of parent-child relationships, a new developmental stage. Our
acceptance of this developmental stage, and the way we model
parentcare for our children, will determine how they, their
children, and future generations perform the tasks of parentcare. It is upon us that our children will bestow that parentcare. What will it be like to have our own children care for us?
That book has not yet been written.

Though the burden of parentcare falls heavily upon more
grown-up children today than ever before, the responsibility

has been with us throughout the ages, as illustrated by a folk-tale of the Brothers Grimm, which can be summarized as follows:

Once upon a time there was an old, old man whose hearing was gone, whose sight had become cloudy, and whose shakiness was plain for all to see. When he sat at the table, he could hardly hold on to his spoon with his shaking fingers: often he would spill the soup on the tablecloth or on his clothes, and sometimes it would even dribble out of his mouth, causing great distress to his son and daughter-in-law. It happened more and more often, until finally they decided to have him eat in the corner behind the stove. They gave him a large bowl with very little food. He used to sit in that corner and look sadly toward the table, but never once said a word. Sometimes, though, his eyes would become moist. One day the bowl slipped from his shaking hands, fell to the floor, and broke. For the next meal he had a cheap wooden bowl, and from then on, that was his only dish.

Some months later, pouring rain confined the family to their house. The old man's grandson was on the floor working with some wooden boards. When asked what he was doing, the boy told his father: "I'm trying to make a trough for you and mother, big enough so you can eat out of it when I'm a grown man." The boy's parents looked at one another for a long time, both began to cry, and they went over to the stove to bring the boy's grandfather back to the table. From that day forward, the old man ate with them at the table, and they barely noticed when he spilled some of his food, or when a little bit of the soup ran down the side of his mouth and dirtied the tablecloth or his clothes.

As we care for our parents, so our children may one day care for us. Perhaps parentcare will become as familiar a term for them as childcare was for us. Meanwhile, some common sense, along with the acceptance that our parents are part of us, an image of what one day we will become, may make us more understanding of their frailties. We can then enjoy and care for that part of them that we do love and never want to give up.

# Appendix 1

## SOME COMMON HEALTH PROBLEMS

The following information is based on *Age Pages*, a handbook published by the National Institute on Aging (see page 127). The information may help adult children assist their parents with common health problems. Many of these health problems also afflict adult children, particularly those in their fifties, sixties, or older, so this information, for many of us, will apply to both generations.

### ALCOHOL ABUSE

Until recently, older problem drinkers tended to be ignored both by health professionals and by the general public. The neglect occurred for several reasons: our elderly population was small and few were identified as alcoholics; chronic problem drinkers (those who abused alcohol off and on for most of their lives) frequently died before old age; and, because they are often retired or have fewer social contacts, many older people have been able to hide drinking problems.

Some adult children may unknowingly encourage their parents' drinking if they have the attitude that excessive drinking should be tolerated because older people have only a limited time left, and therefore should be allowed to "enjoy" themselves. As more people learn that alcohol problems can be successfully treated at any age, more are willing to seek help to stop drinking.

### Physical Effects of Alcohol

Alcohol slows down brain activity. It impairs mental alertness, judgment, physical coordination, and reaction time, increasing the risk of falls and accidents. Over time, heavy drinking can cause permanent damage to the brain and central nervous system, as well as to the liver, heart, kidneys, and stomach.

Alcohol can affect the body in unusual ways, making certain medical problems difficult to diagnose. For example, the effects of alcohol on the heart and blood vessels can mask pain which may otherwise serve as a warning sign of heart attack. Alcoholism can also produce symptoms similar to those of Alzheimer disease—forgetfulness, reduced attention, confusion. If incorrectly identified, such symptoms may lead to unnecessary institutionalization.

Alcohol, itself a drug, mixes unfavorably with many other drugs, including those sold by prescription and those bought over the counter. In addition, use of prescription drugs may intensify the older person's reaction to alcohol, leading to more rapid intoxication. Alcohol can dangerously slow down performance skills (driving, walking, etc.), impair judgment, and reduce alertness when taken with drugs such as the following:

- *"Minor" tranquilizers.* Valium (diazepam), Librium (chlordiazepoxide), Miltown (meprobamate), Xanax (alprazolam), and others.
- *"Major" tranquilizers.* Haldol (haloperidol), Mellaril (thioridazine), and others.
- *Barbiturates.* Luminal (phenobarbital), and others.
- *Painkillers.* Darvon (propoxyphene), Demerol (meperidine), and others.
- *Antihistamines* (both prescription and over-the-counter forms found in cold remedies).

Use of alcohol can cause other drugs to be metabolized more rapidly, producing exaggerated response. Such drugs include anticonvulsants, anticoagulants, and antidiabetes drugs.

In some people, aspirin can cause bleeding in the stomach and intestines. Alcohol also irritates the stomach and can aggravate this bleeding. The combination of alcohol and diuretics can reduce blood pressure in some individuals, producing dizziness.

Anyone who drinks even moderately should check with a physician or pharmacist about possible drug interactions.

### Who Becomes a Problem Drinker?

In old age, problem drinkers seem to be one of two types. The first are chronic abusers, those who have used alcohol heavily throughout life. Although many chronic abusers die by middle age, some survive into old age.

The second type begins excessive drinking late in life, often in response to "situational" factors such as retirement, lowered income, declining health, and the deaths of friends and relatives. In these cases, alcohol is first used for temporary relief but later becomes a problem.

### Detecting Drinking Problems

Not everyone who drinks regularly or heavily is an alcohol abuser, but the following symptoms frequently indicate a problem:

- Drinking to calm nerves, forget worries, or reduce depression
- Losing interest in food
- Gulping drinks and drinking too fast
- Lying about drinking habits
- Drinking alone with increasing frequency
- Injuring oneself or someone else while intoxicated
- Getting drunk often (more than three or four times in the past year)
- Needing to drink increasing amounts of alcohol to get the desired effect
- Frequently acting irritable, resentful, or unreasonable during nondrinking periods
- Experiencing medical, social, or financial problems caused by drinking

### Getting Help

Older problem drinkers and alcoholics may have a good chance for recovery if they stay with treatment programs for the duration. Getting help can begin with a family physician or member of the clergy; through a local health department or social services agency; or with one of the following organizations:

*Alcoholics Anonymous* (*AA*) is a voluntary fellowship of alcoholics whose purpose is to help themselves and each other get—and stay—sober. For information about their programs, call your local chapter or write to the national office at P.O. Box 459, Grand Central Station, New York, NY 10163. They can also send you a free pamphlet on alcoholism and older people entitled *Time to Start Living.*

*National Clearinghouse for Alcohol Information* is a federal information service that answers public inquiries, distributes written materials, and conducts literature searches. For information, write to P.O. Box 2345, Rockville, MD 20852.

*National Council on Alcoholism* distributes literature and can refer you to treatment services in your area. Call your local office (if listed in the telephone book) or write to the national headquarters at 12 West Twenty-first Street, New York, NY 10010.

The article "Liquor May Be Quicker But . . ." from the *FDA Consumer* discusses alcohol and drug interactions. To receive a single free reprint of this article, send a postcard to the Food and Drug Administration, HFE-88, 5600 Fishers Lane, Rockville, MD 20857.

### ARTHRITIS

The word *arthritis* means inflammation of a joint. The diseases commonly known as arthritis—which is also known as *rheumatic disease*—include more than 100 different conditions. They vary in symptoms and probably in cause. Some forms are better understood than others, but the causes of most of them are not yet known. Many effective treatments are used today to control arthritis symptoms, but there are few cures.

Most forms of arthritis are usually chronic, lasting years. The more serious forms involve inflammation—swelling, warmth, redness, and pain. In older people, the two most common forms of arthritis are rheumatoid arthritis and osteoarthritis.

*Rheumatoid arthritis (RA)* is an inflammation of the joint membrane. It varies in severity and can be crippling. RA afflicts three times more women than men, and it usually appears in the middle years, although it can begin at any age.

RA can affect many body systems but most frequently appears in the joints—fingers, wrists, elbows, hips, knees, and ankles. Persistent swelling and pain in joints on both sides of the body are typical symptoms. Morning stiffness is especially common. RA should be treated as soon as it is discovered, because uncontrolled inflammation of joint membranes can damage the joints.

*Osteoarthritis (OA)* is often a mild condition, causing no symptoms in many people and only occasional joint pain and stiffness in others. Still, some people experience considerable pain and disability.

OA is also called *degenerative joint disease*, a more accurate name since "osteoarthritis" implies that inflammation is a part of the disease, which is not usually the case. While wear and tear on the inside surface of the joint is probably a cause of some cases, heredity and overweight may be other possible factors.

Although OA usually affects older people, the condition can occur at any age, especially after a joint injury. Joint stiffness in OA can be brief, is often relieved by activity, and may recur upon rest. The large weight-bearing joints of the body—knees, hips, and spine—are most often affected.

### Treatment

The aim in treating arthritis is to relieve pain and stiffness, stop joint destruction from inflammation, and maintain mobility.

Aspirin is the medicine most often used. It relieves pain and reduces joint inflammation. But aspirin should be taken for arthritis only under medical supervision, since large doses are required to reduce inflammation. In some patients, long-term use of aspirin can cause stomach irritation or other side effects, and may interfere with blood clotting. Some aspirin preparations contain antacids (buffered) or small amounts of other agents, such as caffeine. Acetaminophen—a common aspirin substitute—does not reduce inflammation, although it can relieve aches and pains.

Newer prescription medicines, as well as nonprescription forms of ibuprofen, can be used in place of aspirin. They are nonsteroidal anti-inflammatory drugs (NSAIDs). These are similar to aspirin in their ability to reduce inflammation and may have fewer side effects. Indomethacin, oxyphenbutazone, and phenylbutazone are other NSAIDs that provide relief for patients with arthritis, but they may have more side effects than aspirin. At this time, one of the newest NSAIDs, piroxicam, offers the advantage of a once-daily dosage.

Other stronger or non-aspirin drugs available by prescription for rheumatoid arthritis include antimalarial drugs (such as hydroxychloroquine), gold salts, steroids (including prednisone and cortisone), and penicillamine (not the same as penicillin). These drugs can have more serious side effects than aspirin.

*Physical therapy* is fundamental to treatment. People with arthritis tend to avoid moving around, and while rest can reduce inflammation, too much rest stiffens joints. So rest and exercise must be balanced.

Daily exercise such as walking or swimming can help maintain joint mobility. Good posture and proper eating (to prevent overweight) can help relieve joint strain.

Surgery is sometimes used in patients with RA or OA when joints are severely damaged and the more conservative forms of treatment have failed to control pain. Hip and knee joints are replaced most often. The purpose of surgery is to relieve pain and restore function in patients for whom other forms of treatment have failed.

## Unproven and "Quack" Cures

Arthritis symptoms, especially in RA, may go away by themselves but then reappear weeks, months, or years later. This sudden disappearance of symptoms makes arthritis an ideal target for quack products or gimmicks. Some of the more common unproven or unsafe remedies are the following:

*DMSO (dimethyl sulfoxide).* Currently, this drug is approved only for the treatment of interstitial cystitis, a bladder disorder. Studies are now being conducted to determine the safety and effectiveness of DMSO for the treatment of certain illnesses, but as yet there is no evidence that it is useful for arthritis.

*Special diets.* Recent studies suggest that certain foods such as fatty fish high in omega-3 may benefit patients with rheumatoid arthritis. However, many ads promoting foods, vitamins, or diets as "cures" are misleading, so the consumer must be wary.

*Medical devices.* Magnetic bandages, vibrators, or other gadgets have limited or no proven use in treating arthritis. Be wary of ads that use words such as "cure" or "miracle treatment."

## Warning Signs of Arthritis

Any recurring joint symptoms (lasting longer than six weeks) should be checked by a physician, no matter how mild or "temporary." A physical examination, X-ray studies, and specific laboratory tests can distinguish arthritis from other ailments and can identify the specific type of arthritis. Important signs of arthritis are:

- Pain, tenderness, or swelling in one or more joints.
- Pain and stiffness in the morning.
- Recurring or persistent pain and stiffness in the neck, lower back, or knees.
- Symptoms such as those described above that go away for a week or a month, but return.

### Resources

The American Association of Retired Persons (AARP, 1909 K Street, N.W., Second Floor, Washington, DC 20049) has published *The Gadget Book*. This book is a valuable resource for products that are simple to use and can make everyday tasks easier.

For more information about arthritis treatment and research, write to the Arthritis Foundation (1314 Spring Street, N.W., Atlanta, GA 30309) or the National Institute of Arthritis, Diabetes, and Digestive and Kidney Diseases (NIH, Bethesda, MD 20892).

### CANCER FACTS FOR PEOPLE OVER 50

Most people know something about cancer, but fear keeps many of them from finding out what they can do about it. Because many cancers occur most often in people 50 years of age or older, it is this age group that has the most to gain from learning about symptoms of the disease.

### What Are Common Cancers and Symptoms in People Over 50?

*Lung.* Cough that will not go away; coughing up blood; shortness of breath.

*Breast.* Lump in the breast; change in breast shape; discharge from the nipple.

*Colon and rectum.* Changes in bowel habits; bleeding from the rectum; blood in the stool that appears bright red or black. Persistent abdominal pain can be an early symptom of cancer of the colon.

*Prostate (men).* Difficulty or pain while urinating; the need to urinate often, especially at night. Although these symptoms often occur in benign disorders, they should be investigated whenever they appear.

*Uterus, ovary, and cervix (women).* Vaginal bleeding after menopause; unusual vaginal discharge; enlargement of the abdomen; pain during intercourse.

*Skin.*   Sore that does not heal; change in shape, size, or color of a wart or mole; sudden appearance of a mole.

## What If My Parent Has One of the Symptoms?

Your parent should contact the doctor as soon as possible to find out if an office visit is necessary. The symptoms may indicate an illness other than cancer. Remember, pain is not necessarily an early warning sign of cancer.

Some people, as they age, attribute medical symptoms to "growing older"; many illnesses, therefore, go untreated. Your parents should be sure to mention any suspicious symptoms to their doctor, feel free to ask the doctor questions, and ask for further explanation if they do not understand. It may help to list their questions before an office visit, and take time to record the doctor's answers.

## Are There Regular Medical Tests My Parents or I Should Have?

Even if you or your parents do not have symptoms, certain tests are needed periodically after age 50. It is even advised that some begin at an earlier age.

Doctors can recommend how often a specific test should be done, based on the patient's medical history and generally accepted guidelines for the frequency of these tests. Some may be required more often if the patient has had cancer before, has a family member with cancer, or has other medical conditions. Below is a list of some specific tests:

*Hemoccult test.*   One or more small stool samples are examined for possible traces of blood. Blood in the stool can be a symptom of colon or rectal cancer. Simple kits are available for collecting samples at home and mailing or delivering them to the doctor.

*Rectal exam.*   This test, an examination of the rectum with the doctor's gloved finger, can detect prostate tumors in men and rectal tumors in men and women.

*Sigmoidoscopy.*   This is an examination of the rectum and part of the colon with a lighted instrument.

*Pelvic examination and Pap test.*   The pelvic exam is a check of the female reproductive organs. The doctor, using a special instrument (speculum) and gloved fingers, checks the vagina, uterus, and ovaries for any sign of a problem. A Pap test, also called a Pap smear, is usually done at the same time. It is a painless test that involves removing cells from the cervix and examining them through a microscope to see if they are abnormal. Currently, experts disagree as to the frequency of Pap smears in women over age 60, and each individual should discuss this issue with her physician.

*Breast examination and mammography.*   Women should have their breasts examined periodically to check for such changes as lumps or thickening. A mammogram (an X ray of the breasts), which can detect tumors even before they can be felt, is recommended for all women over 50. Check that the equipment used for mammography exposes you to the lowest dose of radiation. Generally, the amount should be less than 1 rad (a measure of radiation dose) for each breast.

In addition to tests performed by a doctor, women should practice breast self-examination (BSE) monthly to detect lumps or other changes in their breasts. To learn how to do BSE, ask your doctor or nurse, or call the Cancer Information Service (see phone numbers listed below) for a free booklet.

A positive result on any of the above medical tests does not necessarily mean cancer, but it may indicate a need for more testing. If there is a tumor, a test called a biopsy is done. A piece of the tumor is removed surgically and examined microscopically to determine whether it is cancerous (malignant) or noncancerous (benign).

### What If My Parent Has Cancer?

If tests show that your parent has cancer, treatment should begin right away. Cancer is a disease in which cells grow abnormally. If left untreated, the cells continue to grow and eventually invade healthy tissue.

There are a number of treatments that may be used for cancer. To ensure that everyone will be comfortable with the decision to have a particular treatment, you may want to seek the opinion of more than one physician. Ask the doctor if an oncologist (a cancer specialist) should be consulted. It is important to ask questions about the diagnosis and what results are expected from the treatment.

### How Can I Get More Information?

The Cancer Information Service (CIS) is available to answer cancer-related questions. Call, toll-free, 1-800-422-6237 to find the office serving your area.* It is easier to remember that number as 1-800-4-CANCER. CIS staff members can answer your questions confidentially and mail you free booklets about your cancer concerns.

Spanish-speaking CIS staff members are available in the following areas (daytime hours only): California, Florida, Georgia, Illinois, northern New Jersey, New York City, and Texas.

*There are four areas not served by this toll-free number. In New York City, call 212-207-3540; in Alaska, 1-800-638-6070; in Washington, DC (and suburbs in Maryland and Virginia), call 206-467-4675; and in Hawaii, on Oahu, call 808-524-1234 (neighbor islands call collect).

## CONSTIPATION

Constipation is a symptom, not a disease. It is defined as a decrease in the frequency of bowel movements, accompanied by prolonged or difficult passage of stools. There is no accepted rule for the correct number of daily or weekly bowel movements. "Regularity" may be a twice-daily bowel movement for some, or two bowel movements a week for others.

Older people complain of constipation much more often than younger people. Experts agree, however, that older people frequently become overly concerned with having a daily bowel movement, and that constipation is often an overemphasized ailment.

### Who Has Constipation?

Some physicians suggest asking these questions to decide whether a person is really constipated: Are there fewer than two bowel movements each week? Is there difficulty passing stools? Is there pain? Are there other problems, such as bleeding? Unless these are regular symptoms, then your parent is probably not constipated. Changes in bowel movements or habits may signify disease and should be reported to the physician.

### What Causes Constipation?

Physicians do not always know what causes constipation, but an older person who eats an inadequate diet, drinks insufficient fluids, or misuses laxatives can easily become constipated.

Drugs given for other conditions (for example, certain antidepressants, antacids containing aluminum or calcium, antihistamines, diuretics, and antiparkinsonian drugs) can produce constipation in some people, as can lack of exercise.

*The role of diet.* Fiber is the nondigestible portion of plant foods. It retains water as it passes through the system, adding bulk to stools. A shift in dietary habits away from high-fiber foods (vegetables, fruits, and whole grains) to foods that are low in fiber and high in animal fats (meats, dairy products, and eggs) and refined sugars (rich desserts and other sweets) can contribute to constipation. Some studies have suggested that high-fiber diets result in larger stools, more frequent bowel movements, and therefore less constipation.

Lack of interest in eating—a common problem for many who live alone—may lead to heavy use of convenience foods, which tend to be low in fiber. In addition, loss of teeth may force older people to choose soft, processed foods that also contain little, if any, fiber.

Older people sometimes cut back on liquids in their diet, especially if they are not eating regular or balanced meals. Water and other fluids add bulk to stools, making bowel movements easier.

Americans spend an estimated $250 million on over-the-counter (nonprescription) laxatives each year. Many people view them as the cure for constipation. But prolonged use of laxatives is rarely necessary and often can be habit-forming. The body begins to rely on the laxatives to bring on bowel movements, and over time, the natural "emptying" mechanisms fail to work without the help of these drugs. For the same reason, habitual use of enemas can also lead to loss of normal bowel function. Another side effect of heavy laxative use is diarrhea.

Overuse of mineral oil—a popular laxative—may reduce the absorption of certain vitamins (A, D, E, and K). Mineral oil may also interact with drugs such as anticoagulants (given to prevent blood clots) and other laxatives, causing undesired side effects.

*Other causes of constipation.* Lengthy bed rest—for example, after an accident or illness—and lack of exercise may contribute to constipation. For patients who stay in bed and who suffer from chronic constipation, drug therapy may be the best solution.

Ignoring the natural urge to defecate can result in constipation. Some people prefer to have their bowel movements only at home, but holding a bowel movement can cause ill effects if the delay is too long.

In some people, constipation may be caused by abnormalities or blockage of the digestive system. These disorders may affect either the muscles or the nerves responsible for normal defecation. A doctor can perform a series of tests to determine whether constipation is the symptom of an underlying (and often treatable) disorder.

## How to Reduce the Risk of Constipation

If your parent is constipated, the physician should be consulted to rule out a serious problem. If no intestinal disease or abnormality exists and the doctor approves, it may help your parents to:

- Eat more fresh fruits and vegetables, either cooked or raw, and more whole-grain cereals and breads. Dried fruits such as apricots, prunes, and figs are especially high in fiber. Try to cut back on highly processed foods (such as sweets) and food high in fat.

- Drink plenty of liquids (one to two quarts daily) unless there are heart, circulatory, or kidney problems. But be aware that some people become constipated or, more commonly, suffer from gas, bloating, or diarrhea, from drinking large quantities of milk.

- Some doctors recommend adding small amounts of unprocessed bran ("miller's bran") to baked goods, cereals, and fruits as a way of increasing the fiber content of the diet. But if unprocessed bran is used, remember that some people suffer from bloating and gas for several weeks after adding bran to their diet. All changes in the diet should be made slowly, to allow the digestive system to adapt.

- Stay active. Even taking one brisk walk a day can help tone the muscles.

- Try to develop a regular bowel habit. Attempt to have a bowel movement shortly after breakfast or dinner.

- Avoid taking laxatives if at all possible. Although laxatives will usually relieve the constipation, people can quickly come to depend on them, and the natural muscle actions required for defecation may become impaired.

- Limit intake of antacids, since some can cause constipation as well as other health problems.

- Above all, do not expect to have a bowel movement every day or even every other day. "Regularity" differs from person to person. If bowel movements are painless and occur regularly (whether the pattern is twice a day or twice a week), then there is probably no need to be concerned about constipation.

### DIABETES

*Diabetes mellitus* is a disorder in which the body cannot convert foods properly into the energy needed for daily activity. When a person eats sugars and starches, the body always changes them mainly into a specific sugar called glucose. Glucose is a type of "fuel" that circulates in the bloodstream for immediate use, or is stored in the liver as glycogen for future use.

In diabetes, the mechanism that controls the amount of glucose in the blood breaks down. The glucose then builds up to dangerous levels, causing symptoms and damaging body organs. This buildup occurs either because the body does not have enough insulin (the hormone that regulates the glucose level in the blood) or because the insulin is not fully effective on body tissues.

Diabetes tends to run in families, but factors other than heredity are responsible as well. For example, becoming overweight can trigger diabetes in susceptible older people.

There are two main types of diabetes. Type I, or *insulin-dependent diabetes,* is the more severe form of the disease. Although this type of diabetes can appear at any age, it generally starts during childhood or adolescence. Lifelong treatment with insulin is usually required, along with exercise and a controlled diet.

The common form of diabetes among older people is type II or *noninsulin-dependent diabetes*. Previously known as "adult-onset" diabetes, this form accounts for more than 85 percent of all cases. Most people with this type of diabetes do not need insulin injections. They can usually keep their blood glucose levels near normal by controlling their weight, exercising, and following a sensible diet.

Blood glucose levels that are either very high or very low can lead to serious medical emergencies. Diabetics may go into a coma (either the hyperosmolar or diabetic ketoacidotic variety) when their blood sugar levels get very high. Low blood sugar (hypoglycemia) can also lead to unconsciousness. People who have diabetes must know the warning signs of these two conditions and what to do if they occur. In addition, long-term complications that include stroke, blindness, heart disease, kidney failure, gangrene, and nerve damage can result from diabetes. Most experts believe that proper control of blood glucose will help prevent or minimize these complications.

### Detecting Diabetes

Sometimes the first sign of diabetes is found by a physician, who may detect too much sugar in the blood or any in the urine during a routine test. Or the problem may be uncovered by determining the level of glucose in the blood before, and at timed intervals after, drinking a special glucose liquid (glucose tolerance test).

Recent research has shown that some increase in blood glucose levels may occur normally with age. A panel of experts brought together by the National Institutes of Health recently recommended an adjustment in diagnostic standards to take into account that the results of the glucose tolerance test are different for younger and older persons. This recommendation has been widely accepted by doctors specializing in the treatment of diabetes. By changing the interpretation of the glucose tolerance test, fewer people will be incorrectly diagnosed as diabetic.

### Symptoms

Some people with diabetes feel "run down" or have only vague symptoms that may go unrecognized. Others have symptoms such as increased thirst, frequent urination, unexplained weight loss, fatigue, blurred vision, skin infections or itching, and slow-healing cuts and bruises. These problems should be reported promptly to a physician.

### Treatment

Diabetes cannot be cured, but it can be controlled. Adequate control requires a careful blend of diet, exercise, and, if necessary, insulin or oral drugs.

*Diet planning* is vitally important to lowering blood glucose levels. In planning a diet, the physician considers the patient's weight and the amount of daily physical activity. For overweight patients, a weight-reducing plan is essential to achieving proper blood glucose control.

Food-exchange lists to help with meal planning are available from physicians and from the American Diabetes Association.

*Exercise* is also important because it helps the body burn off some of the excess glucose as energy. A doctor can help plan an exercise program that balances the diet and medication needs of the patient. It is important to be consistent, exercising about the same amount each day.

If diet and exercise control diabetes, *drugs* are not needed for certain forms of (noninsulin-dependent) diabetes. But when these measures fail, oral drugs are the treatment of choice. If they fail, insulin injections are used. Sometimes a patient who normally does well without drugs will need one on a short-term basis during acute illnesses.

*Proper foot care* is essential for people with diabetes, since the disease can cut down the blood supply to the feet and reduce feeling. Diabetics should examine their feet every day, taking note of any redness or patches of heat. Any sores, blisters, breaks in the skin, infections, or buildups of calluses should be reported immediately to a podiatrist or family physician.

*Care of the skin* on other parts of the body is also very important. Diabetics are less able than others to tolerate injury and resist infection. They should protect their skin against injury, keep it clean, use skin softeners to treat dryness, and take care of minor cuts and bruises.

*Teeth and gums* must receive special attention, to avoid serious infections. People who have diabetes should inform their dentist they have the disorder, and see him or her when any problems occur in the mouth.

If diabetics adhere to their diets, exercise regularly, take prescribed medications, and observe sensible health practices, they can enjoy normal and productive lives. The American Diabetes Association, National Service Center, Box 25757, 1660 Duke Street, Alexandria, VA 22313, will provide free and low-cost publications with additional information on diabetes.

## DIGESTIVE PROBLEMS

The digestive system performs the amazing task of breaking down the food we eat into the nutrients our bodies need. Most of the time this system stays remarkably free of trouble. As we grow older, however, our bodies begin to work less efficiently in some ways, and our lifestyles may change. As a result, we may have a digestive problem.

During the chemical process of digestion, food is broken down into pieces tiny enough to be taken into the blood. The blood, in turn, carries these food elements to cells in all parts of the body, where they are changed into energy or used to form new structures.

Many body organs are involved in the process of digestion: the esophagus, stomach, pancreas, gallbladder, liver, small intestine, and colon. Most people have few, if any, digestive problems related to aging. Changes that may occur are usually minor and include slower action of the muscles of the digestive system and reduced acid production in some people. Both of these events can affect how fast food travels through the system, slowing down digestion. Such changes, however, usually do not lead to problems.

Changes in lifestyle that can interfere with the workings of the digestive system include increased use of medicines, reduced exercise, and changes in eating habits.

## Taking Care of the System

To keep the digestive system working at its best, the following steps are recommended:

- Eat a well-balanced diet that includes a variety of fresh fruits, vegetables, and whole-grain breads, cereals, and other grain products.
- Eat slowly and, whenever possible, try to relax for 30 minutes after each meal.
- Exercise regularly.
- Drink alcohol in moderation, if at all.
- Avoid large amounts of caffeine.
- Use caution when taking over-the-counter drugs, and always follow the doctor's directions exactly when taking prescribed medications.

## When to See a Doctor

No matter how well we treat our digestive systems, sometimes things go wrong. Often the problem takes care of itself. Symptoms, however, may signal serious illness. Some important warning signs are:

- Stomach pains that are severe, last a long time, are recurring, or come with shaking, chills, and cold, clammy skin.
- Blood in vomit, or recurrent vomiting.
- A sudden change in bowel habits and consistency of stools lasting more than a few days (for example, diarrhea for more than three days, or the sudden onset of constipation).
- Blood in stools, or coal-black stools.
- Jaundice (a yellowing of the skin and the whites of the eyes) or dark, tea-colored urine.
- Pain or any other difficulty in swallowing food.
- Continuing loss of appetite or unplanned weight loss.
- Diarrhea that causes awakening at night.

If your parent has any of the above symptoms, a doctor should be seen at once.

## Digestive Diseases

Disorders of the digestive tract are a frequent cause of hospital admissions, especially of older people. Digestive problems can result from infection, defects present at birth, poisons, stress, and a variety of other diseases. But the causes of many digestive diseases are unknown. Diet may be involved in a few of them. For example, low intake of fiber (the part of a plant that is not digested) is thought to play a role in constipation, cancer of the colon, and diverticulosis, a condition in which small sacs form in the intestine. Alcoholism has been linked to pancreatitis (inflammation of the pancreas), but definite proof still has not been found.

Progress is being made in diagnosing and treating many digestive diseases. In addition to the upper and lower "GI series," which uses X rays and barium to find trouble spots, doctors can use a flexible instrument called the *endoscope* to see inside the esophagus, stomach, duodenum, and colon. The endoscope can be used to perform biopsies and some forms of mini-surgery as well. There are also techniques for getting images of body organs, such as ultrasound and the CT (computerized tomographic) scan, which provide more detailed images.

Treatment advances include new drugs for peptic ulcer, a vaccine to prevent one form of hepatitis, and a drug that can dissolve gallstones in some patients.

Some of the digestive disorders that most commonly cause problems for older people are listed below:

*Constipation* (see earlier discussion).

*Diarrhea.* A condition in which body wastes are discharged from the bowel more often than usual and in a more or less liquid state. There are many possible causes, including infection. Treatment of the underlying disorder is needed, along with replacement of lost fluids.

*Diverticulosis and diverticulitis.* In diverticulosis, which is common in older people, small sacs form on the wall of the large intestine. Although they usually cause no symptoms, occasionally there is pain in the lower left side of the abdomen. Treatment includes a diet high in fiber and liquids. Sometimes the sacs become inflamed, causing fever. The condition is then known as diverticulitis. Treatment consists of bed rest and antibiotics. Occasionally, the sacs rupture, and surgery is required.

*Functional disorders.* Sometimes symptoms such as pain, diarrhea, constipation, bloating, and gas are caused by a "functional" disorder such as irritable bowel syndrome. In these disorders, neither physical examination nor laboratory findings adequately explain the patient's symptoms, yet the intestinal tract still fails to work properly. A functional disorder may cause discomfort but is unlikely to lead to serious disease. A doctor may prescribe medication to relieve symptoms. Because diet and stress are thought to trigger functional disorders, the guidelines for diet and lifestyle given earlier should help control the symptoms (see chapters 5 and 10).

*Gallbladder disease.* In this disease, stones (usually composed of cholesterol) form in the gallbladder. The stones are often "silent," that is, they cause no symptoms or discomfort, but sometimes they cause problems requiring drug treatment or surgery. Severe pain in the upper abdomen may mean that a gallstone has lodged in one of the tubes leading from the gallbladder.

*Gas.* Some gas is normally present in the digestive tract. It is usually caused by swallowing air or eating foods such as cauliflower, brussels sprouts, brown beans, broccoli, bran, and cabbage. The body rids itself of gas by means of belching and flatulence (passing gas through the rectum). However, if the gas collects in some portion of the digestive tract, it can lead to pain and bloating. A change in dietary habits will often relieve extra gas.

*Gastritis.* An inflammation of the stomach, which can be caused by many different digestive ailments. Treatment is aimed at correcting the condition that is causing the gastritis. Alcohol, caffeine, and medications are among the common causes of gastritis, in addition to those mentioned elsewhere.

*Heartburn.* A burning pain felt behind the breastbone that occurs after meals and may last for many minutes to several hours. It is often caused by eating foods such as tomato products, chocolate, fried foods, or peppermint, and by smoking cigarettes. It is relieved by a change in diet, taking an antacid, sleeping with the head of the bed raised 6 inches, or stopping cigarette smoking.

*Peptic ulcer.* A sore on the lining of the stomach or duodenum (the small intestine just below the stomach). An ulcer occurs when the lining is unable to resist the damaging effects of acid and pepsin that are produced by the stomach to digest foods. Antacids, which neutralize acid in the stomach, and drugs that decrease the production of acid or coat the ulcer are very useful in treating peptic ulcer.

*Indigestion.* A common condition involving painful, difficult, or disturbed digestion. Doctors often call it *dyspepsia.* The symptoms may include nausea, regurgitation, vomiting, heartburn, abdominal fullness or bloating after a meal, and stomach discomfort or pain. Overeating or eating the wrong foods can cause symptoms, but they may also be related to other digestive problems such as peptic ulcer, gallbladder disease, or gastritis. Indigestion usually can be controlled through diet or by treating the specific disorder.

*Hemorrhoids.* Veins in and around the rectum and anus that have become weakened and enlarged. The condition is caused by pressure in the rectal veins due to constipation, pregnancy, obesity, or other conditions. The veins may become inflamed, develop blood clots, and bleed. Hemorrhoids are treated with frequent warm baths, creams, or suppositories, and, if necessary, by injections or surgery.

*Hiatal hernia.*   A condition in which part of the stomach slides up through the diaphragm (a thin muscle that separates the abdominal cavity from the chest cavity) into the chest cavity. Hiatal hernias are common after middle age and rarely cause symptoms. Contrary to popular myth, doctors now believe that hiatal hernias do not cause heartburn, although they are sometimes associated with it. Usually they do not need surgical or drug treatment.

*Milk intolerance.*   The inability to properly digest milk and milk products is due to a deficiency of lactase, the intestinal enzyme that digests the sugar found in milk. Some people develop this problem as they grow older. The symptoms, which include cramps, gas, bloating, and diarrhea, appear 15 minutes to several hours after consuming milk or a milk product. Most people can manage by eating fewer dairy products, or taking smaller servings more frequently, or using special milk preparations (acidophilus). If fewer dairy products are eaten, other foods that contain calcium (such as dark green leafy vegetables, salmon, and bean curd) should be substituted to help keep the bones strong. Many people can eat yogurt without having discomfort.

*Ulcerative colitis.*   A chronic disorder that usually develops in young adults, but also appears in older people. In ulcerative colitis, parts of the large intestine become inflamed, causing abdominal cramps and often rectal bleeding. Joint pain and skin rashes may also develop. The symptoms are usually controlled with drugs, but some patients eventually need surgery. Sometimes irritable bowel syndrome (IBS) is incorrectly called "spastic colitis." However, IBS does not cause inflammation and it is not related to ulcerative colitis.

Further information about these and other digestive disorders can be obtained from physicians or the National Digestive Disease Education and Information Clearinghouse, 1801 Rockville Pike, Rockville, MD 20874.

### EYE DISORDERS

Poor eyesight is not inevitable with aging, although some physical changes occur during the normal aging process that can cause a gradual decline in vision. Older people generally need brighter light for such tasks as reading, cooking, or driving a car.

Certain eye disorders and diseases occur more frequently in old age, but a great deal can be done to prevent or correct these conditions. Here are some suggestions for your parents to help protect their eyes:

• Regular health checkups to detect such treatable disease as high blood pressure and diabetes, both of which may cause eye problems.

- A complete eye examination every two or three years, since many eye diseases have no early noticeable symptoms. The examination should include a vision (and glasses) evaluation, eye muscle check, check for glaucoma, and thorough internal and external eye health exams.
- Frequent eye health care, especially if your parent has diabetes or a family history of eye disease. Make arrangements for care immediately if there is loss or dimness in vision, eye pain, excessive discharge from the eye, double vision, or redness or swelling of the eye or eyelid.

### Common Eye Complaints

*Presbyopia (prez-bee-oh'-pe-uh)*—a gradual decline in the ability to focus on close objects or to see small print—is common after the age of 40. People with this condition often hold reading material at arm's length, and some may have headaches or "tired eyes" while reading or doing other close work. There is no known prevention of presbyopia, but the focusing problem can be corrected with glasses or contact lenses.

*Floaters* are tiny spots or specks that float across the field of vision. Most people notice them in well-lighted rooms or outdoors on a bright day. Although floaters are normal and are usually harmless, they may be a warning of certain eye problems, especially if associated with light flashes. If your parent notices sudden changes in the type or number of spots or flashes, a physician should be consulted.

*Dry eyes* occur when the tear glands produce too few tears. The result is itching, burning, or even reduced vision. An eye specialist can prescribe special eye-drop solutions ("artificial tears") to correct the problem.

*Excessive tears* may be a sign of increased sensitivity to light, wind, or temperature changes. In these cases, protective measures (such as sunglasses) may solve the problem. Tearing may also indicate more serious problems such as an eye infection or a blocked tear duct, both of which can be treated and corrected.

### Eye Diseases Common in the Elderly

*Cataracts* are cloudy or opaque areas in part or all of the transparent lens located inside the eye. Normally the lens is clear and allows light to pass through. When a cataract forms, light cannot pass easily through the lens, and this affects vision. Cataracts tend to develop gradually, without pain, redness, or tearing in the eye. Some remain small and do not seriously affect vision. If a cataract becomes larger or denser, however, it can impair vision and may require surgery. Cataract surgery (in which the clouded lens is removed) is a relatively safe procedure that is usually successful. Cataract patients should discuss with their physician the risks and benefits of this elective procedure. Vision is restored by special eyeglasses or contact lenses or by an intraocular lens implant (a plastic lens that is implanted in the eye during surgery).

*Glaucoma* occurs when there is too much fluid pressure in the eye, causing internal eye damage and gradually destroying vision. The underlying cause of glaucoma is often not known, but with early diagnosis and treatment it can usually be controlled and blindness prevented. Treatment consists of special eye drops, oral medications, laser treatments, or, in some cases, other surgery. Glaucoma seldom produces early symptoms and usually there is no pain from the increased pressure. For these reasons, it is important for eye specialists to test for the disease during routine eye examinations in those over 35.

*Retinal disorders* are the leading cause of blindness in the United States. The retina is a thin lining on the back of the eye, made up of nerves that receive visual images and pass them on to the brain. Retinal disorders include senile macular degeneration, diabetic retinopathy, and retinal detachment.

- Senile macular degeneration is a condition in which the macula (a specialized part of the retina responsible for sharp central and reading vision) loses its ability to function efficiently. The first signs may include blurring of reading matter, distortion or loss of central vision (for example, a dark spot in the center of the field of vision), and distortion in vertical lines. Early detection of macular degeneration is important, since some cases may be treated successfully with lasers.

- Diabetic retinopathy, one of the possible complications of diabetes, occurs when small blood vessels that nourish the retina fail to do so properly. In the early stages of the condition, the blood vessels may leak fluid, which distorts vision. In the later stages, new vessels may grow and release blood into the center of the eye, resulting in serious loss of vision.

- Retinal detachment is a separation between the inner and outer layers of the retina. If identified early enough, detached retinas can often be repaired, with full or partial restoration of vision.

### Low-Vision Aids

Many people with visual impairments can be helped by using low-vision aids. These are special devices that provide more power than regular eyeglasses. Low-vision aids include telescopic glasses, light-filtering lenses, and magnifying lenses, along with a variety of electronic devices. Some are designed to be handheld; others rest directly on reading material. Partially sighted individuals often notice surprising improvements with the use of these aids.

## For More Information

- The National Eye Institute, part of the federal government's National Institutes of Health, conducts and supports research on eye disease and the visual system. Write to the Office of Scientific Reporting, National Eye Institute, 9000 Rockville Pike, Bethesda, MD 20892, for free brochures on eye disorders.
- The National Society to Prevent Blindness, 79 Madison Avenue, New York, NY 10016, has several free pamphlets on specific disease affecting the eyes. To receive a free copy of their publication *The Aging Eye: Facts on Eye Care for Older Persons*, send them a self-addressed, stamped envelope. They also have a *Home Eye Test for Adults*, which is available for $1 (to cover the cost of postage and handling).
- The American Foundation for the Blind, 15 East Sixteenth Street, New York, NY 10011, provides a list of their free publications on vision.
- Vision Foundation, 818 Mt. Auburn Street, Watertown, MA 02172, has published a free *Vision Resource List*, which includes information on special products and services for visually impaired people.
- Two professional societies that gather, study, and publish eye-care information are the American Optometric Association, Communications Division, 243 North Lindbergh Boulevard, St. Louis, MO 63141, and the American Academy of Ophthalmology, Box 7424, 655 Beach Street, San Francisco, CA 94120.

## Publications

- "Keeping an Eye on Glaucoma" is a reprint from the June 1980 issue of the *FDA Consumer*. It is available from the Food and Drug Administration, 5600 Fishers Lane, Rockville, MD 20852. Please send your request on a postcard.
- *Cataracts: A Consumer's Guide to Choosing the Best Treatment* is a large-print book available for $3.50 from Public Citizen's Health Research Group, 2000 P Street, N.W., Suite 708, Washington, DC 20036.

### FLU: WHAT TO DO

Each winter, millions of people suffer from the unpleasant effects of the "flu." For most of these people, a few days in bed, a few more days of rest, aspirin, and plenty to drink will be the best treatment.

Flu—the short name for influenza—is usually a mild disease in healthy children, young adults, and middle-aged people. But in older people, or in those of any age who have chronic illnesses, flu can be life-threatening. By lowering a person's resistance, flu may allow more serious infections to occur, especially pneumonia.

It is easy to confuse a common cold with influenza. An important difference is that flu causes fever, usually absent during a cold. However, older people often do not have a fever, even when sick with the flu. Also, nasal congestion occurs more often with a cold than with the flu. Cold symptoms generally are milder and do not last as long as symptoms of the flu.

Flu is a viral infection of the nose, throat, and lungs. It spreads quickly from one person to another, particularly in crowded places such as buses, theaters, hospitals, and schools.

Because of its ability to spread rapidly, flu was once believed to be caused by the influence of the stars and planets. In the 1500s, the Italians gave the disease the name *influenza,* their word for "influence."

### What Causes Flu?

Not until the 1930s and 1940s did scientists discover that flu was caused by constantly changing types of viruses. These tiny organisms invade animals and human beings and begin to multiply rapidly. Disease appears when their number grows so large that the body's immune system can no longer fight it off.

When someone infected with the flu coughs or sneezes, droplets containing the virus particles may reach another person, entering the body through the respiratory system. There, the viruses can multiply and cause flu.

### Symptoms

The effects of a flu infection can differ from person to person. Sometimes flu will cause no obvious symptoms. Often, however, the patient will feel weak and will develop a cough, a headache, and a sudden rise in temperature. The fever can last anywhere from one to six days. Other symptoms include aching muscles, chills, and red, watery eyes.

### Complications of Flu

Flu is rarely a fatal illness. But while the immune system is busy fighting off the flu, a person is less able to resist a second infection. Older people and people with chronic diseases are at great risk of developing secondary infections. The most serious of these is pneumonia, one of the five leading causes of death among people over 65.

Pneumonia—an inflammation of the lungs—may be caused by a flu virus. More often, however, it results from bacteria that multiplied in the system during a flu infection.

The symptoms of pneumonia are somewhat similar to those of the flu, but are much more severe. Shaking chills and chest pain are very common, and coughing becomes more frequent and may produce a colored discharge. The fever that accompanies the flu will continue during pneumonia and will usually stay high. Again, older patients may not have a high fever.

## Treatment

Bacterial pneumonia is treated with antibiotics. During the most serious phase of pneumonia, the body loses essential fluids. Therefore, patients often receive extra fluids to prevent shock, a dangerous condition.

In recent years, the use of an antiviral drug, amantadine, has been recommended for the treatment of many types of influenza, particularly in high-risk individuals. However, the usual recommended treatment is: (1) take aspirin for the aches and pains, (2) drink plenty of fluids, and (3) stay in bed until free of fever for one or two days. It is especially important to stay rested, since the fever may return if the patient becomes too active too soon. If the fever persists, a doctor should be called, since this may mean that a more serious infection is present.

The National Institute of Allergy and Infectious Diseases has prepared a brochure called *Flu*. For free, single copies, write to NIAID, Bethesda, MD 20892.

## Prevention

Because the elderly are prone to develop pneumonia along with the flu, many doctors recommend that their older patients get a flu shot (vaccination) in the early fall. Side effects will sometimes occur, such as a low fever, or a redness at the injection site. But in most people the dangers from getting flu and possibly pneumonia are considered greater than the dangers from the side effects of the flu shot. One exception is people who have allergies to eggs; flu vaccines are made using egg products, and may cause reactions in those with such allergies.

Preventing flu is difficult because flu viruses change constantly and unpredictably. This year's virus usually is slightly different from last year's. The difference generally is just enough to get by the defenses produced by the last flu shot. Therefore, flu shots tend to be effective for only one year.

## FOOT PROBLEMS

In the course of a lifetime, the feet bear a weight equal to several million tons. It is little wonder, then, that in later life feet often hurt.

Many common foot problems may result from disease, long years of wear and tear, ill-fitting or poorly designed shoes, poor circulation to the feet, or toenails that are not properly trimmed.

It is a good idea for your parents to check their feet regularly—or to have them checked by a member of the family—and to care for them properly with good hygiene. Foot checkups can play a key role in the early diagnosis of many illnesses, including diabetes.

## Common Foot Problems

*Fungal and bacterial conditions*—including athlete's foot—occur because the feet are usually enclosed in a dark, damp, warm environment, which is an ideal growing place for fungi and bacteria. Such infections can cause redness, blisters, peeling, and itching. If the infection is not treated promptly, it may become chronic and very difficult to cure. The best preventive measures are to keep the feet—especially the areas between the toes—clean and dry, and to expose the feet to sun and air whenever possible. Fungicidal powders may be dusted on the feet daily.

*Dry skin* sometimes results in itching and burning feet. Dryness can be helped by applying a body lotion to the legs and feet every day, and by using mild soaps, preferably those containing moisturizers. Although bath oils may feel good, their use requires caution because they can make the feet and bathtub slippery.

*Corns and calluses* appear on the skin as a response to repeated friction and pressure from shoes. Some corns and calluses are symptoms of a more serious condition, such as a bone deformity. A podiatrist (a doctor who specializes in the care of feet), a skin specialist, or a family physician can determine the cause of corns and calluses and can recommend treatment. Treating them yourself can be harmful, especially for people who have diabetes or poor circulation (see section on diabetes, page 218). Over-the-counter medicines advertised as cures for corns contain acids that destroy the tissue but do not treat the cause. Nonetheless, when used under proper supervision these medicines will sometimes reduce the need for surgery.

*Warts* are skin growths caused by viruses. They are sometimes painful, and if left untreated, they may spread. When over-the-counter preparations fail to remove warts, professional care should be sought. The doctor may apply medicines, remove the wart surgically, or—using anesthesia—burn or freeze it off.

*Bunions* occur when big toe joints are out of line and become swollen and tender. Bunions may result from ill-fitting shoes pressing on a deformity, or from an inherited weakness in the foot. If a bunion is not severe, wearing shoes that are wide at the instep and the toes may provide relief. Protective pads can also be used to cushion the painful area. There are several methods for treating bunions, including the application or injection of certain drugs, or the use of whirlpool baths. Painful bunions can sometimes be repaired surgically.

*Ingrown toenails* occur when a piece of the nail pierces the skin. This is usually caused by improper trimming of the nails, or by pressure on the nails from nail deformity. It is especially common in large toes. A doctor can remove the part of the nail that is cutting into the skin, and take measures to promote healing and control infection. Ingrown toenails can usually be avoided by cutting the toenail straight across and level with the top of the toe. If your parents have difficulty cutting their toenails, or if they have deformities, it is a good idea to consult a podiatrist. The service is sometimes covered by Medicare or other insurance.

*Diabetes* is a disease that makes people particularly prone to sores and infections on their feet. Because diabetes may impair feeling in the feet, serious injuries can occur more easily. Cuts should receive immediate medical attention. Even minor infections can take months to heal, and complications in severe cases may lead to surgical removal of the limb. Diabetics should be especially careful to avoid extremely hot or cold bath water, to keep their feet clean and dry, and to avoid stepping on sharp objects or dirty surfaces.

### Preventing Foot Trouble

Improving circulation to the feet can help prevent problems. Exposure to cold temperatures, wading or bathing in cold water, pressure on the feet from shoes, long periods of sitting or resting, and smoking can reduce blood flow to the feet. Even sitting with the legs crossed or wearing tight elastic garters or socks (long elastic hose tend to be better) can affect circulation. On the other hand, standing up and stretching, walking, and other forms of exercise promote good circulation. Gentle massage and warm foot baths (95 degrees F./35 degrees C.) can also help increase blood flow to the feet.

Shoes should be chosen carefully. The upper part of the shoe should be made of a soft, flexible material to allow the shoe to conform to the shape of the foot. Soles should provide solid footing and not be slippery. Low-heeled shoes are not only safer and less damaging to the feet than high heels but are more comfortable as well. Shoes made of leather allow the feet to "breathe" and can reduce the possibility of skin irritations.

For more information on foot care, write to the American Podiatric Medical Association, 20 Chevy Chase Circle, N.W., Washington, DC 20015.

### HEARING PROBLEMS

It is easy to take good hearing for granted. In the world of the hearing impaired, words in a conversation may be misunderstood, musical notes might be missed, and a ringing doorbell may go unanswered. Hearing impairment ranges from difficulty understanding words or hearing certain sounds to total deafness.

Because of fear, misinformation, or vanity, some people will not admit to themselves or anyone else that they have a hearing problem. It has been estimated, however, that between 30 percent and 60 percent of adults over age 65, and about 50 percent of those 75 through 79, suffer some degree of hearing loss. In the United States alone, more than 10 million older people are hearing impaired.

If ignored and untreated, hearing problems can grow worse, hindering communication with others, limiting social activities, and reducing constructive use of leisure time. People with hearing impairments often withdraw socially, experience frustration and embarrassment in not being able to understand what is said, and may suffer from periods of isolation and depression. In addition, hearing-impaired people may become suspicious of relatives and friends and may be wrongly labeled as "confused," "unresponsive," or "uncooperative."

While older people today are, in general, demanding greater satisfaction from life, those with hearing impairments often find the quality of their lives diminished. Fortunately, help is often available in the form of surgery, special training, hearing aids or other assistive listening devices.

## Some Common Signs of Hearing Impairment

- Words are difficult to understand.
- Such high-pitched sounds as a whistle, the dripping of a faucet or notes from a violin cannot be heard.
- A hissing or ringing background noise that may be heard continually.
- Another person's speech sounds slurred or mumbled or is difficult to follow, especially when direct eye contact is not made (e.g., while driving an automobile).
- Television programs, concerts, and social gatherings are less enjoyable because much goes unheard.

## Diagnosis of Hearing Problems

Hearing impairments may be caused by exposure to excessively loud noises over a long period of time, viral infections, vascular problems (such as heart conditions or stroke), head injuries, certain drugs, tumors, excessive ear wax, heredity, or age-related changes. In view of the importance of good hearing, it is essential to seek medical help when a problem is suspected.

In some cases, the family physician, internist, or geriatrician can take care of the diagnosis and treatment of a hearing problem. More complicated cases may require the help of specialists known as *otologists* or *otolaryngologists*. These specialists are doctors of medicine or doctors of osteopathy with extensive training in ear problems. They will conduct a thorough examination, take a medical history, ask about hearing problems affecting other family members, and order any other necessary laboratory tests. Many times they will then refer the patient to an audiologist. *Audiologists* specialize in the identification, prevention, and management of hearing problems and in the rehabilitation of people with hearing loss. They do not prescribe drugs or perform surgery, but they can recommend and dispense hearing aids. To test hearing, the audiologist uses an audiometer, a device that electronically generates sounds of different pitches and loudness. The testing is painless, and within a short time the degree of hearing impairment can be determined and treatment recommended.

## Types of Hearing Loss

*Presbycusis (prez-bee-ku'-sis)* is a common type of hearing loss in older people. Changes in the delicate workings of the inner ear lead to difficulties in understanding speech, but not total deafness.

Every year after age 50 we lose some of our hearing ability. The decline is gradual and progressive, so that by age 60 or 70, an estimated 25 percent of people are noticeably hearing impaired. Just as the graying of hair occurs at different rates, so does presbycusis.

Although presbycusis is usually attributed to aging, it does not affect everyone, and some researchers view it as a disease. Environmental noise, certain drugs, improper diet, and genetic makeup may contribute to this disorder. Although the condition is permanent, there is much that a person can do to function well despite the impairment.

*Conduction deafness* is another form of hearing loss sometimes experienced by the elderly. It involves blockage or impairment of the mechanical movement in the outer or middle ear, so that sound waves are not able to travel properly through the ear. This may be caused by packed ear wax, extra fluid, abnormal bone growth in the ear, or infection. People with this problem often find that voices and other sounds seem muffled, but their own voices sound louder than normal. As a result, they often speak softly. Depending on the cause, flushing of the ear, medicines, or surgery will prove successful in most cases.

*Central deafness* is a third type of hearing loss that occurs in the elderly, although it is rare even in this age group. It is caused by damage to the nerve centers within the brain. Hearing tests alone cannot reliably find the damaged part of the brain. The causes include extended illness with a high fever, lengthy exposure to loud noises, use of certain drugs, head injuries, vascular problems, or tumors. Central deafness cannot be treated medically or surgically, but for some, special training by an audiologist or speech therapist can be beneficial.

## Treatment

Examination and test results from the family physician, ear specialist, and/or audiologist will determine the most effective treatment for a specific hearing problem. In some cases, medical treatment, such as flushing the ear canal to remove packed ear wax, or surgery, may restore some or all hearing ability.

At other times, a hearing aid may be recommended. A hearing aid is a small device designed to amplify sounds. Although hearing aids are not recommended for all hearing difficulties, some persons can benefit from a properly used device.

Should a hearing aid be the recommended form of treatment, there are several things to know about buying one. An informed consumer should shop for a hearing aid just as for any other product. There are many models on the market, offering different kinds of help for different kinds of problems. Before deciding where to buy an aid, consider the quality of service as well as the quality of merchandise.

When buying a hearing aid, keep in mind that the most expensive one may not be the best. Buy an aid with only those features needed. Also, be aware that the controls for many of the special features are tiny and may be difficult to adjust. Choose an aid that can be operated easily. Many hearing aid dealers (usually called "dispensers") offer a free trial period of up to 30 days so that the consumer may wear the aid before making a decision. It is a good idea to take advantage of the trial period, since it often takes at least a month to become comfortable with a new hearing aid. The dispenser should have the patience and skill to help you through the adjustment period.

At times, people with certain types of hearing impairments may need special training. One form, speech-reading, trains a person to receive visual clues from lip movements as well as from facial expressions, body posture and gestures, and the environment. Auditory training may include hearing aid orientation, but it is also designed to help hearing-impaired persons identify their specific communication problems. Although neither speech-reading nor auditory training can improve damaged hearing, both can reduce the handicapping effects of hearing impairment by making the best use of the hearing ability that remains. If needed, counseling is also available so that hearing-impaired people are able to maintain a positive self-image while understanding their communication abilities and limitations.

## Cost

Because hearing impairments have so many causes, it is important to be examined by a doctor as soon as a hearing problem is suspected. Too often, people with hearing problems fail to get medical attention until the condition is beyond help. Unfortunately, the high cost of hearing health care contributes to this neglect. Medicare will pay for the diagnosis and evaluation of hearing loss if requested by a physician, but it will often not pay for the means to correct it. In some states, Medicaid covers some of the costs.

## If Your Parents Have Problems Hearing, They Should:

- See a physician to determine the cause. Ask if a specialist should be consulted.
- Not hesitate to ask people to repeat what they just said.
- Try to limit background noise (stereo, television, etc.) during conversation.
- Not hesitate to tell people about the hearing problem and what others can do to make communication easier.

## If You Know Someone with a Hearing Problem

- Speak slightly louder than normal. However, shouting will not make the message any clearer, and may sometimes distort it. Speak at your normal rate, but not too rapidly. Do not over-articulate. This distorts the sounds of speech and makes use of visual clues more difficult.
- Speak to the person at a distance of three to six feet. Position yourself near good light so that your lip movements, facial expressions, and gestures may be seen clearly. Wait until you are visible to the hearing-impaired person before speaking. Avoid chewing, eating, or covering your mouth when speaking.
- Never speak directly into the person's ear. This prevents the listener from making use of visual clues.
- If the listener does not understand what was said, rephrase the idea in short, simple sentences.
- Arrange living rooms or meeting rooms so that seats are no more than six feet apart and everyone is completely visible. In meetings or group activities where there is a speaker presenting information, ask the speaker to use the public address system.
- Treat the hearing-impaired person with respect. Include the person in all discussions about him or her. This helps to alleviate the feelings of isolation common in hearing-impaired persons.

## For Your Reference

If you would like further information about hearing problems, you may contact the following organizations:

- American Academy of Otolaryngology (Head and Neck Surgery), Suite 302, 1101 Vermont Avenue, N.W., Washington, DC 20005. The academy is a professional society of medical doctors specializing in diseases of the ear and related areas. They can provide information on hearing and balance disorders.
- American Speech-Language-Hearing Association, 10801 Rockville Pike, Rockville, MD 20852; or call 1-800-638-8255 for the National Association for Hearing and Speech Action. Either organization can answer questions or mail information on hearing aids or hearing loss and communication problems in the elderly. They can also provide a list of certified audiologists in each state.
- Office of Scientific and Health Reports, National Institute of Neurological and Communicative Disorders and Stroke, 9000 Rockville Pike, Bethesda, MD 20892. The Institute is the focal point within the federal government for research on hearing loss and other communication disorders. Ask for the institute's pamphlet "Hearing Loss: Hope Through Research."
- Self Help for Hard of Hearing People (SHHH), 7800 Wisconsin Avenue, Bethesda, MD 20814. SHHH is a nationwide organization for the hard of hearing. The national office publishes a bimonthly journal reporting the experiences of those with hearing impairments, as well as new developments in the field of hearing loss. A number of publications and reprints are available for the hard of hearing.

### HEAT-RELATED ILLNESS

As we get older, our bodies become less able to respond to prolonged exposure to heat or cold. In cold weather, some older people may develop accidental hypothermia, a drop in internal body temperature that can be fatal if not detected and treated promptly. During hot and humid weather, a buildup in body heat can cause heatstroke or heat exhaustion in the elderly. This is especially true of those with heart and circulatory disease, stroke, or diabetes.

*Accidental hypothermia.* Hypothermia is a condition of below-normal body temperature. Accidental hypothermia may occur in anyone who is exposed to severe cold without enough protection. However, some older people can develop accidental hypothermia after exposure to relatively mild cold.

Among the elderly, those most likely to develop accidental hypothermia are the chronically ill, the poor who are unable to afford enough heating fuel, and those who do not take the appropriate steps to keep warm. The small number of aged persons whose temperature regulation is impaired face the greatest danger. For unknown reasons, these people do not feel cold and do not shiver. Thus they cannot produce body heat when they need it. Many people who have "felt cold" for years may actually have a lower risk of accidental hypothermia.

The only sure way to detect hypothermia is to use a special low-reading thermometer, available in most hospitals. A regular thermometer will do, as long as you shake it down well. If the temperature is below 95 degrees F. (35 degrees C.) or does not register, get emergency medical help. Other signs include an unusual change in appearance or behavior during cold weather; slow, sometimes irregular, heartbeat; slurred speech; shallow, very slow breathing; sluggishness; and confusion. Treatment consists of rewarming the person under a doctor's supervision, preferably in a hospital.

*Heatstroke.* This is a medical emergency requiring immediate attention and treatment by a doctor. Among the symptoms are faintness, dizziness, headache, nausea, loss of consciousness, body temperature of 104 degrees F. (40 degrees C.) or higher (measured rectally), rapid pulse, and flushed skin.

*Heat exhaustion.* This results from a loss of body water and salt, and takes longer to develop than other heat-related illnesses. The symptoms include weakness, heavy sweating, nausea, and giddiness. Heat exhaustion is treated by resting in bed away from the heat and drinking cool liquids.

### Protective Measures

*In cold weather.* There is no strong scientific basis for recommending specific room temperatures for older people. However, setting the heat at 65 degrees F. (18.3 degrees C.) in living and sleeping areas should be adequate in most cases, although sick people may need more heat.

Measures to prevent accidental hypothermia include the following:

- Dressing warmly even when indoors, eating enough food, and staying as active as possible.
- Because hypothermia may start during sleep, keeping warm in bed by wearing enough clothing and using blankets.
- Asking the doctor whether specific medications might affect the control of body temperature, such as medicines to treat anxiety, depression, nervousness, or nausea.
- Asking friends or neighbors to look in once or twice a day, particularly during cold spells. Seeing if the community has a telephone check-in or personal visit service for the elderly or homebound.

*In hot weather.* The best precaution during hot spells is to remain indoors in an air-conditioned room. If the home is not air-conditioned, going to a cool public place (like a library, movie theater, or store) during the hottest hours is helpful.

Other ways to cool off include taking cool baths or showers, placing icebags or wet towels on the body, and using electric fans (being careful to avoid getting an electrical shock). In addition, it is wise to:

- Stay out of direct sunlight and avoid strenuous activity.
- Wear lightweight, light-colored, loose-fitting clothing that permits sweat to evaporate.
- Drink plenty of liquids such as water, fruit and vegetable juice, and iced tea to replace the fluids lost by sweating. Avoid alcoholic beverages or fluids that have too much salt, since salt can complicate existing medical problems, such as high blood pressure. Salt tablets should be used only with the doctor's approval.
- Above all, take the heat seriously and pay attention to danger signs such as nausea, dizziness, and fatigue.

### Contact for Assistance

People trying to save on fuel costs can protect against hypothermia by dressing warmly and heating only one or two rooms of the home. There are government-funded programs to help low-income families pay high energy bills, weatherize (insulate) their homes, or even get emergency repairs of heating/cooling units. Local community-action agencies or the Area Agency on Aging should know the proper source of assistance.

Caution, common sense, and prompt medical attention can help older people avoid illnesses due to heat and cold. For the brochure "A Winter Hazard for the Old: Accidental Hypothermia," write to the National Institute on Aging/Hypo, 9000 Rockville Pike, Bethesda, MD 20892.

### HIGH BLOOD PRESSURE: A COMMON BUT CONTROLLABLE DISORDER

You or your parent may be surprised if the doctor says your parent has high blood pressure, because it produces no obvious symptoms and can occur in an otherwise healthy person. Although scientists do not yet know how to prevent high blood pressure, there are ways to control the condition by bringing blood pressure (BP) readings down to safe levels.

What is high BP? As blood flows from the heart out to the blood vessels, it creates pressure against the blood vessel walls. Your BP reading is a way of measuring this pressure, and it tells you if the pressure is normal (normotensive), high (hypertensive), or low (hypotensive). Another name for high BP is hypertension.

BP readings are given in two numbers, such as 120/80. Although the average BP reading for adults is 120/80, a slightly higher or lower reading (for either number) is not necessarily abnormal or unsafe. Lower BP readings (for example, 110/70) are considered safe for most people. For older people, many experts feel that readings up to 140/90 are acceptable. Once the BP goes above this level, however, some form of treatment is generally considered.

When the doctor takes a BP reading, he or she may want the patient to stand, sit, or both. The BP test is painless and takes only a few minutes. Unless the BP is very high, the doctor usually takes several readings on different days before deciding if the BP is too high. All of these steps are necessary because BP changes so quickly and is affected by many factors, including the normal feelings of tension during a visit to the doctor.

It is estimated that 60 million Americans may have high BP. About 40 percent of whites and more than 50 percent of blacks over the age of 65 suffer from some form of high BP. Because this disease is so common, a BP test is recommended at least once a year.

Although in some patients high BP is caused by specific illnesses, these cases account for only about 5 to 10 percent of the total number of patients with high BP. This kind of high BP is referred to as "secondary hypertension" and is often cured by treating the original medical problem. Most forms of high BP, however, cannot be cured, but can be controlled by continuous treatment. These cases of high BP fall into the category known as *essential* or *primary* hypertension. The causes of primary hypertension are not known, but most experts agree on certain risk factors.

For example, it appears that high BP runs in families, and is more common as well as more severe in blacks than in whites. Other risk factors include obesity and diets high in salt. Many doctors now feel that not just one but a combination of several factors may be responsible for high BP.

BP will go up not only in tense people during periods of stress or increased physical activity. Usually calm, relaxed persons can also have high BP.

The good news about high BP is that for most people it can be controlled by drugs and sometimes by changes in daily habits. The type and severity of a patient's high BP, as well as his or her other medical problems, will determine which drug, or combination of drugs, is used.

Some patients incorrectly believe that once BP is brought down to normal levels, medicine is no longer needed. If the doctor has prescribed an antihypertensive drug, it probably means that the medicine is needed for a prolonged period of time, although patients should check with their physicians several times a year.

Sometimes it is possible to lower BP simply by losing weight, eating less salt, or getting more exercise. The physician may suggest these changes in daily habits if drugs are needed to control the BP.

Facts about high BP or hypertension:

- People with hypertension may not feel sick, but hypertension is serious and should be treated by a doctor.
- Research shows that the treatment of mild hypertension can be beneficial.
- BP can be lowered with medicines, but it will probably rise again if the medicine is not used. If one day's dose is missed, the next day's dose should not be doubled. Instead, the doctor should be called for advice.
- Medicine is best taken at the same time each day, for example, in the morning or evening after brushing teeth. This will help establish a regular and easily remembered routine. The doctor should be asked about the best times to take the medications.
- Weight reduction, reduced salt intake, and exercise may be helpful, but should be supervised by the doctor. These actions are not substitutes for drugs unless the doctor specifically says they are.

High BP can lead to many serious conditions in older people, including stroke, heart disease, and kidney failure. The risk of developing these problems can be reduced by getting proper treatment if a BP test shows hypertension.

For more information on high BP, write to the High Blood Pressure Information Center, 120/80 National Institutes of Health, Bethesda, MD 20892.

### OSTEOPOROSIS: THE BONE THINNER

All women should know about osteoporosis. This bone-thinning condition affects one in four women over age 60 and is a major cause of fractures of the spine, hip, wrist, and other parts of the skeleton. Treatment may help older women who have the disorder. And steps can be taken in the middle years, and earlier, to help prevent it.

Osteoporosis develops silently over a period of many years. Gradually and without discomfort, the bones thin out until some of them break, causing pain and disability.

Bones maintain themselves throughout life by a process known as remodeling, in which small amounts of old bone are removed and new bone is formed in its place. Beginning at about age 35, however, a little more bone is lost than is gained. The bone loss continues throughout life, but is not likely to cause problems until after menopause.

Why osteoporosis develops is not fully understood. Decreasing hormone levels, not enough calcium in the diet, inadequate exposure to sunlight (which helps the body manufacture vitamin D), and inactivity all may play a role.

## Who Gets It?

Fair-skinned white women are affected most often. Those who are thin and have smaller frames are more susceptible than larger, heavier people. Women who have a family history of osteoporosis, or who have had their ovaries removed at an early age, have an increased risk of developing the disease. Because of their denser bone structure and other factors, men are much less likely than women to get osteoporosis.

## Diagnosis

An early sign of the disorder is loss of height. This happens when weakened bones of the spine (vertebrae) become compressed. Later, as the vertebrae fracture and collapse, a curving of the spine (often called "dowager's hump") may occur.

Osteoporosis may go unrecognized until the spine becomes noticeably curved or until a hip, wrist, or other bone breaks. A minor fall can result in a broken bone. Or a hip bone may fracture, causing a fall. There may be no back pain until a fracture occurs, but when it does, the discomfort may be severe and last several months.

A number of methods are available for diagnosing osteoporosis, including X rays and sophisticated new medical devices that can assess bone loss.

## Prevention

The methods of both prevention and treatment of osteoporosis are controversial. Certain dietary and exercise habits can help prevent osteoporosis. The daily diet should include foods that are high in calcium. Milk and dairy products such as cheese, yogurt, and ice cream are the best sources of this mineral. (Choose low-fat products, such as skim milk, when possible.) Other sources include dark green leafy vegetables (such as collards, turnip greens, spinach, and broccoli), salmon, sardines, oysters, and tofu (soybean curd).

Although the current recommended dietary allowance (RDA) for calcium is 800 milligrams (mg) per day, most researchers believe that women past the age of 40 need 1,000 to 1,500 mg daily. One cup of milk has about 300 mg of calcium. Other foods provide the mineral in smaller amounts. If the daily diet does not provide enough calcium, doctors often recommend supplements such as oyster-shell calcium (calcium carbonate) or calcium citrate preparation, which may be more desirable for the elderly because it can be absorbed even when the stomach acid is low. (Some people—for example, those who form kidney stones—need to be cautious about increasing their calcium intake, although calcium citrate may create less of a problem than calcium carbonate.)

It is also important to get adequate amounts of vitamin D each day. Scientists recommend 400 IU (international units) daily. Vitamin-fortified milk and cereals, egg yolk, saltwater fish, and liver have this vitamin. One cup of fortified milk provides 100 IU. Fifteen minutes to one hour of midday sunshine also will meet the daily need for this vitamin. However, exposure to the midday sun is not recommended, especially for older people, and use of sunscreens cancels the effect of sunshine on vitamin D formation. Also, many older persons on low-fat diets do not consume enough vitamin D (see the "Sun-Damaged Skin" section of chapter 10). As a result, older people are prone to vitamin D deficiency.

Regular exercise is another important preventive measure. Activities that place moderate stress on the spine and the long bones of the body, such as walking, jogging, dancing, and bicycle riding, are good. Simple exercises to maintain strength in the shoulders, chest, back, and arms also are helpful.

Although protein is an important daily requirement, large quantities can lead to loss of calcium through the urine. Women whose diets are very high in protein should consider cutting back. Protein is found primarily in meats, poultry, fish, and dairy products. (However, since dairy products also are important sources of calcium, this may not be the place to cut back.) Forty-four grams of protein each day are recommended for adult women, 56 grams for adult men. One chicken breast has 26 grams of protein; a three-ounce sirloin steak has 20 grams.

Drinking alcoholic beverages or drinks containing caffeine increases the body's requirement for calcium, as does smoking.

Women in their forties should ask their doctor about tests to evaluate bone mass. And, at the time of menopause, they should ask whether an estrogen supplement is advisable, weighing the risks against the potential benefits.

### Treatment

The goal in treating osteoporosis is to stop further bone loss. The same principles apply in treating the disorder as in preventing it. People who have osteoporosis should eat foods that are high in calcium. Excess protein should be avoided, since too much of it can lead to bone loss. Doctors usually prescribe calcium tablets, possibly with added vitamin D, which helps supply the body with calcium. Both calcium and vitamin D preparations can be purchased in health food and other stores without prescription. Because both can be harmful in large quantities, and because the amounts of other substances are important—for example, the calcium to phosphorous ratio—it is important to consult a physician. Calcium and vitamin D may slow the rate of bone loss, but they will not cause new bone to form.

Exercise does stimulate formation of new bone. In a person who already has fractures, a doctor should determine the type and amount of activity to be done.

Many doctors prescribe the hormone estrogen, which also slows the rate of bone loss. However, there is controversy over its safety. Other agents are being tested. Fluoride, for example, may increase bone density. In high doses, however, it may have severe side effects. Investigators are studying combinations of calcium, vitamin D, estrogen, and fluoride in the hope of finding a way to stop bone loss.

Fractures are more severe in people who have osteoporosis; however, the healing process and treatment are much the same as in those without the condition. Wrist fractures may be treated with a cast, and metal parts can be used to replace or strengthen broken hips. Little can be done about collapsed vertebrae, but physical therapy and muscle-strengthening exercises are important means to rehabilitate the patient.

## PROSTATE PROBLEMS

The prostate is a small organ about the size of a walnut. It is located next to the bladder (where urine is stored) and surrounds the urethra (the canal through which urine passes out of the body). During sexual activity, it secretes fluid that helps transport sperm.

Prostate problems are common in men over 50. Because it surrounds the urethra, an enlarged prostate can make urination difficult. Most problems can be treated effectively without harming sexual function.

### Common Prostate Problems

*Acute prostatitis*, a bacterial infection of the prostate, is relatively uncommon but can occur in men at any age. Symptoms include fever, chills, painful or difficult urination, and pain in the lower back and between the legs. It can usually be treated successfully with antibiotics.

*Chronic prostatitis* is a recurring prostate infection. The symptoms are similar to those of acute prostatitis but are usually milder. Fever is uncommon. Chronic prostatitis can be difficult to treat. Antibiotics, which may be used for up to three months, are often effective when the infection is due to bacteria. Sometimes no disease-causing bacteria can be found. In some of these cases, massaging the prostate to release fluids is helpful. Often the condition clears up by itself, but symptoms may last a long time.

*Benign prostatic hypertrophy (BPH)* is an enlargement of the prostate. It is caused by small, noncancerous tumors that grow inside the prostate. It is not known what causes these growths, but they may be related to hormone changes with aging.

An enlarged prostate may eventually obstruct the urethra and cause difficulty urinating. Dribbling after urination, and the urge to urinate frequently, even at night, are common symptoms. In rare cases, the patient is unable to urinate.

A doctor usually can detect an enlarged prostate by rectal examination. The doctor may also measure how much urine is left in the bladder after urination, since even small amounts of residual can cause infections and possibly kidney damage. Usually, the amount of residual urine can be readily determined by inserting a catheter into the bladder. If there is a problem, such as inability to pass the catheter because of obstruction, the patient is usually referred to a urologist for cystoscopy (a procedure for looking into the bladder through a special instrument). Sometimes a dye is injected into a vein; it eventually appears in the urine and causes urine remaining in the bladder to show up on X-ray. Some people are allergic to the dye. Therefore, it is important to find out what dye will be used. The doctor may also examine the prostate and bladder by inserting an instrument called a cystoscope into the penis.

Drugs have not yet been successful in treating BPH, but current studies are investigating new compounds. Surgery may be necessary to remove the overgrown portion of the prostate.

## Prostate Cancer

In early stages of prostate cancer, the disease stays localized (in the prostate) and does not endanger life. But without treatment the cancer can spread to other tissues and eventually cause death. Prostate cancer usually progresses slowly.

Regular physical checkups that include a rectal examination increase the chances of detecting prostate cancer before symptoms appear, when it is in its early, most curable states. When symptoms do appear, they are usually similar to those caused by BPH.

A urologist (a specialist in diseases of the urinary system) is the best-qualified doctor to diagnose the problem and perform any necessary surgery. If a suspicious area is found in the prostate, the urologist may recommend a biopsy (a procedure in which a tiny piece of prostate tissue is removed with a needle and examined under a microscope). If the biopsy shows prostate cancer, other tests may be done to determine the type of treatment necessary. The urologist often consults an oncologist to decide on the most appropriate form of treatment. When the cancer is confined to the prostate, the cure rate is high. Even when the cancer is more advanced, it is still often possible to control it for long periods of time. For more information about prostate cancer, write to the National Cancer Institute, Bethesda, MD 20892.

## Prostate Surgery

Prostate surgery is often done to treat BPH and prostate cancer. Patients usually recover rapidly.

For BPH, it is common to remove only the portions of the prostate obstructing the urethra. This is sometimes called a simple prostatectomy. It does not damage the nerves that cause erection of the penis, and men can usually resume normal sexual activity soon after the operation. However, some men may experience problems, sometimes psychological, that can lead to impotence. In these cases, counseling can help restore confidence and normal sexual functioning.

*Transurethral resection of the prostate (TURP)* is the most common procedure for slightly or moderately enlarged prostates. An instrument inserted in the penis trims away the excess tissue, which is flushed out through the penis. A catheter (tube) remains in the bladder for several days to drain out urine during healing. No incision is made through the skin, and the patient usually recovers rapidly. After this operation, semen released during sexual activity may flow into the bladder rather than out of the penis, but the sensation of orgasm is reported to be the same.

When the prostate is much enlarged, an incision is made in the abdomen to remove the prostate growths (transabdominal prostatectomy). This surgery is more uncomfortable for the patient, but the long-term effects generally are similar to those of TURP.

During surgery for prostate cancer, the entire prostate and adjacent structures may be removed. This is called a *radical prostatectomy*. Many patients are impotent after this surgery, but special prosthetic devices inserted into the penis can restore the ability to make the penis firm for insertion. New surgical techniques are being developed to preserve the nerves going to the penis so that the patient will be able to have an erection after prostate removal.

Incontinence, the inability to hold urine, is a rare complication after surgery for BPH, but is common after radical surgery for cancer. Fortunately, most men regain urinary control within several weeks, and only a few continue to have problems that require them to wear a device to collect urine.

## URINARY INCONTINENCE

Loss of urine control, or urinary incontinence, is especially common in older women, but occurs in men as well. The overall frequency is said to be at least one in ten persons age 65 or older. Incontinence can range from the discomfort of slight losses of urine to the disability and shame of severe, frequent wetting.

Persons who are incontinent often withdraw from social life and try to hide the problem from their families, their friends, and even their doctors. The relatives of an incontinent person often do not know about available treatments and may believe that nursing home care is the only option.

These reactions are unfortunate, because in many cases incontinence can be treated and controlled, if not cured. Incontinence is not an inevitable result of aging. It is caused by specific changes in body function that often result from diseases or use of medications. If untreated, incontinence can increase the chance of skin irritation and might raise the risk of developing bedsores.

Persons having problems in controlling urine should seek prompt medical attention to determine the cause and lessen the chance of complications. Even in cases where incontinence cannot be completely eliminated, modern products and ways of managing the condition can ease the discomfort and inconvenience it causes.

Incontinence may be brought on by an illness that is accompanied by fatigue, confusion, or hospital admission. It is sometimes the first and only symptom of a urinary tract infection. Curing the illness will usually relieve or clear up the incontinence.

### Types of Incontinence

When incontinence is persistent, it may be one or more of the following types:

*Stress incontinence* describes the leakage of urine during exercise, coughing, sneezing, laughing, or other body movements that put pressure on the bladder. It occurs most often in women.

*Urge incontinence* refers to the inability to hold urine long enough to reach a toilet. It is often associated with conditions such as stroke, dementia, Parkinson disease, and multiple sclerosis, but it can occur in otherwise normal elderly persons.

Many older people with normal urine control may have difficulty reaching a toilet in time because of arthritis or other crippling disorders. A person who is not always able to reach a toilet in time to avoid wetting should not be considered incontinent. Instead, every effort should be made to make reaching the toilet easier.

*Overflow incontinence* describes the leakage of small amounts of urine from a constantly filled bladder. A common cause in older men is blockage of urine outflow from the bladder by an enlarged prostate gland. Another cause is loss of normal contraction of the bladder in some people with diabetes.

### Diagnosis

The first and most important step in treating incontinence is to see a doctor for a complete medical examination. This generally involves giving a detailed history as well as undergoing a physical examination that focuses on the urinary and nervous systems and reproductive organs. The doctor will probably also want to do an analysis of urine samples. In many cases, patients will then be referred to a urologist.

### Treatment

Treatment of urinary incontinence should be tailored to each patient's needs.

- Several medications can be used to treat incontinence. However, these drugs may cause such side effects as a dry mouth, eye problems, and buildup of urine, and therefore must be used carefully under a doctor's supervision.
- Certain behavioral management techniques, including biofeedback and "bladder retraining," have proved helpful in the control of urination. These can help a person sense bladder filling and delay voiding until he or she can reach a toilet.
- Exercises can be used to strengthen the muscles that help close the bladder outlet.
- Several types of surgery can improve or even cure incontinence that is related to a structural problem such as an abnormally positioned bladder or blockage owing to an enlarged prostate.
- Artificial devices that replace or aid the muscles that control urine flow have been tried in the management of incontinence. Many of these prosthetic devices require surgical implantation.
- Sometimes incontinence is treated by inserting a catheter into the urethra and collecting urine in a container. However, long-term catheterization—although sometimes necessary—creates many problems, particularly urinary infections. In men, an alternative to the indwelling catheter is an external collecting device. This is fitted over the penis (like a condom) and connected to a drainage bag.
- Specially designed absorbent underclothing is available. Many of these garments are no more bulky than normal underwear, can be worn easily under everyday clothing, and free a person from discomfort and embarrassment.

It is important to remember that incontinence can be treated and often cured after a thorough medical evaluation. Even incurable problems can be managed to reduce complications, anxiety, and family stresses.

# Appendix 2

## WHAT CAN YOU DO IF YOUR PARENT HAS ALZHEIMER DISEASE?

One of the most widely discussed and tragically debilitating illnesses is Alzheimer disease. Physicians have known about it for more than 80 years, ever since Alois Alzheimer delivered his famous report to a meeting of German psychiatrists. Until the 1980s, however, few people had heard of the disease, or could even pronounce its name. An estimated 1 million people are victims of the disease in the United States today, and the cost of their care was approximately $40 billion in 1986. As many as 25 percent of persons over the age of 85 may be suffering from this disease, including up to one-half of nursing home residents.

Alzheimer disease has become a popular media story, which has heightened public awareness. Many adult children and their parents live in constant fear that they will eventually become disabled by the illness. Some basic knowledge about the problem, and how to cope with it if it strikes your family, will help you and your parents allay some of that anxiety.

Alzheimer disease, the commonest form of mental decline in old age, causes a gradual deterioration of nearly all mental functions. A person may first experience forgetfulness and later more severe memory loss and difficulty learning anything new. Then patients become disoriented, and their personalities and moods change. They get lost in familiar surroundings and become suspicious and misidentify people whom they previously knew. They may become agitated, paranoid, and withdrawn, or have almost any other change in personality and behavior. Eventually they lose control of their basic body functions and usually die from infection, especially pneumonia.

Though our chances of suffering from this illness increase with age, less than 5 percent of people 65 years of age and older develop the illness. If a parent or sibling has Alzheimer disease, the risk of developing the illness is three times greater than that for the general population, but even in Alzheimer families, at least half the family members or more will *not* be affected.

Not all forgetfulness, or even serious memory loss, means your parent has Alzheimer disease. In fact, mild forgetfulness affects many people in their fifties and sixties. Such physical illnesses as thyroid disease or heart failure, as well as medications, can also cause memory loss. Depression, too, may make your parent confused and forgetful. If you or your parents are concerned about such symptoms, it is essential to see a physician, preferably one with experience in evaluating and treating patients with Alzheimer disease.

If the diagnosis is Alzheimer disease, the course is unpredictable. Symptoms usually worsen with time, but at varying rates. Some symptoms, particularly agitation, paranoia, and depression, can be treated with medications. Others respond to changes in the patient's environment. Patients with Alzheimer disease do best in familiar and constant surroundings. Daily routines increase their sense of security. Prominent displays of clocks and calendars, night lights, checklists, and diaries all aid in their orientation and memory. Medication schedules should be kept as simple as possible. Moves should be avoided, but, if necessary, photographs and other familiar objects from the patient's previous home should be moved along with the patient, to help maintain constancy.

Alzheimer disease affects the entire family, and family members usually provide the direct care of patients. Many support and therapy groups have been formed to aid them in their long ordeal. About a decade ago, a group of family caregivers created the Alzheimer's Disease and Related Disorders Association, now a national organization with local chapters throughout the country. The organization provides help through support groups, education and contributions to research. To find your local chapter, write to ADRDA National Headquarters, Suite 600, 70 East Lake Street, Chicago, IL 60601, or telephone 1-312-853-3060.

## Suggested Readings

Alzheimer, A. *About a peculiar disease of the cerebral cortex.* Translated by L. Jarvik and H. Greenson. *Alzheimer Disease and Associated Disorders: An International Journal 1* (1987): 3–8.

Mace, N. L., and P. V. Rabins. *The 36-Hour Day.* Baltimore: Johns Hopkins University Press, 1981.

Winograd, C., and L. F. Jarvik. *Treating the Alzheimer Patient: The Long Haul.* New York: Springer Publishing, in press.

U.S. Congress, Office of Technology Assessment. *Losing a Million Minds: Confronting the Tragedy of Alzheimer's Disease and Other Dementias.* OTA-BA. 323, Government Printing Office: Washington, DC, April 1987.

# Appendix 3

## WHO'S WHO IN HEALTH CARE

(based on *Age Pages*, the National Institute on Aging. See page 127.)

In many cases, the family physician is no longer the sole provider of medical care and advice for older Americans. Often the elderly are treated by a variety of health providers; it is important to understand which professionals can offer the best and least costly care for a specific problem and which services normally will be covered by Medicare. The following definitions include some, but not all, of the health practitioners frequently seen by older people.

### General Care

*Doctors of medicine* (M.D.) practice all accepted methods of medical care. They treat diseases and injuries, provide preventive care, do routine checkups, prescribe drugs, and perform some surgery. M.D.'s must complete medical school plus three to seven years of graduate medical education. They must be licensed by the state in which they practice.

*Doctors of osteopathic medicine* (D.O.) also provide general health care to individuals and families. The training they receive is similar to that of an M.D. In addition to drugs, surgery, and other treatments, a D.O. may manipulate muscles and bones to treat specific problems. In most states, doctors of medicine and osteopathy have the same practice privileges.

*Internists* (M.D.) specialize in the diagnosis and medical treatment of diseases in adults. Internists do not perform surgery or deliver babies.

*Family practitioners* (M.D.) specialize in providing comprehensive health care for all members of a family, on a continuing basis, regardless of age or sex.

The above doctors might refer patients to a number of medical specialists, including the following:

- Cardiologist—a heart specialist
- Dermatologist—a skin specialist
- Endocrinologist—a specialist in disorders of the glands of internal secretion, such as diabetes

250

- Gastroenterologist—a specialist in diseases of the digestive tract
- Geriatrician—a specialist treating the illnesses of the elderly
- Geriatric psychiatrist—a psychiatrist specializing in illnesses of the elderly, including dementias, such as Alzheimer disease
- Gynecologist—a specialist in the female reproductive system
- Neurologist—a specialist in disorders of the nervous system
- Oncologist—a specialist in tumors and cancer
- Ophthalmologist—an eye specialist
- Orthopedist—a surgeon who specializes in bones, joints, and muscles
- Proctologist—a specialist in rectal and colonic diseases
- Psychiatrist—a specialist in mental, emotional, and behavioral disorders
- Rheumatologist—a specialist in arthritis and rheumatism
- Urologist—a specialist in the urinary system, including the bladder and kidneys in both sexes and the male reproductive system

Most of the services of M.D.'s, D.O.'s, or specialists who have M.D. or D.O. degrees are covered by Medicare.

*Physician assistants* (*P.A.*) most often work in doctors' offices or hospitals, doing some of the tasks traditionally performed by physicians. They do physical examinations, take medical histories, carry out diagnostic tests, and develop treatment plans for patients. Their education includes two to four years of college, followed by a two-year period of specialized training. P.A.'s must always work under the supervision of a physician, but, depending on the state laws, the supervision can be by telephone rather than in person. In some states, P.A.'s can prescribe certain drugs. Medicare will pay for the services provided by a P.A. only if they are performed in a hospital or doctor's office under the supervision of a physician.

*Registered nurses* (*R.N.*) have two to four years of education in nursing school. In addition to performing bedside nursing duties, such as giving medicine, administering treatments, and educating patients, R.N.'s often hold supervisory and teaching positions in hospitals, long-term care facilities, and colleges. R.N.'s also work in doctors' offices, clinics, and community health agencies. Medicare does not cover private-duty nursing. It helps pay for general nursing services by reimbursing hospitals, skilled nursing facilities, and home health agencies for part of the nurses' salaries.

*Nurse practitioners* (*R.N., N.P*) are registered nurses with training beyond basic nursing education. Nurse practitioners perform physical examinations and diagnostic tests, counsel patients, and develop treatment programs. Regulations regarding their duties vary from state to state. Nurse practitioners may work independently, as they do in rural clinics, or may be staff members at hospitals and other health facilities. Medicare will help pay for services performed under the supervision of a physician.

*Registered dietitians (R.D.)* provide nutritional care and dietary counseling. Most of them work in hospitals or doctors' offices, but some have private practices. R.D.'s complete a bachelor's degree and an internship (or an approved coordinated undergraduate program) and, in addition, pass an examination. Medicare generally will not pay for a dietitian's services. However, it does reimburse hospitals and skilled nursing facilities for a portion of dietitians' salaries.

*Physical therapists (P.T.)* help people whose strength, ability to move, sensation, or range of motion is impaired. They may use exercise; heat, cold, or water therapy; or other treatments to control pain, strengthen muscles, and improve coordination. All P.T.'s complete a program leading to a bachelor's degree, and some of them receive postgraduate training. Patients are usually referred by a doctor, and Medicare pays some of the costs of outpatient treatments. Physical therapy performed in a hospital or skilled nursing facility is covered by Medicare.

*Occupational therapists (O.T.)* assist patients with handicaps to function more independently. They may provide exercise programs; heat, cold, and whirlpool treatments to relieve pain; and hand splints and adaptive equipment to improve function and independence. O.T.'s have a bachelor's degree plus five months of specialized training. The costs of occupational therapy will be paid in part by Medicare if the patient is referred as an outpatient by a doctor, or in full if the patient is in a hospital or skilled nursing facility.

*Speech-language pathologists* are concerned with speech and language problems, while *audiologists* evaluate hearing disorders. Some specialists work in both areas. They test and evaluate patients, and they plan therapy to restore as much normal function as possible. Many speech-language pathologists work with stroke victims, patients who have dementia, patients with diseases of the nervous system, and people who have had their vocal cords removed. Many audiologists work with older people whose hearing is failing. They recommend hearing aids when needed, and sometimes dispense them. Speech-language pathologists and audiologists have at least a master's degree. Most of them are licensed by the state in which they practice. Medicare generally will cover the services of speech-language pathologists and audiologists.

*Social workers* in health-care settings alert patients to potentially useful services, arrange for counseling when necessary, and help patients and their families handle problems related to physical and mental illness and disability. Older people might be referred to social workers by various health providers. A social worker's education may range from a bachelor's degree to a doctorate. Most of them have a master's degree (M.S.W.). Medicare does not cover services provided by social workers unless they work in a hospital setting.

### Dental Care

*Dentists (D.D.S. or D.M.D.)* treat oral conditions such as gum disease and tooth decay. They do regular checkups, give routine dental and preventive care, fill cavities, remove teeth, provide dentures, and check for cancers in the mouth. Dentists can prescribe medication and perform oral surgery. A general dentist might refer patients to a specialist such as an oral surgeon, who does difficult tooth removals and surgery on the jaw; an endodontist, who is an expert on root canals; or a periodontist, who is especially knowledgeable about gum diseases. Medicare will not pay for any dental care except surgery on the jaw or facial bones.

*Dental hygienists (R.D.H.)* examine, clean, and polish teeth. They also take X rays and teach patients about proper dental care. Although hygienists' duties vary according to state law, they almost always work under the supervision of a dentist. Most hygienists have at least two years of formal training, and all are licensed by the states in which they practice. Medicare does not pay for their services.

*Dental assistants* help dentists and dental hygienists in the dental office. They may process X rays, prepare the patient for examination, schedule appointments, or assist the dentist while he or she works. Dental assistants may have some formal training, or they may learn their responsibilities on the job. Their services are not covered by Medicare.

### Eye Care

*Ophthalmologists (M.D.)* specialize in the diagnosis and treatment of diseases of the eye. They also prescribe eyeglasses and contact lenses. They often treat older people who have glaucoma and cataracts. Medicare helps pay for all medically necessary surgery or treatment of eye diseases, and for examinations and eyeglasses to correct vision after cataract surgery. But it will not pay for routine examinations, eyeglasses, or contact lenses.

*Optometrists (O.D.)* generally have a bachelor's degree plus four years of graduate training in a school of optometry. They are trained to diagnose eye abnormalities and prescribe, supply, and adjust eyeglasses and contact lenses. In several states, optometrists are authorized to use drugs to treat eye disease, and in most states they can use drugs to diagnose abnormalities of the eyes. An optometrist may refer patients to an ophthalmologist or other medical specialist when medication or surgery is required. Medicare pays for only a limited number of optometric services.

*Opticians* fit, supply, and adjust eyeglasses and contact lenses that have been prescribed by an ophthalmologist or optometrist. They cannot examine or test the eyes, or prescribe glasses or drugs. Opticians are licensed in 22 states and may have formal training. Traditionally, however, most opticians learn their skills during on-the-job training.

## Muscle, Bone, and Foot Care

*Orthopedists* (see page 251).

*Podiatrists (D.P.M.)* diagnose, treat, and prevent disease and injuries of the foot. They may do surgery, make devices to correct or prevent foot problems, provide toenail care, and prescribe certain drugs. A podiatrist is not licensed to treat disease or injuries of any other part of the body. Podiatrists complete four years of professional school, and, once they have been licensed, Medicare will cover the cost of their services except for routine foot care. (However, routine foot care is covered if it is necessary because of diabetic complications.)

## Mental Health Care

*Psychiatrists (M.D.)* treat people with mental, behavioral, and emotional difficulties. They prescribe medication, treat and counsel patients, and can perform diagnostic tests to determine whether physical problems are causing or complicating the mental, behavioral, and emotional problems. Medicare will pay for a portion of both inpatient and outpatient psychiatric costs, and most, if not all, of the costs for diagnosis and treatment of conditions such as Alzheimer disease.

*Clinical psychologists (Ph.D.)* are called doctor because they have a doctoral degree in psychology. They are not medical doctors, but they counsel people with mental and emotional problems. (Some clinical psychologists who have a master's degree, but not a Ph.D., also work with patients, but they do not use the title doctor.) The services of a clinical psychologist are not covered by Medicare except when they are performed in connection with the services of a psychiatrist or other M.D.

Psychiatrists and psychologists are not the only professionals who treat mental, behavioral, and emotional difficulties. Psychiatric social workers (M.S.W.'s) and psychiatric nurses (R.N.'s) are just two examples of other health-care professionals who specialize in treating mental and behavioral problems.

## Pharmacists (D. Pharm.)

Pharmacists are knowledgeable about the chemical makeup and correct use of medicines—the names, ingredients, possible side effects, and uses in the treatment of medical problems. Pharmacists have legal authority to dispense drugs according to formal instructions issued by physicians, surgeons, dentists, or podiatrists. They can also provide information on nonprescription products that are sold in pharmacies. Pharmacists must complete five or six years of college, fulfill a practical experience requirement, and pass a state licensure examination to practice.

These are only some of the health professionals who provide care to people of all ages. They are especially important to the elderly, who may require a great deal of medical attention. Ideally, all health professionals will work together to provide older people with care that is comprehensive, efficient, cost effective, and compassionate.

# Appendix 4

# SIDE EFFECTS OF ANTIDEPRESSANTS

Antidepressants, like all medications, have their undesirable as well as desirable effects. Do not let them scare you or your parents. It is important to remember that these are excellent medications for treating depression. In fact, they are often life-saving, but they must be used properly. Many of their side effects can be modified by adjusting the timing and the amount taken, or, when necessary, by changing from one medication to another. Even with our sophisticated knowledge of psychopharmacology, using antidepressant drugs is still more of an art than a science. And, whether we like it or not, dealing with psychological factors remains vitally important. Do not forget to keep the physician informed of any discomforts that may develop, whether or not you think they might be due to the medication. Take an active role in working together with your parent and physician in adjusting medications so that side effects can be minimized and therapeutic effects maximized.

The table on page 258 lists some of the commonly prescribed antidepressants with their most frequent side effects. As the table indicates, there are three major areas to be concerned about: anticholinergic effects, sedation, and blood pressure changes.

*Anticholinergic effects.* These effects are named for *acetylcholine,* the specific chemical brain messenger they involve. They include dry mouth, blurring of vision, hesitancy in urinating, constipation, and rapid heartbeat. Dry mouth is perhaps the most frequent complaint, and often improves over time, even if the dosage of medication is not changed. Some people have difficulty with dentures because of dry mouth, and some find lozenges helpful. Problems in urinating can range from being just a nuisance to more serious complications, such as bladder infections or complete inability to pass urine. Anyone with a predisposition to bladder or prostate problems should be given these medications very cautiously, and preferably an antidepressant rated low in anticholinergic effects. Rapid heart rate is of special concern to people with heart failure; low dosages and close monitoring by a physician are in order. Elderly persons are also prone to develop confusion. For example, when getting up in the middle of the night, they may not recognize where they are, get lost on the way to the bathroom, and become frightened.

*Sedation.* Although listed as a side effect, sedation is often just what is wanted by the depressed person who is restless, agitated, and has difficulty sleeping. In such situations, taking the medication at bedtime will help reduce insomnia. When sedation becomes a problem during the day, lower dosages or switching to a less sedating medication may be indicated.

*Blood pressure changes.* The most frequent problem that people experience is a drop in blood pressure when they arise from a horizontal or sitting position to a standing one. Technically, this is called *orthostatic hypotension.* If the change is sudden, they may experience lightheadedness, faintness, or dizziness. If your parent complains of such symptoms, it is important to make sure he or she gets up gradually, especially when arising in the morning. Sometimes dangling the feet at the foot of the bed can help. This side effect may be most serious. It can lead to falls and possibly fractures, and lack of blood supply to vital areas of the brain or heart. Therefore, drugs with a high frequency of inducing blood pressure changes should be avoided unless it has been established that the particular patient—*your* parent—does not respond that way. Lowering the dose of the drug usually does not help reduce orthostatic hypotension.

One group of antidepressants, called *monoamine oxidase inhibitors,* requires restriction of certain foods and medications, to avoid a potentially dangerous increase in blood pressure. Although these drugs also cause orthostatic hypotension, the more dangerous complication of hypertensive crisis is brought about by foods such as aged cheeses, pickled herring, chicken liver, yeast extract, and broad beans. They are just some of the foods that are rich in *tyramine,* a substance in some foods that should be avoided by people taking monoamine oxidase inhibitors. The psychiatrist can supply you with a detailed list of other such foods.

Medications containing epinephrine or similar drugs, such as nose drops, decongestants, and cold remedies must also be avoided. It is helpful to get a complete list from the physician. The following classes of drugs may cause problems in the presence of monoamine oxidase inhibitors: antihypertensives, diuretics, sedatives, antihistamines, anesthetics, narcotics, amphetamines, alcohol, and too much caffeine. In addition, the drugs listed in the table on page 259 (except trazodone), levodopa (used in the treatment of Parkinson disease), dopamine, cyclobenzazepine (used to treat muscle spasms), and carbamazepine (an anticonvulsant) may also cause problems.

Patients should avoid nonprescription cold remedies, antihistamines, and weight-loss agents without a doctor's approval.

As with most other medications, antidepressants have numerous side effects. The *cardiovascular* side effects are among the most worrisome. Many other side effects are relatively uncommon. If you thumb through a *PDR (Physicians' Desk Reference)*, you may read what appears to be a frighteningly long list. Again, most of these are relatively rare. If you have specific concerns, or if your parent experiences any new or unusual symptom, do not hesitate to contact your physician, day or night.

### SOME SIDE EFFECTS OF COMMONLY USED ANTIDEPRESSANTS

| | Anticholinergic Effect | Sedation | Blood Pressure Changes |
|---|---|---|---|
| Amitriptyline | ++++ | ++++ | ++++* |
| Amoxapine | +++ | +++ | ++ |
| Desipramine | + | + | ++ |
| Doxepin | ++ | +++ | ++ |
| Imipramine | +++ | ++ | ++++ |
| Isocarboxazid | — | + | ++++ |
| Maprotiline | + | ++ | ++ |
| Nortriptyline | ++ | + | ++ |
| Phenelzine | — | ++ | ++++ |
| Protriptyline | ++++ | + | ++ |
| Tranylcypromine | — | + | ++++ |
| Trazodone | — | +++ | ++ |
| Trimipramine | ++++ | ++ | ++ |

*++++ = most severe; + = least severe

## SOME MANUFACTURERS' NAMES
## FOR SOME ANTIDEPRESSANTS

| Generic Name | Manufacturers' Name |
| --- | --- |
| Amitriptyline | Elavil |
| | Endep |
| | Etrafon (combination with antipsychotic drug) |
| | Limbitrol (combination with antianxiety drug) |
| | Triavil (combination with antipsychotic drug) |
| Amoxapine | Asendin |
| Desipramine | Norpramin |
| | Pertofrane |
| Doxepin | Adapin |
| | Sinequan |
| Imipramine | Janimine |
| | Presamine |
| | SK-Pramine |
| | Tofranil |
| Isocarboxazid | Marplan |
| Maprotiline | Ludiomil |
| Nortriptyline | Aventyl |
| | Pamelor |
| Pargyline | Eutonyl |
| Phenelzine | Nardil |
| Protriptyline | Vivactil |
| Tranylcypromine | Parnate |
| Trazodone | Desyrel |
| Trimipramine | Surmontil |

# Appendix 5

## DURABLE POWER OF ATTORNEY

(Discussion of California Durable Power
of Attorney for Health Care adapted from
California Medical Association, 1986)

Most states have statutes authorizing a durable power of attorney. This legal document allows a person (the "principal") to designate someone else (the "attorney-in-fact") to make decisions on his or her behalf, if for some reason the principal becomes unable to make decisions. In the event that the principal becomes mentally incapacitated, the attorney-in-fact can have limited or broad powers, depending on how the document is drafted. Powers may include financial decisions, such as purchasing properties or establishing trusts, or decisions about medical treatments, such as whether or not to use a respirator. The durable power of attorney allows the principal to choose ahead of time someone whom he or she trusts to make future decisions. Often people take advantage of this law to prevent heroic medical treatments in the face of catastrophic illness.

For an example of this law, we have reprinted a form "Durable Power of Attorney for Health Care" developed by the California Medical Association to comply with California's laws governing durable powers for health care decision making. The form can be completed without the assistance of an attorney, although legal consultation may avoid future complications. The person chosen to make health-care decisions may be any adult—a son or daughter or friend, or anyone you trust. Before filling out the form, you should discuss the matter thoroughly with the person you have chosen. More than one person may be identified, as a safeguard if the first person cannot be found. The law does prohibit your own doctor or someone who operates or is employed by community care facilities from being appointed, unless that person is related to you by blood, adoption, or marriage.

This form complies with California law. The laws in other states may vary. Legal advice should be obtained before attempting to use this form outside of California. Also, other powers of attorney often are specifically invalidated by the mental incapacitation of the principal and are, therefore, not durable.

# DURABLE POWER OF ATTORNEY
# FOR HEALTH CARE©

*(California Civil Code Sections 2410-2443)*

This is a Durable Power of Attorney for Health Care form. By filling in this form, you can select someone to make health care decisions for you if for some reason you become unable to make those decisions for yourself. A properly completed form provides the best legal protection available to help ensure that your wishes will be respected.

**READ THIS FORM CAREFULLY BEFORE FILLING IT OUT. EACH PARAGRAPH IN THE FORM CONTAINS INSTRUCTIONS. IT IS IMPORTANT THAT YOU FOLLOW THESE INSTRUCTIONS SO THAT YOUR WISHES MAY BE CARRIED OUT.**

The following checklist is provided to help you fill out this form correctly. You may use this checklist to double check sections you may be unsure of as you fill in the form. You may also use this checklist to help make sure you have completed the form properly. If you have properly completed this form, you should be able to answer **yes** to each question in the checklist.

_____ 1. I am a California resident who is at least 18 years old, of sound mind and acting of my own free will.

_____ 2. The individuals I have selected as my agent and alternate agents to make health care decisions for me are at least 18 years old and are *not:*

- my *treating* health care provider.

- an employee of my *treating* health care provider, unless the employee is related to me by blood, marriage or adoption.

- an operator of a community care facility (Community care facilities are sometimes called board and care homes. If you are unsure whether a person you are thinking of selecting operates a community care facility, you should ask that person.)

- an employee of a community care facility, unless the employee is related to me by blood, marriage or adoption.

_____ 3. I have talked with the individuals I have selected as my agent and alternate agents and these individuals have agreed to participate. (You may select someone who is not a California resident to act as your agent or alternate agent, but you should consider whether someone who lives far away will be available to make decisions for you if and when that may become necessary.)

_____ 4. I have read the instructions and completed paragraphs 4, 5, 6, 7, 8, and 9 to reflect my desires.

_____ 5. I have *signed* and *dated* the form.

_____ 6. I have either _____ had the form notarized; *or* _____ had the form properly witnessed:

_____ 1. I have obtained the signatures of two adult witnesses who personally know me.

_____ 2. Neither witness is:

- my agent or alternate agent designated in this form.

- a health care provider, or the employee of a health care provider.

- a person who operates or is employed by a community care facility.

_____ 3. At least one witness is not related to me by blood, marriage, or adoption, and is not named in my will or so far as I know entitled to any part of my estate when I die.

_____ 7. I HAVE GIVEN A COPY OF THE COMPLETED FORM TO THOSE PEOPLE INCLUDING MY AGENT, ALTERNATE AGENTS, FAMILY MEMBERS AND DOCTOR, WHO MAY NEED THIS FORM IN CASE AN EMERGENCY REQUIRES A DECISION CONCERNING MY HEALTH CARE.

## SPECIAL REQUIREMENTS

_____ **8. Patients in Skilled Nursing Facilities.**
If I am a patient in a skilled nursing facility, I have obtained the signature of a patient advocate or ombudsman. (If you are not sure whether you are in a skilled nursing facility, you should ask the people taking care of you.)

_____ **9. Conservatees under the Lanterman-Petris-Short Act.**
If I am a conservatee under the Lanterman-Petris-Short Act and want to select my conservator as my agent or alternate agent to make health care decisions, I have obtained a laywer's certification. (If you are not sure whether the person you wish to select as your agent is your conservator under the Lanterman-Petris-Short Act, you should ask that person.)

If you change your mind about who you would like to make health care decisions for you, or about any of the other statements you have made in this form, you should take all of the following steps: 1. Complete a new form with the changes you desire; 2. Tell everyone who got a copy of the old form that it is no longer valid and ask that copies of the old form be returned to you so you may destroy them; 3. Give copies of the new form to the people who may need the form to carry out your wishes as described above in number 7. If after reading this material you still have unanswered questions, you should talk to your doctor or a lawyer.

     ©California Medical Association 1986 (revised)   ▷

# DURABLE POWER OF ATTORNEY
# FOR HEALTH CARE DECISIONS

*(California Civil Code Sections 2410-2443)*

## WARNING TO PERSON EXECUTING THIS DOCUMENT

This is an important legal document. Before executing this document, you should know these important facts:

This document gives the person you designate as your agent (the attorney-in-fact) the power to make health care decisions for you. Your agent must act consistently with your desires as stated in this document or otherwise made known.

Except as you otherwise specify in this document, this document gives your agent the power to consent to your doctor not giving treatment or stopping treatment necessary to keep you alive.

Notwithstanding this document, you have the right to make medical and other health care decisions for yourself so long as you can give informed consent with respect to the particular decision. In addition, no treatment may be given to you over your objection, and health care necessary to keep you alive may not be stopped or withheld if you object at the time.

This document gives your agent authority to consent, to refuse to consent, or to withdraw consent to any care, treatment, service, or procedure to maintain diagnose, or treat a physical or mental condition. This power is subject to any statement of your desires and any limitations that you include in this document. You may state in this document any types of treatment that you do not desire. In addition, a court can take away the power of your agent to make health care decisions for you if your agent (1) authorizes anything that is illegal, (2) acts contrary to your known desires or (3) where your desires are not known, does anything that is clearly contrary to your best interests.

Unless you specify a shorter period in this document, this power will exist for seven years from the date you execute this document and, if you are unable to make health care decisions for yourself at the time when this seven-year period ends, this power will continue to exist until the time when you become able to make health care decisions for yourself.

You have the right to revoke the authority of your agent by notifying your agent or your treating doctor, hospital, or other health care provider orally or in writing of the revocation.

Your agent has the right to examine your medical records and to consent to their disclosure unless you limit this right in this document.

Unless you otherwise specify in this document, this document gives your agent the power after you die to (1) authorize an autopsy, (2) donate your body or parts thereof for transplant or therapeutic or educational or scientific purposes, and (3) direct the disposition of your remains.

If there is anything in this document that you do not understand, you should ask a lawyer to explain it to you.

## 1. CREATION OF DURABLE POWER OF ATTORNEY FOR HEALTH CARE

By this document I intend to create a durable power of attorney by appointing the person designated above to make health care decisions for me as allowed by Sections 2410 to 2443, inclusive, of the California Civil Code. This power of attorney shall not be affected by my subsequent incapacity.

## 2. DESIGNATION OF HEALTH CARE AGENT

*(Insert the name and address of the person you wish to designate as your agent to make health care decisions for you. None of the following may be designated as your agent: (1) your treating health care provider, (2) a nonrelative employee of your treating health care provider, (3) an operator of a community care facility, or (4) a nonrelative employee of an operator of a community care facility.)*

I, _____
(insert your name)

do hereby designate and appoint: Name: _____

Address: _____

Telephone Number: _____ as my attorney-in-fact (agent)
to make health care decisions for me as authorized in this document.

## 3. GENERAL STATEMENT OF AUTHORITY GRANTED

If I become incapable of giving informed consent to health care decisions, I hereby grant to my agent full power and authority to make health care decisions for me including the right to consent, refuse consent, or withdraw consent to any care, treatment, service, or procedure to maintain, diagnose or treat a physical or mental condition, and to receive and to consent to the release of medical information, subject to the statement of desires, special provisions and limitations set out in paragraph 4.

## 4. STATEMENT OF DESIRES, SPECIAL PROVISIONS, AND LIMITATIONS

*(Your agent must make health care decisions that are consistent with your known desires. You can, but are not required to, state your desires in the space provided below. You should consider whether you want to include a statement of your desires concerning decisions to withhold or remove life-sustaining treatment. For your convenience, some general statements concerning the withholding and removal of life-sustaining treatment are set out below. If you agree with one of these statements, you may INITIAL that statement. READ ALL OF THESE STATEMENTS CAREFULLY BEFORE YOU SELECT ONE TO INITIAL. You can also write your own statement concerning life-sustaining treatment and/or other matters relating to your health care. BY LAW, YOUR AGENT IS NOT PERMITTED TO CONSENT ON YOUR BEHALF TO ANY OF THE FOLLOWING: COMMITMENT TO OR PLACEMENT IN A MENTAL HEALTH TREATMENT FACILITY, CONVULSIVE TREATMENT, PSYCHOSURGERY, STERILIZATION OR ABORTION. In every other respect, your agent may make health care decisions for you to the same extent you could make them for yourself if you were capable of doing so. If you want to limit in any other way the authority given your agent by this document, you should state the limits in the space below. If you do not initial one of the printed statements or write your own statement, your agent will have the broad powers to make health care decisions on your behalf which are set forth in Paragraph 3, except to the extent that there are limits provided by law.)*

I do **not** want my life to be prolonged and I do **not** want life-sustaining treatment to be provided or continued if the burdens of the treatment outweigh the expected benefits. I want my agent to consider the relief of suffering and the quality as well as the extent of the possible extension of my life in making decisions concerning life-sustaining treatment.

I want my life to be prolonged and I want life-sustaining treatment to be provided **unless I am in a coma** which my doctors reasonably believe to be irreversible. Once my doctors have reasonably concluded I am in an irreversible coma, I do **not** want life-sustaining treatment to be provided or continued.

I want my life to be prolonged to the greatest extent possible without regard to my condition, the chances I have for recovery or the cost of the procedures.

*If this statement reflects your desires, initial here _____ .*

*If this statement reflects your desires, initial here _____ .*

*If this statement reflects your desires, initial here _____ .*

Other or additional statements or desires, special provisions, or limitations.

_____

_____

_____

(You may attach additional pages if you need more space to complete your statement. If you attach additional pages, you must DATE and SIGN EACH PAGE.)

## 5. CONTRIBUTION OF ANATOMICAL GIFT

*(You may choose to make a gift of all or part of your body to a hospital, physician, or medical school for scientific, educational, therapeutic or transplant purposes. Such a gift is allowed by California's Uniform Anatomical Gift Act. If you do not make such a gift, you may authorize your agent to do so, or a member of your family may make a gift unless you give them notice that you do not want a gift made. In the space below you may make a gift yourself or state that you do not want to make a gift. If you do not complete this section, your agent will have the authority to make a gift of all or a part of your body under the Uniform Anatomical Gift Act.)*

If either statement reflects your desires, sign on the line next to the statement. **You do not have to sign either statement.** If you do not sign either statement, your agent and your family will have the authority to make a gift of all or part of your body under the Uniform Anatomical Gift Act.

(_____)
        *(signature)*

Pursuant to the Uniform Anatomical Gift Act, I hereby give, effective upon my death:

☐ Any needed organ or parts; or

☐ The parts or organs listed:

_____
_____
_____

(_____)
        *(signature)*

I do not want to make a gift under the Uniform Anatomical Gift Act, nor do I want my agent or family to do so.

## 6. AUTOPSY AND DISPOSITION OF MY REMAINS

I understand that my agent will be able to authorize an autopsy (an examination of my body after my death to determine the cause of my death) and to direct the disposition of my remains unless I limit that authority in this document. I also understand that my agent or any other person who directs the disposition of my remains must follow any instructions I have given in a written contract for funeral services, my will or by some other method.

*(OPTIONAL: If you do not want your agent to be involved in these matters, you should state your desires concerning an autopsy and the person you would like to direct the disposition of your remains. If any of the statements below reflect your desires, sign next to that statement. If none of these statements reflect your desires and you want to limit the authority of your agent to consent to an autopsy and/or to dispose of your remains, you should write your own statement in paragraph 4, above.)*

*Autopsy*

(_____)
        *(signature)*

I hereby consent to an examination of my body after my death to determine the cause of my death.

(_____)
        *(signature)*

My agent may not authorize an autopsy.

**Disposition of Remains**

(_____)
        *(signature)*

My agent may not direct the disposition of my remains and I would prefer that _____
                     *(name and address)*

direct the disposition of my remains.

(_____)
        *(signature)*

I have described the way I want my remains disposed of in (circle one):

1. A written contract for funeral services with _____
_____
        *(name of mortuary cemetery)*

2. My will

3. Other: _____

## 7. DESIGNATION OF ALTERNATE AGENTS

*(You are not required to designate any alternate agents but you may do so. Any alternative agent you designate will be able to make the same health care decisions as the agent designated in Paragraph 2, above, in the event that agent is unable or unwilling to act as your agent. Also, if the agent designated in Paragraph 2 is your spouse, his or her designation as your agent is automatically revoked by law if your marriage is dissolved.)*

If the person designated in Paragraph 2 as my agent is not available and willing to make a health care decision for me, then I designate the following persons to serve as my agent to make health care decisions for me as authorized in this document, such persons to serve in the order listed below:

A. First Alternative Agent

Name: _____

Address: _____

Telephone Number: _____

B. Second Alternative Agent

Name: _____

Address: _____

Telephone Number: _____

## 8. DURATION

I understand that this power of attorney will exist for seven years from the date I execute this document unless I establish a shorter time. If I am unable to make health care decisions for myself when this power of attorney expires, the authority I have granted my agent will continue to exist until the time when I become able to make health care decisions for myself.

*(Optional)* I wish to have this power of attorney end before seven years on the following date: _____ .
(Fill in this space ONLY if you want the authority of your agent to end EARLIER than the seven-year period described above.)

## 9. NOMINATION OF CONSERVATOR OF MY PERSON

*(A conservator of the person may be appointed for you if a court decides that you are unable properly to provide for your personal needs for physical health, food, clothing or shelter. The appointment of a conservator may affect, or transfer to the conservator your right to control your physical care, including under some circumstances your right to make health care decisions. You are not required to nominate a conservator but you may do so. The court will appoint the person you nominate unless that would be contrary to your best interests. You may, but are not required to, nominate as your conservator the same person you named in paragraph 2 as your health care agent. You can nominate an individual as your conservator by completing the space below.)*

If a conservator of the person is to be appointed for me, I nominate the following individual to serve as conservator of the person:

Name: _____

Address: _____

Telephone Number: _____

## 10. PRIOR DESIGNATIONS REVOKED

I revoke any prior durable power of attorney for health care.

### Date and Signature of Principal

## (YOU MUST DATE AND SIGN THIS POWER OF ATTORNEY)

I sign my name to this Durable Power of Attorney for Health Care on _____ at

*(Date)*

_____ ,     _____

*(City)*                                                   *(State)*

_____

*(Signature of Principal)*

(THIS POWER OF ATTORNEY WILL NOT BE VALID FOR MAKING HEALTH CARE DECISIONS UNLESS IT IS EITHER: (1) SIGNED BY TWO QUALIFIED ADULT WITNESSES WHO ARE PERSONALLY KNOWN TO YOU AND WHO ARE PRESENT WHEN YOU SIGN OR ACKNOWLEDGE YOUR SIGNATURE OR (2) ACKNOWLEDGED BEFORE A NOTARY PUBLIC IN CALIFORNIA.)

## CERTIFICATE OF ACKNOWLEDGEMENT OF NOTARY PUBLIC

*(You may use acknowledgment before a notary public instead of the statement of witnesses which appears on the following page.)*

State of California                              )

                                              ) ss.

County of _____ )

    On this _____ day of _____ , in the year _____ ,

before me, _____

*(here insert name of notary public)*

    personally appeared _____ ,

*(here insert name of principal)*

personally known to me (or proved to me on the basis of satisfactory evidence) to be the person whose name is subscribed to this instrument, and acknowledged that he or she executed it. I declare under penalty of perjury that the person whose name is subscribed to this instrument appears to be of sound mind and under no duress, fraud, or undue influence.

NOTARY SEAL

_____

*(Signature of Notary Public)*

## STATEMENT OF WITNESSES

*(If you elect to use witnesses instead of having this document notarized, you must use two qualified adult witnesses. None of the following may be used as a witness: (1) a person you designate as your agent or alternate agent, (2) a health care provider, (3) an employee of a health care provider, (4) the operator of a community care facility, (5) an employee of an operator of a community care facility. At least one of the witnesses must make the additional declaration set out following the place where the witnesses sign.)*

I declare under penalty of perjury under the laws of California that the person who signed or acknowledged this document is personally known to me to be the principal, that the principal signed or acknowledged this durable power of attorney in my presence, that the principal appears to be of sound mind and under no duress, fraud, or undue influence, that I am not the person appointed as attorney-in-fact by this document, and that I am not a health care provider, an employee of a health care provider, the operator of a community care facility, nor an employee of an operator of a community care facility.

Signature: _____     Residence Address: _____

Print Name: _____     _____

Date: _____     _____

Signature: _____     Residence Address: _____

Print Name: _____     _____

Date: _____     _____

(AT LEAST ONE OF THE ABOVE WITNESSES MUST ALSO SIGN THE FOLLOWING DECLARATION.)

I further declare under penalty of perjury under the laws of California that I am not related to the principal by blood, marriage, or adoption, and, to the best of my knowledge I am not entitled to any part of the estate of the principal upon the death of the principal under a will now existing or by operation of law.

Signature: _____

*(Optional Second Signature):* _____

## COPIES

**YOUR AGENT MAY NEED THIS DOCUMENT IMMEDIATELY IN CASE OF AN EMERGENCY THAT REQUIRES A DECISION CONCERNING YOUR HEALTH CARE. YOU SHOULD KEEP THE EXECUTED ORIGINAL DOCUMENT AND GIVE A COPY OF THE EXECUTED ORIGINAL TO YOUR AGENT AND ANY ALTERNATE AGENTS. YOU SHOULD ALSO GIVE A COPY TO YOUR DOCTOR, MEMBERS OF YOUR FAMILY, AND ANY OTHER PEOPLE WHO WOULD BE LIKELY TO NEED A COPY OF THIS FORM TO CARRY OUT YOUR WISHES. PHOTOCOPIES OF THIS DOCUMENT CAN BE RELIED UPON AS THOUGH THEY WERE ORIGINALS.**

## SPECIAL REQUIREMENTS

*(Special additional requirements must be satisfied for this document to be valid if (1) you are a patient in a skilled nursing facility or (2) you are a conservatee under the Lanterman-Petris-Short Act and you are appointing the conservator as your agent to make health care decisions for you. If you are not sure whether you are in a skilled nursing facility, which is a special type of nursing home, ask the facility staff. If you are not sure whether the person you want to choose as your health care agent is your conservator under the Lanterman-Petris-Short Act, ask that person.)*

1. If you are a patient in a skilled nursing facility (as defined in Health and Safety Code Section 1250(c)) at least one of the witnesses must be a patient advocate or ombudsman. The patient advocate or ombudsman must sign the witness statement **and** must also sign the following declaration:

I further declare under penalty of perjury under the laws of California that I am a patient advocate or ombudsman as designated by the State Department of Aging and am serving as a witness as required by subdivision (f) of Civil Code 2432.

Signature: _____   Address: _____

Print Name: _____   _____

Date: _____   _____

2. If you are a conservatee under the Lanterman-Petris-Short Act (of Division 5 of the Welfare and Institutions Code) and you wish to designate your conservator as your agent to make health care decisions, you must be represented by legal counsel. Your lawyer must also sign the following statement:

I am a lawyer authorized to practice law in the state where this power of attorney was executed, and the principal was my client at the time this power of attorney was executed. I have advised my client concerning his or her rights in connection with this power of attorney and the applicable law and the consequences of signing or not signing this power of attorney, and my client, after being so advised, has executed this power of attorney.

Signature: _____   Address: _____

Print Name: _____   _____

Date: _____   _____

California Medical Association
P.O. Box 7690, San Francisco 94103-7690

The person you select may make health-care decisions for you only if you are in a coma or mentally incapacitated. The document is generally valid for a maximum of seven years. You must complete a new form to be covered after the expiration date unless you are incompetent, in which case the form remains valid until you regain competency or die. You may include written instructions that specify how you want the attorney-in-fact to carry out decisions. If this person decides to remove or withhold life-sustaining treatment, your doctor must attempt to discover if you object, and may not withhold or remove treatment if you object. If a particular decision is not specified in your instructions, the appointed person must make decisions based on your "best interests."

# Appendix 6

## THE LIVING WILL

The living will gives you the opportunity to state your desire not to be given "extraordinary" treatment if you are terminally ill and if the treatment would only artificially prolong the process of dying. Each state varies as to whether a living will is considered a legal document there. The document ultimately has been upheld in every state court where it has been tested, whether or not that state was one of the 38 that has passed some form of living will legislation. For further information regarding the living will and other advance directives, contact Concern for Dying, 250 West Fifty-seventh Street, New York, NY 10107.

At the end of this appendix is an example of a living will. To make best use of a living will, be sure to do the following:

1. Sign and date it before two witnesses. (This is to ensure that you signed of your own free will and not under any pressure.)

2. If you have a doctor, give him or her a copy for your medical file and discuss it to make sure the doctor is in agreement.

   Give copies to those most likely to be concerned if the time comes when you can no longer take part in decisions for your own future. Enter their names on the bottom line of the living will. Keep the original nearby, easily and readily available.

3. Above all, discuss your intentions with those closest to you.

4. It is a good idea to look over your living will once a year and redate it and initial the new date to make it clear that your wishes are unchanged.

Declarants may also wish to add specific statements to the living will to be inserted in the space provided for that purpose above the signature. Possible additional provisions are suggested below:

1. (a) I appoint _____
to make binding decisions concerning my medical treatment.

    Or:

    (b) I have discussed my views as to life-sustaining measures with the following, who understand my wishes:

_____

_____

2. Measures of artificial life support in the face of impending death that are especially abhorrent to me are:

    (a) Electrical or mechanical resuscitation of my heart when it has stopped beating.

    (b) Nasogastric tube feedings when I am unable to swallow.

    (c) Mechanical respiration by machine when my brain can no longer sustain my own breathing.

3. If it does not jeopardize the chance of my recovery to a meaningful and sentient life or impose an undue burden on my family, I would like to live out my last days at home rather than in a hospital.

4. If any of my tissues are sound and would be of value as transplants to help other people, I freely give my permission for such donation.

### EXAMPLE OF LIVING WILL

To my family, my physician, my lawyer, and all others whom it may concern:

Death is as much a reality as birth, growth, maturity and old age; it is the one certainty of life. If the time comes when I can no longer take part in decisions for my own future, let this statement stand as an expression of my wishes and directions, while I am still of sound mind.

If at such a time the situation should arise in which there is no reasonable expectation of my recovery from extreme physical or mental disability, I direct that I be allowed to die and not be kept alive by medications, artificial means, or "heroic measures." I do, however, ask that medication be mercifully administered to me to alleviate suffering, even though this may shorten my remaining life.

This statement is made after careful consideration and is in accordance with my strong convictions and beliefs. I want the wishes and directions here expressed carried out to the extent permitted by law. Insofar as they are not legally enforceable, I hope that those to whom this Will is addressed will regard themselves as morally bound by these provisions.

Signed _____

Date _____

Witness _____

Witness _____

Copies of this request have been given to _____

_____

_____

_____

# Appendix 7

# OTHER RESOURCES

## REGIONAL GERIATRIC PROGRAMS

The UCLA Multicampus Division of Geriatric Medicine compiled the following listing of active training programs in geriatric medicine and psychiatry, scheduled to be in operation as of July 1987. These are largely university-affiliated programs that train and educate physician-specialists to evaluate and treat the health problems of the elderly. Contact persons from these programs may be helpful in finding a geriatric internist or geriatric psychiatrist in your area. Not all geriatric training programs and treatment centers are listed, but those included should provide a reasonable start in finding a specialist near you. The status of some programs changes, so you may want to write to the American Geriatrics Society for an updated directory of programs (American Geriatrics Society, 770 Lexington Avenue, Suite 400, New York, NY 10021; or telephone 212-308-1414).

## GERIATRIC MEDICINE FELLOWSHIP TRAINING PROGRAMS

ARIZONA

William Jerry Carter, M.D.
(University of Arkansas)
Geriatric Medicine
VA Medical Center
300 East Roosevelt
Little Rock, AR 72206

CALIFORNIA

Elizabeth Barrett-Conner, M.D.
Chair, Dept. of Community and Family Medicine
UC San Diego
School of Medicine
La Jolla, CA 92093

Harold Brownstein, M.D.
(University of California, San Francisco)
Mount Zion Hospital and Medical Center
P.O. Box 7921
San Francisco, CA 94120

Thomas Cesario, M.D., Director
Dept. of Medicine
UC Irvine
California College of Medicine
101 The City Drive
Building 53, Route 81
Orange, CA 92668

Joan T. Gnadt, M.D.
Chief, Geriatric
    Section
VA Medical Center
150 Muir Road
Martinez, CA 94553


Joe Ramsdell, M.D.
General Internal
    Medicine/Geriatrics
Academic Geriatric
    Resource Center
    (M-031G)
UC San Diego
School of Medicine
La Jolla, CA 92093


Gerald M. Reaven,
    M.D.
(Stanford University)
Division of
    Gerontology
Dept. of Internal
    Medicine
GRECC 182B, VA
    Medical Center
3801 Miranda Avenue
Palo Alto, CA 94304


Mary Elizabeth Roth,
    M.D.
Dept. of Family
    Medicine
UC Irvine
California College of
    Medicine
101 The City Drive
Building 29A,
    Route 81
Orange, CA 92668


Philip Weiler, M.D.
Dept. of Community
    Health TB168
UC Davis
School of Medicine
Davis, CA 95616

Thomas T. Yoshikawa,
    M.D.
c/o Rosemary Brittain
UCLA Multicampus
    Division of Geriatric
    Medicine
Department of
    Medicine
32-144 CHS
10833 Le Conte
Los Angeles, CA
    90024


COLORADO

F. Marc LaForce, M.D.
(University of
    Colorado)
VA Medical Center
1055 Claremont Street
Denver, CO 80220


CONNECTICUT

Richard W. Besdine,
    M.D.
Director,
Travelers Center on
    Aging
University of
    Connecticut
    Health Center
Farmington, CT
    06032-9984

Leo Cooney, M.D.
Department of
    Medicine
Yale University School
    of Medicine
333 Cedar Street
P.O. Box 3333
New Haven, CT 06510

WASHINGTON, D.C.

L. Gregory Pawlson,
M.D.
George Washington
University
School of Medicine
and Health Sciences
Room 322
1229 Twenty-fifth
Street, N.W.
Washington, DC 20037

FLORIDA

William Reefe, M.D.
University of Miami
School of Medicine
VA Medical Center
(11A)
1201 N.W. Sixteenth
Street
Miami, FL 33125

Bruce E. Robinson,
M.D.
University of South
Florida
12901 North Thirtieth
Street
P.O. Box 19
Tampa, FL 33612

William C. Thomas,
Jr., M.D.
George J. Caranasos,
M.D.
University of Florida,
Gainesville
VA Medical Center
573/182
Gainesville, FL 32602

GEORGIA

Herbert R. Karp, M.D.
(Emory University)
Wesley Woods Center,
Inc.
1817 Clifton Road,
N.E.
Atlanta, GA 30029

HAWAII

Patricia Blanchette,
M.D.
Dept. of Medicine
John A. Burns School
of Medicine
University of Hawaii
Division of Geriatric
Medicine
Building HPM
347 North Kuakini
Street
Honolulu, HI 96817

IDAHO

Robert E. Vestal, M.D.
(University of
Washington)
Clinical Pharmacology
and
Geriatrics Units (151)
VA Medical Center
Fifth and Fort Streets
Boise, ID 83702

ILLINOIS

Christine K. Cassel,
M.D.
Chief, Section of
General Internal
Medicine
Dept. of Medicine
Pritzker School of
Medicine
University of Chicago
BH Box 12
5841 South Maryland
Avenue
Chicago, IL 60637

Morton Creditor, M.D.
Geriatric Medicine
Program
Dept. of Medicine
University of Illinois
College of Medicine
P.O. Box 6998
Chicago, IL 60680

James N. Kvale, M.D.
Division of Geriatrics
Dept. of Family
  Practice
Southern Illinois
  University
P.O. Box 3926
Springfield, IL 62708

Donald F. Pochyly,
  M.D.
Section, General
  Internal Medicine
Loyola University
  Medical Center
2160 South First
  Avenue
Maywood, IL 60153

Daniel Rudman, M.D.
Chief, Division of
  Geriatric Medicine
(Chicago Medical
  School)
VA Medical Center,
  556/111J
North Chicago, IL
  60064

Thomas J. Schnitzer,
  M.D., Ph.D.
(Rush Medical College)
Sect./Geriatric
  Medicine
Rush-Presbyterian-
  St. Luke's
  Medical Center
1753 West Congress
  Parkway
Chicago, IL 60612


IOWA

Ian M. Smith, M.D.
Geriatric Medicine
Dept. of Internal
  Medicine
University of Iowa
Iowa City, IA 52242

Glenys O. Williams,
  M.D.
Director, Geriatrics
  Program
Dept. of Family
  Practice
University of Iowa
Iowa City, IA 52242

KANSAS

Frederick F. Holmes,
  M.D.
University of Kansas
  Medical Center
Division of General
  and Geriatric
  Medicine
39th and Rainbow
Kansas City, KS 66103

KENTUCKY

Carole Gardner, M.D.
Geriatric Medicine
Lexington VA Medical
  Center
Lexington, KY 40507

MARYLAND

John R. Burton, M.D.
Johns Hopkins
  University School of
  Medicine
Baltimore City
  Hospitals
Francis Scott Key
  Medical Center
4940 Eastern Avenue
Baltimore, MD 21224

William Reichel, M.D.
(Georgetown
  University)
Dept. of Community
  and Family Practice
Franklin Square
  Hospital
9000 Franklin Square
  Drive
Baltimore, MD 21237

MASSACHUSETTS

Patricia Barry, M.D.
Boston University
  School of Medicine
Doctors Office
  Building
720 Harrison Avenue
Suite 1101
Boston, MA 02118

Edgar S. Cathcart,
  M.D.
(Boston University)
VA Hospital
200 Springs Road
Bedford, MA 01730

Janice Hitzhusen, M.D.
Division of General
  Medicine and
  Geriatrics
Department of
  Medicine
University of
  Massachusetts
  Medical School
55 Lake Avenue North
Worcester, MA 01605

Lewis Lipsitz, M.D.
Fellowship Director
Harvard Division of
  Aging
643 Huntington Ave.
Boston, MA 02115

MICHIGAN

Jeffrey B. Halter, M.D.
Division of Geriatric
  Medicine
University of Michigan
  Hospital
1010 Wall Street
Ann Arbor, MI 48109

James O'Brien, M.D.
Dept. of Family
  Practice
B-100 Clinical Center
Michigan State
  University
College of Human
  Medicine
East Lansing, MI
  48824-1313

MINNESOTA

Richard H. Bick, M.D.
Dept. of Family
  Practice and
  Community Health
University of
  Minnesota Medical
  School
6-240 Phillips-
  Wangensteen Bldg.
516 Delaware Street,
  S.E.
Box 381 Mayo
Minneapolis, MN
  55455

Robert Breitenbucher,
  M.D.
(Univ. of Minnesota)
Geriatric Medicine
Hennepin County
  Medical Center
701 Park Avenue
  South
Minneapolis, MN
  55416

Patrick Irvine, M.D.
(Univ. of Minnesota)
St. Paul-Ramsay
  Medical Center
640 Jackson Street
St. Paul, MN 55101

## MISSOURI

Coy D. Fitch, M.D.
Dept. of Medicine
St. Louis University
  School of Medicine
1325 South Grand
  Boulevard
St. Louis, MO 63104

Stanley R. Ingman,
  Ph.D.
(John L. Winnacker,
  M.D.)
Dept. of Family and
  Community
  Medicine
University of Missouri
  School of Medicine
Columbia, MO 65201

William A. Peck, M.D.
(Washington
  University)
Jewish Hospital
Program on Aging
216 South
  Kingshighway
St. Louis, MO 63110

## NEBRASKA

Jane F. Potter, M.D.,
  Chief
Section of Geriatrics
  and Gerontology
Dept. of Internal
  Medicine
Univ. of Nebraska
  Medical Center
42nd and Dewey
  Avenue
Omaha, NE 68105

## NEW JERSEY

Marian R. Stewart,
  Ph.D.
Dept. of Family
  Medicine
Robert Wood Johnson
  Medical School
1 Robert Wood
  Johnson Place CN19
New Brunswick, NJ
  08903

## NEW MEXICO

Robert F. Thompson,
  M.D.
Director, Geriatric
  Programs
Dept. of Family,
  Community and
  Emergency Medicine
University of New
  Mexico
School of Medicine
2400 Tucker Avenue,
  N.E.
Albuquerque, NM
  87131

## NEW YORK

Ray Bissonette, M.D.
Dept. of Family
  Medicine
State Univ. of New
  York (SUNY)
at Buffalo School of
  Medicine
Deaconess Hospital
1001 Humboldt
  Parkway
Buffalo, NY 14208

Evan Calkins, M.D.
(SUNY Buffalo)
Dept. of Medicine,
   Division of
   Geriatrics-
   Gerontology
VA Medical Center
Room 602-C
3495 Bailey Avenue
Buffalo, NY 14215

Conn J. Foley, M.D.
Stephen Wener, M.D.
(SUNY Stonybrook)
Jewish Institute for
   Geriatric Care
271-11 Seventy-sixth
   Avenue
New Hyde Park, NY
   11042

Michael L. Freedman,
   M.D.
New York University
   School of Medicine
Dept. of Medicine
550 First Avenue
New York, NY 10016

Steven R. Gambert,
   M.D.
Geriatric Medicine
New York Medical
   College
Westchester City
   Medical Center
Valhalla, NY 10545

Richard J. Ham, M.D.
SUNY Health Science
   Center at Syracuse
Program in Geriatrics
Weiskotten Hall, Room
   125
766 Irving Avenue
Syracuse, NY 13210

Donald Jue, M.D.
Division of General
   Internal Medicine
Dept. of Med.
Albany Med. College
Albany, NY 12208

Timothy Kaiser, M.D.
(Univ. of Rochester)
Geriatric Medicine
Monroe Community
   Hospital
435 East Henrietta
   Road
Rochester, NY 14603

Robert Kennedy, M.D.
(Albert Einstein
   College of Medicine)
Director, Geriatrics
Dept. of Medicine
Montefiore Medical
   Center
111 East 210 Street
Bronx, NY 10467

Leslie S. Libow, M.D.
Mount Sinai School of
   Medicine
One Gustave L. Levy
   Place
Annenberg 13-30
New York, NY 10029

Kenneth P. Scileppi,
   M.D.
(Cornell Univ.)
New York Hospital
Division of Geriatric
   Medicine
Department of
   Medicine
535 East Sixty-eighth
   Street
New York, NY 10021

NORTH CAROLINA

Harvey Jay Cohen,
M.D.
Director, Center for
the Study of Aging
and Human
Development
Box 3003
Duke University
Medical Center
Durham, NC 27710

William R. Hazzard,
M.D.
Professor and
Chairman
Dept. of Medicine
Bowman Gray School
of Medicine
Wake Forest
University
300 South Hawthorne
Road
Winston-Salem, NC
27103

Harold Kallman, M.D.
Dept. of Family
Medicine
East Carolina
University School of
Medicine
P.O. Box 1846
Greenville, NC 27835-
1846

OHIO

J. D. Frengley, M.D.
(Case Western
Reserve Univ.)
Cleveland
Metropolitan
General/Highland
View Hospital
3395 Scranton Road
Cleveland, OH 44109

Dennis Jahnigen, M.D.
Geriatric Medicine
Cleveland Clinic
Foundation (A-91)
9500 Euclid Avenue
Cleveland, OH 44106

Jerome Kowal, M.D.
(Case Western
Reserve Univ.)
Director, Geriatric
Care Center
University Hospitals of
Cleveland
2074 Abington Road
Cleveland, OH 44106

Gregg Warshaw, M.D.
Dept. of Family
Medicine
University of
Cincinnati College
of Medicine
231 Bethesda Avenue,
ML582
Cincinnati, OH 45267

OREGON

John R. Walsh, M.D.
(University of Oregon)
Chief, Gerontology
Section
VA Medical Center
3710 S.W. U.S. Veterans
Hospital Road
Portland, OR 97201

PENNSYLVANIA

Laurence H. Beck,
M.D.
Director
Program in Geriatric
Medicine
University of
Pennsylvania
Room 321R, Nursing
Education Bldg.
420 Service Drive
Philadelphia, PA
19104-6095

Mark Blossom, M.D.
(Medical College of
  Pennsylvania)
Philadelphia Geriatric
  Center
5301 Old York Road
Philadelphia, PA 19141

RHODE ISLAND

Marsha D. Fretwell,
  M.D.
(Brown University)
Department of
  Medicine
Roger Williams
  General Hospital
825 Chalkstone
  Avenue
Providence, RI 02908

TENNESSEE

William B. Applegate,
  M.D., M.P.H.
(Matthew Ochs, M.D.)
Section of Geriatrics/
  Gerontology
Dept. of Medicine and
  Community
  Medicine
University of
  Tennessee Center
  for Health Sciences
66 North Pauline
Memphis, TN 38163

Ron Hamdy, M.D.
Dept. of Medicine
East Tennessee State
  University
Quillen-Dishner
  College of Medicine
P.O. Box 23320A
Johnson City, TN
  37614

TEXAS

Judy Hill, M.D.
(University of Texas
  Health Science
  Center)
Audie L. Murphy
  Memorial VA
(11C)
7400 Merton Minton
  Street
San Antonio, TX
  78284

Robert J. Luchi, M.D.
Program in Aging
Baylor College of
  Medicine
Texas Medical Center
One Baylor Plaza
Houston, TX 77030

Derek M. Prinsley,
  M.D.
Director, Geriatric
  Medicine B-37
Dept. of Internal
  Medicine
University of Texas
  Medical Branch
Galveston, TX 77550-
  2775

VIRGINIA

Richard W. Lindsay,
  M.D.
Division of Geriatrics
Dept. of Medicine
University of Virginia
  School of Medicine
Box 157
Univ. of Virginia
  Hospital
Charlottesville, VA
  22908

Thomas M. Mulligan, M.D.
(Medical College of Virginia)
McGuire VA Hospital
1201 Broad Rock Blvd.
Richmond, VA 23249

WASHINGTON

Itamar B. Abrass, M.D.
University of Washington
Harborview Medical Center
325 Ninth Avenue (ZA-87)
Seattle, WA 98104

WISCONSIN

William A. Craig, M.D.
Molly Carnes, M.D.
William S. Middleton Memorial VA Hospital
2500 Overlook Terrace
Madison, WI 53705

Edmund H. Duthie, Jr., M.D., Chief of Geriatrics
Medical College of Wisconsin
5000 West National Avenue
Milwaukee, WI 53295

Elaine A. Leventhal, M.D., Ph.D.
Department of Medicine
H6/372 Clinical Sciences Center
University of Wisconsin
600 Highland Avenue
Madison, WI 53792

## GERIATRIC PSYCHIATRY FELLOWSHIP TRAINING PROGRAMS

ALABAMA

David Folks, M.D.
Dept. of Psychiatry
University of Alabama at Birmingham
University Station
Birmingham, AL 35294

CALIFORNIA

Thomas Cesario, M.D., Director
Mary Watson, Ph.D., Administrator
Academic Geriatric Resource Center
UC Irvine
101 The City Drive, Building 53
Orange, CA 92668

Jeste V. Dilip, M.D.
Director, Neuropsych.
  and Geropsych.
Dept. of Psychiatry
  (M003)
UC San Diego
School of Medicine
La Jolla, CA 92093

Lon S. Schneider,
  M.D.
Dept. of Psychiatry
Univ. of Southern
  California
School of Medicine
2025 Zonal Avenue
Los Angeles, CA
  90033

J. Edward Spar, M.D.
UCLA
  Neuropsychiatric
  Institute
760 Westwood Plaza
Los Angeles, CA
  90024

Jerome A. Yesavage,
  M.D.
Dept. of Psychiatry,
  TD114
Stanford University
  School of Medicine
Stanford, CA 94305

CONNECTICUT

Harry Morgan, M.D.
The Institute of Living
400 Washington Street
Hartford, CT 06106

FLORIDA

Eugene M. Dagon,
  M.D.
(Univ. of South
  Florida)
Dept. of Psychiatry
James Haley VAMC
13000 Bruce Down
  Boulevard
Tampa, FL 33612

ILLINOIS

Lawrence W. Lazarus,
  M.D.
(Rush Medical College)
Johnston R. Bowman
  Center for
  the Elderly
1725 West Harrison
  Street
Chicago, IL 60612

Kenneth Sakauye,
  M.D.
Director, Older Adult
  Program
Geriatric Psychiatry
  Services
Institute of Psychiatry
Northwestern
  Memorial Hospital
  STE446
259 East Erie Street
Chicago, IL 60611

MARYLAND

Brian Hepburn, M.D.
Paul Ruskin, M.D.
Geropsychiatry
University of Maryland
  Medical School
645 West Redwood
  Street
Baltimore, MD 21201

Paul McHugh, M.D.
Peter Rabins, M.D.
Dept. of Psychiatry
Johns Hopkins
  Hospital
600 North Wolfe
  Street
Baltimore, MD 21205


MASSACHUSETTS

Bennett S. Gurian,
  M.D.
Director of
  Geropsychiatry
Dept. of Psychiatry
Harvard Medical
  School
74 Fenwood Road
Boston, MA 02115

Janice E. Knoefel,
  M.D.
(Boston University)
Neurology Div. 127
VA Medical Center
150 South Huntington
  Avenue
Boston, MA 01230

Orlando B. Lightfoot,
  M.D. (Boston
  University)
Dept. of Psychiatry
ACC Building, 4 South
  33
Boston City Hospital
818 Harrison Avenue
Boston, MA 02118

Benjamin Liptzin,
  M.D.
(Harvard Medical
  School)
McLean Hospital
115 Mill Street
Belmont, MA 02178

MINNESOTA

Gabe Maletta, M.D.,
  Ph.D.
(University of
  Minnesota)
Director, GRECC
VA Medical Center
Minneapolis, MN
  55417


MISSOURI

George T. Grossberg,
  M.D.
(St. Louis University)
Director, Division of
  Geropsychiatry
David P. Wohl, Sr.,
  Memorial Institute
1221 South Grand
  Boulevard
St. Louis, MO 63104


NEW YORK

David D. Bonacci,
  M.D.
Director, Geriatric
  Psychiatry Program
Department of
  Psychiatry
University of
  Rochester
300 Crittenden Road
Rochester, NY 14642

Carl I. Cohen, M.D.
Dept. of Psychiatry
SUNY Downstate
  Medical Center
450 Clarkson Avenue
Brooklyn, NY 11203

Jeffrey R. Foster, M.D.
Dept. of Psychiatry
New York University
  Medical Center
550 First Avenue
New York, NY 10016

Ahmed Mobarak, M.D.
Director,
  Geropsychiatry
Dept. of Psychiatry
  and Behavioral
  Sciences
New York Medical
  College
Valhalla, NY 10595

Charles A. Shamoian,
  Ph.D., M.D.
New York Hospital-
  Cornell Medical
  Center
Westchester Division
21 Bloomingdale Road
White Plains, NY
  10605

NORTH CAROLINA

Dan Blazer, M.D.
Professor of Psychiatry
P.O. Box 3215
Duke University
  Medical Center
Durham, NC 27710

OHIO

David Bienenfeld,
  M.D.
Director, Division of
  Geriatric Psychiatry
Dept. of Psychiatry
  (ML559)
University of
  Cincinnati
231 Bethesda Avenue
Cincinnati, OH 45267-
  0559

PENNSYLVANIA

Erwin A. Carner,
  Ed.D.
Patricia A. J. Kay,
  M.D.
Geropsychiatry
Thomas Jefferson
  College of Medicine
1015 Walnut Street,
  3rd Floor
Philadelphia, PA 19107

Gary L. Gottlieb, M.D.
Director of
  Geropsychiatry
3rd Floor Piersol
Hospital of the
  University of
  Pennsylvania
3400 Spruce Street
Philadelphia, PA
  19104-4283

John P. Nelson, M.D.
(Univ. of Pittsburgh)
Medical Director,
  Geriatric Psychiatry
  and Behavioral
  Neurology Module
Western Psychiatric
  Institute and Clinic
3811 O'Hara Street
Pittsburgh, PA 15213

WASHINGTON

Murray Raskind, M.D.
GRECC (182-B)
Seattle VA Medical
  Center
1550 Columbian Way
  South
Seattle, WA 98108

## OTHER ORGANIZATIONS

ADMINISTRATION ON AGING
330 Independence Avenue, S.W.
Washington, DC 20201
(202) 245-0724

Acts as advocate for the elderly; serves as the principal agency for implementing programs of the Older Americans Act.

ALZHEIMER'S DISEASE AND RELATED DISORDERS
ASSOCIATION, INC.
700 East Lake Street
Chicago, IL 60601
(312) 853-3060

National organization of Alzheimer family members with 164 local chapters throughout the country; provides help through support groups, education, and contributions to research.

AMERICAN ASSOCIATION FOR GERIATRIC PSYCHIATRY
P.O. Box 376A
Greenbelt, MD 20770
(301) 220-0952

An association of about 800 psychiatrists throughout the United States who specialize in treating mental disorders of the older patient.

AMERICAN ASSOCIATION OF HOMES FOR THE AGING
1129 Twentieth Street, N.W., Suite 400
Washington, DC 20036
(202) 296-5960

Comprises 3200 nonprofit long-term care institutions that provide housing, congregate housing, skilled nursing, and related services to more than 500,000 elderly Americans.

AMERICAN ASSOCIATION OF RETIRED PERSONS
1909 K Street, N.W.
Washington, DC 20049
(202) 872-4700

National organization of 24 million older Americans (not all retired); provides a wide range of member benefits and service programs.

AMERICAN GERIATRICS SOCIETY
770 Lexington Avenue, Suite 400
New York, NY 10021
(212) 308-1414

Approximately 5,400 health-care professionals, primarily physicians
from all parts of the world, who are devoted to the clinical care of the
elderly.

AMERICAN HEALTH CARE ASSOCIATION
1200 Fifteenth Street, N.W.
Washington, DC 20005
(202) 833-2050

Nonprofit federation of associations from each of the 50 states plus
Washington, DC, serving 950,000 residents of nearly 9,500 licensed
nursing homes and allied facilities.

AMERICAN PSYCHIATRIC ASSOCIATION
1400 K Street, N.W.
Washington, DC 20005
(202) 682-6000

Professional association of approximately 36,000 psychiatrists
throughout the United States.

AMERICAN PSYCHOLOGICAL ASSOCIATION
1200 Seventeenth Street, N.W.
Washington, DC 20036
(202) 955-7600

Professional society of over 65,000 psychologists throughout the
United States.

AMERICAN SOCIETY FOR GERIATRIC DENTISTRY
211 East Chicago Avenue
Chicago, IL 60611
(312) 353-6547, (312) 664-8270

AMERICAN SOCIETY ON AGING
833 Market Street, Suite 512
San Francisco, CA 94103
(415) 543-2617

A national, nonprofit membership organization of practitioners, ed-
ucators, researchers, and others in the field of aging.

ASSOCIATION FOR GERONTOLOGY
IN HIGHER EDUCATION
600 Maryland Avenue, S.W.
West Wing 204
Washington, DC 20024
(202) 484-7505

Membership of over 200 colleges and universities whose purpose is to foster the development and increase the commitment of higher education in the field of aging through education, research, and public service.

CHILDREN OF AGING PARENTS
2761 Trenton Road
Levittown, PA 19056
(215) 547-1070

CAPS is an organization of adult children involved in parentcare; it can help find support groups in your area.

GERONTOLOGICAL SOCIETY OF AMERICA
1411 K Street, N.W.
Suite 300
Washington, DC 20005
(202) 393-1411

A 6,500-member, multidisciplinary professional organization devoted to bettering the condition of the aged through research and education.

GRAY PANTHERS
311 South Juniper Street, Suite 601
Philadelphia, PA 19107
(215) 545-6555

National group with 75,000 or more members in over 100 chapters focused on activities aimed to improve health, social, economic, and political conditions in the United States, especially for older Americans.

HUNTINGTON'S DISEASE SOCIETY OF AMERICA, INC.
140 West Twenty-second Street
New York, NY 10011-2420
(212) 242-1968

NATIONAL ASSOCIATION FOR HOME CARE
519 C Street, N.E., Stanton Park
Washington, DC 20002
(202) 547-7424

NAHC is a national clearinghouse of information on home-care agencies.

NATIONAL ASSOCIATION FOR SPANISH
SPEAKING ELDERLY
2025 I Street, N.W., Suite 219
Washington, DC 20006
(202) 293-9329

NATIONAL ASSOCIATION OF MEAL PROGRAMS
204 E Street, N.E.
Washington, DC 20002
(202) 547-6157

Over 800 individual, organization, and corporate members active in delivery of meals to older persons at home and in group settings; provides technical assistance, information exchange, and leadership in legislative action.

NATIONAL ASSOCIATION OF SOCIAL WORKERS
7981 Eastern Avenue
Silver Spring, MD 20910
(301) 565-0333

Professional society of approximately 109,000 social workers throughout the United States.

NATIONAL COUNCIL ON THE AGING, INC.
600 Maryland Avenue, S.W.
West Wing 100
Washington, DC 20024
(202) 479-1200

NATIONAL INSTITUTE OF MENTAL HEALTH
Mental Disorders of the Aging Research Branch, DCR
Room 11C-03
5600 Fishers Lane
Rockville, MD 20857
(301) 443-1185

NATIONAL INSTITUTES OF HEALTH
9000 Rockville Pike
Bethesda, MD 20814
(301) 496-4000
National Institute on Aging
(301) 496-1752

OFFICE OF HUMAN DEVELOPMENT SERVICES
200 Independence Avenue, S.W., Room 309F
Washington, DC 20201
(202) 245-7246

VETERANS ADMINISTRATION (VA)
810 Vermont Avenue, N.W.
Washington, DC 20420
(202) 233-4000

# NOTES

## Chapter 3

1. U.S. Senate Special Committee on Aging, in conjunction with the American Association of Retired Persons, *Aging America: Trends and Projections* (Washington, DC, 1984), 44–45.

## Chapter 4

1. U.S. Senate Special Committee on Aging, *Aging America*, 78–79.

2. Ibid., 26–42.

3. Ibid.

4. Ibid.

## Chapter 5

1. Fleg, J. L., and E. G. Lakatta, "Cardiovascular Disease in Old Age," *Clinical Geriatrics*, 3rd edition, edited by I. Rossman (New York: Lippincott, 1986).

2. Durnin, J.V.G.A., "The Gastrointestinal System—Nutrition," *Textbook of Geriatric Medicine and Gerontology*, edited by J. C. Brocklehurst (London: Churchill Livingstone, 1985).

3. Davis, I., "Facts About Fast Food," *Consumers' Research* (August 1984), 11–16.

## Chapter 6

1. Frank, E., C. Anderson, and D. Rubinstein, "Frequency of Sexual Dysfunction in "Normal" Couples," *New England Journal of Medicine* (1978), 299:111–115.

2. Gruman, G. J., "A History of Ideas About the Prolongation of Life," *Transactions of the American Philosophical Society* (1966), vol. 56, part 9.

3. Maspero, H., "Les Procédés de 'Nouvir le Principe Vital' dans la Religion Taoiste Ancienne," *Jour Asiatique* (1937), 229:382.

4.   Kinsey, A. C., W. B. Pomeroy, and C. R. Martin, *Sexual Behavior in the Human Male* (Philadelphia: W. B. Saunders, 1948); Kinsey, A. C., W. B. Pomeroy and C. R. Martin, *Sexual Behavior in the Human Female* (Philadelphia: W. B. Saunders, 1953); Masters, W. H., and V. E. Johnson, *Human Sexual Response* (Boston: Little, Brown, 1966).

5.   Starr, B. D., "Sexuality and Aging," *Annual Review of Gerontology and Geriatrics,* vol. 5, edited by C. Eisdorfer (New York: Springer Publishing, 1985).

6.   Ibid.

7.   Starr, B. D., and M. B. Weiner, *The Starr-Weiner Report on Sex and Sexuality in the Mature Years* (New York: McGraw-Hill, 1981).

8.   U.S. Senate Special Committee on Aging, *Aging America,* 80–81.

9.   Spengler, A., "Sexuality and Aging: The Role of Severe Illness" (Paper presented at the XII International Congress of Gerontology, Hamburg, 1981).

10.   Kinsey et al., *Sexual Behavior in the Human Male.*

11.   Hellerstein, H. K., and E. H. Friedman, "Sexual Activity and the Postcoronary Patient," *Archives of Internal Medicine* (1970), 125:987–999.

12.   Sjögren, K., and A. R. Fugl-Meyer, "Some Factors Influencing Quality of Sexual Life After Myocardial Infarction," *International Rehabilitation Medicine* (1983), 5:197–201.

13.   Newman, G., and C. R. Nichols, "Sexual Activities and Attitudes of Older Persons," *Journal of the American Medical Association* (1960), 173:33–35.

14.   Brecher, E., *Love, Sex and Aging* (Boston: Little, Brown, 1984); Starr, *Starr-Weiner Report.*

*Chapter 7*

1.   U.S. Senate Special Committee on Aging, *Aging America,* 84–85.

2.   Ibid.

3.   Shanas, E., "Social Myth as Hypothesis: The Case of the Family Relations of Old People," *The Gerontologist* (1979), 19:3–9.

4.   Cicirelli, V. G., *Helping Elderly Parents: The Role of Adult Children* (Boston: Auburn House, 1981).

5.   Schooler, K. K., *National Senior Citizens Survey, 1968* (Ann Arbor: Inter-University Consortium for Political Social Research, 1979).

6. Gelfand, D. E., *The Aging Network Programs and Services*, 2nd ed. (New York: Springer Publishing, 1984).

7. U.S. Senate Special Committee on Aging, *Aging America*, 73.

8. Gelfand, *The Aging Network*.

*Chapter 9*

1. U.S. Senate Special Committee on Aging, *Aging America*, 44–49.

2. Ibid.

3. Kimmel, D., K. Price, and J. Walker, "Retirement Choice and Retirement Satisfaction," *Journal of Gerontology* (1978), 33:575–585; Peretti, P. O., and C. Wilson, "Voluntary and Involuntary Retirement of Aged Males and Their Effect on Emotional Satisfaction, Usefulness, Self-image, Emotional Stability, and Interpersonal Relationships," *International Journal of Aging and Human Development* (1975), 6:131–138.

4. Shaw, L. B., "Retirement Plans of Middle-aged Married Women," *The Gerontologist* (1984), 24:154–159.

5. Neugarten, B. L., "Personality Changes in Late Life: A Developmental Perspective," *The Psychology of Adult Development and Aging* edited by C. Eisdorfer and M. P. Lawton (American Psychological Association, 1973).

6. Atchley, R. C., and S. J. Miller, "Older People and Their Families," *Annual Review of Gerontology and Geriatrics*, vol. 1 (1980), 337–369.

7. Palmore, E., "Why Do People Retire?", *International Journal of Aging and Human Development* (1971), 2:264–283.

8. Palmore, E. B., B. M. Burchett, G. G. Fillenbaum, L. K. George, and L. M. Wallman, *Retirement: Causes and Consequences* (New York: Springer Publishing, 1985).

9. McGuire, F. A., D. Dottavio, and J. T. O'Leary, "Constraints to Participation in Outdoor Recreation Across the Life Span: A Nationwide Study of Limitors and Prohibitors," *The Gerontologist* (1986), 26:538–544.

10. Greenough, W. C., "The Future of Employer Pension," *Retirement Policy in an Aging Society*, edited by R. L. Clark (Durham, NC: Duke University Press, 1980).

*Chapter 11*

1. Gersh, B. J., R. A. Kronmal, H. V. Schaff et al., "Long-term (5-

year) Results of Coronary Bypass Surgery in Patients 65 Years Old or Older: A Report from the Coronary Artery Surgery Study" *Circulation* (1983), 68(II):II190–II199; Kolata, G., "Some Bypass Surgery Unnecessary," *Science* (1983), 218: 605.

2.  Gersh et al., *Circulation*.

3.  Gibson, R. M., K. R. Levit, H. Lazenby, and D. R. Waldo, "National Health Expenditures, 1983," *Health Care Financing Review* (1984), 6:1–29.

4.  Schroeder, S. A., "Doctors and the Medical Cost Crisis: Culprits, Victims, or Solution?" *Pharos* (1985), 48:12–18.

5.  Gibson et al., *Health Care*.

6.  Kemp, K. B., ed., *The Implications of Cost-Effectiveness Analysis of Medical Technology, Background Paper No. 4: The Management of Health Care Technology in Ten Countries* (Congress of the United States, Office of Technology Assessment, U.S. Government Printing Office, 1980), 119–140.

7.  Vestal, R. E., "Clinical Pharmacology," *Principles of Geriatric Medicine,* edited by R. Andres, E. L. Bierman, and W. R. Harand (New York: McGraw-Hill, 1984).

8.  Ibid.

9.  Chien, C. P., E. J. Townsend, and A. Ross-Townsend, "Substance Use and Abuse Among the Community Elderly: The Medical Aspect," *Drug Use Among the Aged,* edited by D. M. Peterson (New York: Spectrum Publications, 1979) 357–372.

10.  Federal Council on Aging, *National Health Expenditures, 1980. Health Care Financing Review,* HCFA Publication No. 03123 (Health Care Financing Administration, Office of Research, Demonstration, and Statistics, Washington, DC: U.S. Government Printing Office, 1981).

11.  Lunn, J. N., "Anesthetic Mortality in Britain and France—Methods and Results of the British Study," *Mortality in Anesthesia,* edited by V. D. Vickers and J. N. Lunn (New York: Springer-Verlag, 1983), 19–24.

12.  Committee on Leadership for Academic Geriatric Medicine, *Academic Geriatrics for the Year 2000* (Division of Health Promotion and Disease Prevention, Institute of Medicine, Washington, DC: National Academy Press, December 1986).

13.  Holmes, A. W., and B. A. Winch, "Have a Good Rest in the Hospital," *New England Journal of Medicine* (1984), 310:1396–1397.

14. U.S. Senate Special Committee on Aging, *Aging America*, 64.

15. Schwartz, J., "Demographic Trends and Hospital Utilization: The Elderly Population," *Office of Public Policy Analysis, Policy Brief No. 41* (Chicago: American Hospital Association, 1982).

16. Natelson, B. H., C. DeRoshia, and B. E. Levin, "Physiological Effects of Bed Rest," *Lancet* (1982), i:51.

17. Popkin, M. K., T. B. Mackenzie, and A. L. Callies, "Psychiatric Consultation to Geriatric Medically Ill Patients in a University Hospital," *Archives of General Psychiatry* (1984), 41:703–707; Rabins, P., M. J. Lucas, M. Teitelbaum, S. R. Mark, and M. Folstein, "Utilization of Psychiatric Consultation for Elderly Patients," *Journal of the American Geriatrics Association* (1983), 31:581–584.

## Chapter 12

1. Office of Technology Assessment, *Technology and Aging in America* (U.S. Congress, OTA-BA-264, Washington, DC, June 1985), 54.

2. Ibid., 29.

3. Brocklehurst, J. C., *Textbook of Geriatric Medicine and Gerontology*, 3rd ed. (London: Churchill Livingstone, 1985), chapter 22.

4. American Academy of Ophthalmology, "Public Need for Eye Care," *Eye Care for the American People, Supplement to Ophthalmology* (April 1987), 23.

5. Shanas, E., "Older People and Their Families: The New Pioneers," *Journal of Marriage and the Family* (February 1980), 3–9.

## Chapter 13

1. Myers, G. C., and K. G. Manton, "Recent Changes in the U.S. Age at Death Distribution: Further Observations," *The Gerontologist* (1984), 24:572–575.

2. Plotkin, D. A., S. C. Gerson, and L. F. Jarvik, "Antidepressant Drug Treatment in the Elderly," *Psychopharmacology, the Third Generation of Progress: The Emergence of Molecular Biology and Biological Psychiatry*, edited by H. Y. Meltzer (New York: Raven Press, 1987).

# SUGGESTED READINGS

*Chapter 4*

Koff, G. J. *The Jacoby & Meyers Practical Guide to Everyday Law*. New York: Simon & Schuster, 1985.

Matthews, J. L., and D. M. Berman. *Sourcebook for Older Americans: Income, Rights and Benefits*. Berkeley: Noto, 1984.

Ross, M. J., and J. S. Ross. *Handbook of Everyday Law*. New York: Gramercy, 1986.

*Chapter 5*

Feldman, E. B., ed. *Nutrition in the Middle and Later Years*. New York: Warner Books, 1986.

Hendler, S. *The Complete Guide to Anti-Aging Nutrients*. New York: Simon & Schuster, 1985.

Piscattela, J. C. *Don't Eat Your Heart Out*. New York: Workman, 1982.

Walford, R. *The 120-Year Diet: How to Double Your Vital Years*. New York: Simon & Schuster, 1986.

Winch, M. *Your Personalized Health Profile: Nutrition to Prevent Disease*. New York: Ballantine Books, 1985.

*Chapter 6*

Butler, R. N., and M. I. Lewis. *Sex After Sixty*. New York: Harper & Row, 1976.

Comfort, A. *The Joy of Sex*. New York: Crown, 1972.

Drakeford, J. *Growing Old, Feeling Young*. New York: Ballantine Books, 1986.

## Chapter 7

American Association of Retired Persons. *Housing Choices for Older Homeowners.* A Publication of the Housing Program, Program Department. For a copy of this educational booklet, write to AARP, 1900 K Street, N.W., Washington, DC 20049.

Lawton, M. P. *Environment and Aging.* Monterey, California: Brooks/ Cole, 1980.

Spitz, L. A., and S. Leader. *A Consumer Guide to Life-Care Communities.* Washington: National Consumers League, 1986. For a copy of this pamphlet, contact National Consumers League, 815 Fifteenth Street, N.W., Suite 516, Washington, DC 20005.

## Chapter 8

Bengtson, V. L., and J. F. Robertson, eds. *Grandparenthood.* London: Sage, 1985.

Cherlin, A. J., and F. F. Furstenberg, Jr. *The New American Grandparent: A Place in the Family, a Life Apart.* New York: Basic Books, 1986.

## Chapter 9

American Association of Retired Persons. *Meaningful Use of Time— Retirement Planning Seminar.* For a copy of this pamphlet, write to Action for Maturity, AARP, 1909 K Street, N.W., Washington, DC 20049.

Hartford, M. E. *Making the Best of the Rest of Your Life.* Pacific Palisades, California: Personal Strengths Publishing, 1982.

## Chapter 10

Higdon, H. *Fitness After Forty.* Mountain View, California: World Publications, 1971.

Rosenfeld, I. *Modern Prevention: The New Medicine.* New York: Linden Press, 1986.

## Chapter 11

Coombs, R. H., D. S. May, and G. W. Small, eds. *Inside Doctoring.* New York: Praeger, 1986.

National Institute on Drug Abuse. *Using Your Medicines Wisely: A Guide for the Elderly.* Single copies are available free by writing to Elder-Ed, P.O. Box 416, Kensington, MD 20795.

U.S. Food and Drug Administration. "Food and Drug Interactions," *FDA Consumer Magazine*. For a free copy of this large-type reprint, send a postcard to FDA, HFE-88, 5600 Fishers Lane, Rockville, MD 20857.

## Chapter 12

Cary, J. R. *How to Create Interiors for the Disabled*. New York: Pantheon, 1978.

*How to Hire Helpers: A Guide for Elders and Their Families*. Seattle: Church Council of Greater Seattle, 1985. For a copy of this pamphlet, write to Church Council of Greater Seattle, 4759 Fifteenth Street, N.E., Seattle, WA 98105.

## Chapter 13

Cain, L. *Widow*. New York: Morrow, 1974.

Griest, J. H., and J. W. Jefferson. *Depression and Its Treatment*. New York: Warner Books, 1984.

Stearns, A. K. *Living Through Personal Crisis*. New York: Ballantine, 1984.

Worden, J. W. *Grief Counseling and Grief Therapy: A Handbook for the Mental Health Practitioner*. New York: Springer Publishing, 1982.

# ACKNOWLEDGMENTS

We thank our families—especially Laurence A. Jarvik; Jeffrey G. Jarvik, M.D.; Murray E. Jarvik, Ph.D., M.D.; Amy Gandin; Jeff Gandin; Mindy Gandin; Robert Gandin, D.D.S.; Max S. Small, M.D.; and Rena Small—for their support throughout all the years we have been together. We are indebted to L. Jolyon West, M.D., and our colleagues at UCLA for providing an intellectually stimulating atmosphere; to our patients and the many volunteers in our research studies on aging for contributing immeasurably to whatever expertise we can now claim; to Jessy Sandoval, our word-processor; and to Robert H. Gerner, M.D.; Martin J. Gorbien, M.D.; Hildi Greenson; Janice Hackman, M.B.B.S.; Ross R. Hart, Esq.; Sheldon Hendler, M.D.; Bayu Kalayam, M.D.; Judith Hornung-Kalla, M.B.B.S.; Marie Liston, M.S.W., M.S.G.; Joseph G. Ouslander, M.D.; Kay Russell; Harry W. Saperstein, M.D.; Ursula Springer; Donald P. Tashkin, M.D.; Mary C. Territo, M.D.; Sandra Westerman; Alisa Weyman, M.B.B.S.; and William C. Wirshing, M.D., for reviewing various sections and drafts of the manuscript and offering valuable comments.

Most of all, our thanks go to Gertrude Small, M.A., M.F.C.C., without whose help this book would not have been possible.

# INDEX